Devotional Islam in Contemporary South Asia

The Muslim shrine is at the crossroad of many processes involving society and culture. It is the place where a saint – often a Sufi – is buried, and it works as a main social factor, with the power of integrating or rejecting people and groups, and as a mirror reflecting the intricacies of a society.

This book discusses the role of popular Islam in structuring individual and collective identities in contemporary South Asia. It identifies similarities and differences between the worship of saints and the pattern of religious attendance to tombs and mausoleums in South Asian Sufism and Shi'ism. Inspired by new advances in the field of ritual and pilgrimage studies, this book demonstrates that religious gatherings are spaces of negotiation and redefinitions of religious identity and of the notion of sainthood. Drawing from a large corpus of vernacular and colonial sources, as well as popular literature and ethnographic observation, the authors describe how religious identities are co-constructed through the management of rituals and are constantly renegotiated through discourses and religious practices.

By enabling students, researchers and academics to critically understand the complexity of religious places within the world of popular and devotional Islam, this geographical re-mapping of Muslim religious gatherings in contemporary South Asia contributes to a new understanding of South Asian and Islamic Studies.

Michel Boivin is the Director of Research at the French National Center for Scientific Research (CNRS) and a member of the Centre for South Asian Studies at the School for Advanced Studies in the Social Sciences (EHESS), France.

Rémy Delage is a research fellow at the French National Center for Scientific Research (CNRS), France and an associate researcher at the French Institute of Pondicherry in India.

Routledge Contemporary South Asia Series

1 **Pakistan**
Social and cultural transformations in a Muslim nation
Mohammad A. Qadeer

2 **Labor, Democratization and Development in India and Pakistan**
Christopher Candland

3 **China–India Relations**
Contemporary dynamics
Amardeep Athwal

4 **Madrasas in South Asia**
Teaching terror?
Jamal Malik

5 **Labor, Globalization and the State**
Workers, women and migrants confront neoliberalism
Edited by Debdas Banerjee and Michael Goldfield

6 **Indian Literature and Popular Cinema**
Recasting classics
Edited by Heidi R.M. Pauwels

7 **Islamist Militancy in Bangladesh**
A complex web
Ali Riaz

8 **Regionalism in South Asia**
Negotiating cooperation, institutional structures
Kishore C. Dash

9 **Federalism, Nationalism and Development**
India and the Punjab economy
Pritam Singh

10 **Human Development and Social Power**
Perspectives from South Asia
Ananya Mukherjee Reed

11 **The South Asian Diaspora**
Transnational networks and changing identities
Edited by Rajesh Rai and Peter Reeves

12 **Pakistan–Japan Relations**
Continuity and change in economic relations and security interests
Ahmad Rashid Malik

13 **Himalayan Frontiers of India**
Historical, geo-political and strategic perspectives
K. Warikoo

14 India's Open-Economy Policy
Globalism, rivalry, continuity
Jalal Alamgir

15 The Separatist Conflict in Sri Lanka
Terrorism, ethnicity, political economy
Asoka Bandarage

16 India's Energy Security
Edited by Ligia Noronha and Anant Sudarshan

17 Globalization and the Middle Classes in India
The social and cultural impact of neoliberal reforms
Ruchira Ganguly-Scrase and Timothy J. Scrase

18 Water Policy Processes in India
Discourses of power and resistance
Vandana Asthana

19 Minority Governments in India
The puzzle of elusive majorities
Csaba Nikolenyi

20 The Maoist Insurgency in Nepal
Revolution in the twenty-first century
Edited by Mahendra Lawoti and Anup K. Pahari

21 Global Capital and Peripheral Labour
The history and political economy of plantation workers in India
K. Ravi Raman

22 Maoism in India
Reincarnation of ultra-left wing extremism in the twenty-first century
Bidyut Chakrabarty and Rajat Kujur

23 Economic and Human Development in Contemporary India
Cronyism and fragility
Debdas Banerjee

24 Culture and the Environment in the Himalaya
Arjun Guneratne

25 The Rise of Ethnic Politics in Nepal
Democracy in the margins
Susan I. Hangen

26 The Multiplex in India
A cultural economy of urban leisure
Adrian Athique and Douglas Hill

27 Tsunami Recovery in Sri Lanka
Ethnic and regional dimensions
Dennis B. McGilvray and Michele R. Gamburd

28 Development, Democracy and the State
Critiquing the Kerala model of development
K. Ravi Raman

29 Mohajir Militancy in Pakistan
Violence and transformation in the Karachi conflict
Nichola Khan

30 Nationbuilding, Gender and War Crimes in South Asia
Bina D'Costa

31 The State in India after Liberalization
Interdisciplinary perspectives
Edited by Akhil Gupta and K. Sivaramakrishnan

32 National Identities in Pakistan
The 1971 war in contemporary Pakistani fiction
Cara Cilano

33 Political Islam and Governance in Bangladesh
Edited by Ali Riaz and C. Christine Fair

34 Bengali Cinema
'An other nation'
Sharmistha Gooptu

35 NGOs in India
The challenges of women's empowerment and accountability
Patrick Kilby

36 The Labour Movement in the Global South
Trade unions in Sri Lanka
S. Janaka Biyanwila

37 Building Bangalore
Architecture and urban transformation in India's Silicon Valley
John C. Stallmeyer

38 Conflict and Peacebuilding in Sri Lanka
Caught in the peace trap?
Edited by Jonathan Goodhand, Jonathan Spencer and Benedict Korf

39 Microcredit and Women's Empowerment
A case study of Bangladesh
Amunui Faraizi, Jim McAllister and Taskinur Rahman

40 South Asia in the New World Order
The role of regional cooperation
Shahid Javed Burki

41 Explaining Pakistan's Foreign Policy
Escaping India
Aparna Pande

42 Development-induced Displacement, Rehabilitation and Resettlement in India
Current issues and challenges
Edited by Sakarama Somayaji and Smrithi Talwar

43 The Politics of Belonging in India
Becoming Adivasi
Edited by Daniel J. Rycroft and Sangeeta Dasgupta

44 Re-Orientalism and South Asian Identity Politics
The oriental Other within
Edited by Lisa Lau and Ana Cristina Mendes

45 Islamic Revival in Nepal
Religion and a new nation
Megan Adamson Sijapati

46 Education and Inequality in India
A classroom view
Manabi Majumdar and Jos Mooij

47 The Culturalization of Caste in India
Identity and inequality in a multicultural age
Balmurli Natrajan

48 Corporate Social Responsibility in India
Bidyut Chakrabarty

49 Pakistan's Stability Paradox
Domestic, regional and international dimensions
Edited by Ashutosh Misra and Michael E. Clarke

50 Transforming Urban Water Supplies in India
The role of reform and partnerships in globalization
Govind Gopakumar

51 South Asian Security
Twenty-first century discourse
Sagarika Dutt and Alok Bansal

52 Non-discrimination and Equality in India
Contesting boundaries of social justice
Vidhu Verma

53 Being Middle-class in India
A way of life
Henrike Donner

54 Kashmir's Right to Secede
A critical examination of contemporary theories of secession
Matthew J. Webb

55 Bollywood Travels
Culture, diaspora and border crossings in popular Hindi cinema
Rajinder Dudrah

56 Nation, Territory, and Globalization in Pakistan
Traversing the margins
Chad Haines

57 The Politics of Ethnicity in Pakistan
The Baloch, Sindhi and Mohajir ethnic movements
Farhan Hanif Siddiqi

58 Nationalism and Ethnic Conflict
Identities and mobilization after 1990
Edited by Mahendra Lawoti and Susan Hangen

59 Islam and Higher Education
Concepts, challenges and opportunities
Marodsilton Muborakshoeva

60 Religious Freedom in India
Sovereignty and (anti) conversion
Goldie Osuri

61 Everyday Ethnicity in Sri Lanka
Up-country Tamil identity politics
Daniel Bass

62 Ritual and Recovery in Post-Conflict Sri Lanka
Eloquent bodies
Jane Derges

63 Bollywood and Globalisation
The global power of popular Hindi cinema
Edited by David J. Schaefer and Kavita Karan

64 Regional Economic Integration in South Asia
Trapped in conflict?
Amita Batra

65 Architecture and Nationalism in Sri Lanka
The trouser under the cloth
Anoma Pieris

66 **Civil Society and Democratization in India**
Institutions, ideologies and interests
Sarbeswar Sahoo

67 **Contemporary Pakistani Fiction in English**
Idea, nation, state
Cara N. Cilano

68 **Transitional Justice in South Asia**
A study of Afghanistan and Nepal
Tazreena Sajjad

69 **Displacement and Resettlement in India**
The human cost of development
Hari Mohan Mathur

70 **Water, Democracy and Neoliberalism in India**
The power to reform
Vicky Walters

71 **Capitalist Development in India's Informal Economy**
Elisabetta Basile

72 **Nation, Constitutionalism and Buddhism in Sri Lanka**
Roshan de Silva Wijeyeratne

73 **Counterinsurgency, Democracy, and the Politics of Identity in India**
From warfare to welfare?
Mona Bhan

74 **Enterprise Culture in Neoliberal India**
Studies in youth, class, work and media
Edited by Nandini Gooptu

75 **The Politics of Economic Restructuring in India**
Economic governance and state spatial rescaling
Loraine Kennedy

76 **The Other in South Asian Religion, Literature and Film**
Perspectives on Otherism and Otherness
Edited by Diana Dimitrova

77 **Being Bengali**
At home and in the world
Edited by Mridula Nath Chakraborty

78 **The Political Economy of Ethnic Conflict in Sri Lanka**
Nikolaos Biziouras

79 **Indian Arranged Marriages**
A social psychological perspective
Tulika Jaiswal

80 **Writing the City in British Asian Diasporas**
Edited by Seán McLoughlin, William Gould, Ananya Jahanara Kabir and Emma Tomalin

81 **Post-9/11 Espionage Fiction in the US and Pakistan**
Spies and 'terrorists'
Cara Cilano

82 **Left Radicalism in India**
Bidyut Chakrabarty

83 **"Nation-State" and Minority Rights in India**
Comparative perspectives on Muslim and Sikh identities
Tanweer Fazal

84 **Pakistan's Nuclear Policy**
A minimum credible deterrence
Zafar Khan

85 **Imagining Muslims in South Asia and the Diaspora**
Secularism, religion, representations
Claire Chambers and Caroline Herbert

86 **Indian Foreign Policy in Transition**
Relations with South Asia
Arijit Mazumdar

87 **Corporate Social Responsibility and Development in Pakistan**
Nadeem Malik

88 **Indian Capitalism in Development**
Barbara Harriss-White and Judith Heyer

89 **Bangladesh Cinema and National Identity**
In search of the modern?
Zakir Hossain Raju

90 **Suicide in Sri Lanka**
The anthropology of an epidemic
Tom Widger

91 **Epigraphy and Islamic Culture**
Inscriptions of the early Muslim rulers of Bengal (1205–1494)
Mohammad Yusuf Siddiq

92 **Reshaping City Governance**
London, Mumbai, Kolkata, Hyderabad
Nirmala Rao

93 **The Indian Partition in Literature and Films**
History, politics and aesthetics
Rini Bhattacharya Mehta and Debali Mookerjea-Leonard

94 **Development, Poverty and Power in Pakistan**
The impact of state and donor interventions on farmers
Syed Mohammad Ali

95 **Ethnic Subnationalist Insurgencies in South Asia**
Identities, interests and challenges to state authority
Edited by Jugdep S. Chima

96 **International Migration and Development in South Asia**
Edited by Md Mizanur Rahman and Tan Tai Yong

97 **Twenty-First Century Bollywood**
Ajay Gehlawat

98 **Political Economy of Development in India**
Indigeneity in transition in the state of Kerala
Darley Kjosavik and Nadarajah Shanmugaratnam

99 **State and Nation-Building in Pakistan**
Beyond Islam and security
Edited by Roger D. Long, Gurharpal Singh, Yunas Samad, and Ian Talbot

100 Subaltern Movements in India
Gendered geographies of struggle against neoliberal development
Manisha Desai

101 Islamic Banking in Pakistan
Shariah-compliant finance and the quest to make Pakistan more Islamic
Feisal Khan

102 The Bengal Diaspora
Rethinking Muslim migration
Claire Alexander, Joya Chatterji, and Annu Jalais

103 Mobilizing Religion and Gender in India
The role of activism
Nandini Deo

104 Social Movements and the Indian Diaspora
Movindri Reddy

105 Identity Politics and Elections in Malaysia and Indonesia
Ethnic engineering in Borneo
Karolina Prasad

106 Religion and Modernity in the Himalaya
Edited by Megan Adamson Sijapati and Jessica Vantine Birkenholtz

107 Devotional Islam in Contemporary South Asia
Shrines, journeys and wanderers
Edited by Michel Boivin and Rémy Delage

108 Women and Resistance in Contemporary Bengali Cinema
A freedom incomplete
Srimati Mukherjee

109 Islamic NGOs in Bangladesh
Development, piety and neoliberal governmentality
Mohammad Musfequs Salehin

Devotional Islam in Contemporary South Asia

Shrines, journeys and wanderers

Edited by
Michel Boivin and Rémy Delage

Routledge
Taylor & Francis Group
LONDON AND NEW YORK

First published 2016
by Routledge

2 Park Square, Milton Park, Abingdon, Oxfordshire OX14 4RN
711 Third Avenue, New York, NY 10017

Routledge is an imprint of the Taylor & Francis Group, an informa business

First issued in paperback 2018

British Library Cataloguing in Publication Data
A catalogue record for this book is available from the British Library

Library of Congress Cataloging-in-Publication Data
Devotional Islam in contemporary South Asia : shrines, journeys and wanderers / edited by Michel Boivin and Rémy Delage.
pages cm. — (Routledge contemporary South Asia series)
Includes bibliographical references and index.
ISBN 978-0-415-65750-1 (hardback) — ISBN 978-1-315-67471-1 (ebook) 1. Islam—South Asia. 2. Muslim saints—South Asia. 3. Islamic shrines—South Asia. I. Boivin, Michel. II. Delage, Rémy.
BP63.A37D48 2016
297.3'554—dc23
2015027350

ISBN: 978-0-415-65750-1 (hbk)
ISBN: 978-1-138-61107-8 (pbk)

Typeset in Times New Roman
by Apex CoVantage, LLC

Contents

Contributors xiii
Acknowledgements xvi

1 **Authority, shrines and spaces: scrutinizing devotional Islam from South Asia** 1
MICHEL BOIVIN

PART I
Authority and the figures of sainthood 13

2 **Vagrancy and pilgrimage according to the Sufi qalandari path: the illusions of anti-structure** 15
ALEXANDRE PAPAS

3 **Qalandars and Ahl-e Haqq** 31
MOJAN MEMBRADO

4 **Women [un-]like women: the question of spiritual authority among female fakirs of Sehwan Sharīf** 47
OMAR KASMANI

5 **Negotiating religious authority at a shrine inhabited by a living saint: the dargāh of 'Zinda' Shāh Madār** 63
UTE FALASCH

6 **How discourses and rituals construct figures of holiness: the example of the Indo-Muslim martyr Ghāzī Miyān (Uttar Pradesh, North India)** 79
DELPHINE ORTIS

PART II
Shrine and circulation 101

7 **Meditative practice, aesthetics and entertainment music in an Indian Sufi shrine** 103
MIKKO VIITAMÄKI

8 **Evolution of the Chishtī shrine and the Chishtīs in Pakpattan (Pakistan)** 119
MUHAMMAD MUBEEN

9 **The mother and the other: tourism and pilgrimage at the shrine of Hiṅglāj Devī/Bībī Nānī in Baluchistan** 138
JÜRGEN SCHAFLECHNER

10 **Sacred journeys, worship and reverence: the Sufi legitimation of the *ziyārat* in Hyderabad** 156
MAURO VALDINOCI

11 **An ambiguous and contentious politicization of Sufi shrines and Pilgrimages in Pakistan** 174
ALIX PHILIPPON

Index 191

Contributors

Michel Boivin is Director of Research in the CNRS and member of the Centre for South Asian Studies (CEIAS). Trained in History, Islamic Studies and Ethnology, he teaches historical anthropology of the nineteenth through twenty-first century Muslim societies and cultures in South Asia at the Advanced School in Social Sciences (EHESS). In 2015, he has published *Historical Dictionary of the Sufi Culture of Sindh in Pakistan and in India* (Karachi, OUP) and *Le Pakistan et l'islam. Anthropologie d'une république islamique* (Paris, Téraèdre).

Ute Falasch graduated in South Asian Studies, Islamic Studies and Cultural Studies from Humboldt-University of Berlin and completed her Ph.D. in South Asian Studies from the same university. She is currently a staff member at the Institute of Indology and Central Asian Studies at Leipzig University. Academic publications include: *Heiligkeit und Mobilität*, Berlin: Lit 2015; and "Regulating Rapture: 'The *malang* in the Madāriyya', in *Oriente Moderno*, 92, 2/2012, S. 369–92.

Omar Kasmani is a social and cultural anthropologist. He recently completed his doctoral research on the fakirs of Sehwan Sharif, Pakistan. His research and creative interests lie at the intersections of gender, queer subjectivities and performances of religious devotion. He is currently based at the Berlin Graduate School Muslim Cultures and Societies (BGSMCS) and teaches at the Institut für Ethnologie, Freie Universität, Berlin.

Mojan Membrado teaches History of Religions in the Eurasia Department, National Institute of Oriental Languages and Civilizations (INALCO). Her focus in Religious Studies is on Islamic 'heterodoxies' in the Persianate world. Her research interests are 'normativity' in esoteric and syncretistic communities; religious groups facing the modernity; and the status of women in religious communities. Her publications include: 'Ḥājj Ne'mat-Allāh Jayḥūnābādī (1871–1920) and His Mystical Path Within the Ahl-e Ḥaqq Order', in Khanna Omarkhali (ed.); and *Religious Minorities in Kurdistan: Beyond the Mainstream*. Series: Studies in Oriental Religions 68. Wiesbaden: Harrassowitz. 2014, pp. 13–45.

Muhammad Mubeen is currently serving as Assistant Professor of History at Quaid-i-Azam University, Islamabad. He holds a Ph.D. in History and Civilizations from EHESS – Paris. His research interests include the history of the Sufi shrine culture in the Indian subcontinent with a major focus on the history of the Chishti Sufism and the Chishti shrine cult in the Punjab.

Delphine Ortis obtained her Ph.D. in social anthropology and ethnology in 2008 at EHESS. Her doctoral dissertation, which dealt with the organization of the shrine of a Muslim Indian saint, was entitled 'Ethnographie d'un islam indien. Organisation cultuelle et sociale d'une institution musulmane : la dargāh du martyr Ghāzī Miyān (Bahraich, Uttar Pradesh, Inde du Nord)'. After focusing on the cult of martyrs, she is doing research on Sufism and Shiism in Pakistan. She is preparing a book on the cult of the great Saint of the Sindh, Lāl Shahbaz Qalandar, with other French scholars. She is currently a lecturer in anthropology and ethnology at ESSEC and EHESS.

Alexandre Papas is Research Fellow at the National Center for Scientific Research in Paris. A historian of Sufism and Central Asia, he has published: *Soufisme et politique entre Chine, Tibet et Turkestan* (J. Maisonneuve, 2005); *Mystiques et vagabonds en islam* (Cerf, 2010); *Central Asian Pilgrims* (Klaus Schwarz, 2011, co-ed.); *Family Portraits with Saints* (Klaus Schwarz, 2013, co-ed.); and *L'autorité religieuse et ses limites en terres d'islam* (Brill, 2013, co-ed.).

Alix Philippon is Associate Professor (Maître de conférences) in Sociology at Sciences Po Aix. She has completed a Ph.D. at Aix-en-Provence and published it under the title of *Soufisme et politique au Pakistan. Le movement Barelvi à l'heure de la guerre contre le terrorisme* (Karthalla-Sciences Po Aix, 2011). She is also co-organizing a seminar at EHESS on "Politics and Authority in Contemporary Sufism". Her work focuses on the political dimension of Sufism in Pakistan. She has notably analyzed the re-composition and mobilization of (neo) Sufi orders. She has also authored a number of papers in academic journals and directed a documentary on dance in Pakistan with Faizan Peerzada (Laatoo, 2002).

Jürgen Schaflechner is Assistant Professor at the Department of Modern South Asian Languages and Literatures at the South Asia Institute, University of Heidelberg. He is a research associate at the Cluster of Excellence "Asia and Europe in a Global Context" and holds a Ph.D. in Modern South Asian Languages and Literatures and Anthropology, also from the University of Heidelberg. His research interests include religious minorities in Pakistan with a special focus on Pakistani Hindus, gender and women's right, nationalism and social movements in South Asia, and critical theory. Jürgen teaches classes in postcolonial and literary theory at the South Asia Institute and produces documentary films relating to his research interest.

Mauro Valdinoci is currently an independent researcher. During the academic year 2013/2014, he was Postdoctoral Fellow at the Oriental Institute of the Academy of Sciences of the Czech Republic in Prague. In 2012, he received his Ph.D. in Anthropology from the Department of Sciences of Language and Culture at the University of Modena and Reggio Emilia. He did extensive fieldwork in Hyderabad, India. His research interests include Muslim cultures and societies in South Asia, Sufism, Islam and modernity, Islamic reformism, identity, transmission of knowledge, and ritual.

Mikko Viitamäki completed his doctoral studies at the University of Helsinki in 2015. His dissertation analyses the usages of poetry in South Asian Sufi practice with special reference to qawwali music. His other research interests include Sufism in colonial and post-colonial periods and the popularization of Ibn Arabi's thought in the Indian Subcontinent. At present, he works as the university lecturer of South Asian studies at the University of Helsinki, teaching Hindi and Urdu and conducting research.

Acknowledgements

The present volume is made of the proceedings of a conference held at the Centre for Indian and South Asian Studies (CEIAS), School of Advanced Studios in Social Sciences (EHESS) in Paris. The international conference was organized by Michel Boivin and Rémy Delage as members of the CEIAS research group *History and Sufism in the Indus Valley* with the title of *Shrines, Pilgrimages and Wanderers in Muslim South Asia* on September 23–24, 2010. We would like to thank the CEIAS, the CNRS Institute of Social Sciences, the Centre de Sciences Humaines (CSH) and the Maison des Sciences de l'Homme (MSH) for their supports. Finally, we are most grateful to Rémy Delage for the responsibility he took in an earlier stage of the book making. We warmly thank Carole Le Cloiérec, for the help she was able to provide for the index. The transliteration was not harmonized.

1 Authority, shrines and spaces

Scrutinizing devotional Islam from South Asia

Michel Boivin

This book discusses the role of popular Islam in structuring individual and collective identities in contemporary South Asia. We are aware of the difficulties arisen by the use of words such as 'popular'[1], and even 'devotional', the one we have chosen for the main title. Although the approach is multidisciplinary, anthropology frames most of the papers. In this field, the building of the object under study results from observation. The main behavior observed by the contributors was related to devotion. From Latin, devotion interestingly refers to the vow, the promise made by a believer to God. Such practices of making vows are still a basic ritual in the shrines in South Asia. It implies that devotion plays a leading role in framing the religiosity and piety of such places.

Regarding devotion, a main issue is related to the translation. When we use the Western word devotion, to what vernacular are we referring? In South Asian languages, devotion is expressed as *ibadat*, *bandagi*, *bhagti/bhakti*, etc. For many believers from South Asia, devotion will not be distinguished from spiritual love (*pyar*, *ishq*). The notion of love is the most widespread in locality to express the link between the devotees and a spiritual master. Furthermore, the semantic field of devotion is usually close to two other notions: that of service (*khidmat*) and that of sacrifice (*qurban*).[2] The relation between a devotee and the saint is conceived as an exchange of services. The devotee asks something and in return, he is supposed to perform some services or duties. The service can be a donation in cash, but also the sweeping of the shrines, or other material services for the maintenance or improvement of the shrine. It shows the complexity of the notion of devotion in Muslim South Asian context, beyond the difficulty coming from the translation, since there is not a single word for expressing the single idea of devotion.

Another point to be raised is that it is well known that devotion, which can also encompass veneration, is for many Muslims restricted to the Prophet Muhammad. All over the Muslim world, the Prophet Muhammad is undoubtedly the main figure to which devotion is directed.[3] In the second part of the *shahada*, it is clearly stated that he is the second after Allah to be the recipient of the prayers. Since our work was not on the mosques, which are the most common places where God and the Prophet Muhammad are praised, but on the shrines, we observed that logically, only a few shrines are devoted to the Prophet Muhammad.[4] It is also well known that the devotional literature dedicated to him is huge.[5] Furthermore, a number of reformist movements centers piety on the devotion towards the Prophet Muhammad, from the well-named Tariqa-e Muhamadiyya which was created in the beginning of the twentieth century.[6] Since the veneration of the Prophet Muhammad is a distinct and separate topic, we have decided not to include the devotion. A main reason would be that the topic will require a whole book devoted to it.

However, a discussion on devotional Islam will imply two main issues: the issue of visitation of the holy tombs and the issue of sainthood, which are in both cases focusing on the shrines. In the Muslim context, visitation and sainthood are reminiscent of the *ziyarat*,[7] from the Arabic verb *zâra*, 'to see somebody or something, to pay a visit', sometimes translated as 'pilgrimage',[8] although it is also used to translate the *hajj*, which I will discuss more later in this book. This said, the *ziyarat* is very often understood as a substitute for the *hajj*, when people are prevented from performing the pillar of Islam (Boissevain and Boivin forthcoming). It is true it is a commonly studied topic, mostly in relation with Sufism. In the eleventh volume of the *Encyclopedia of Islam* (2002), Bearman, Bianquis, Bosworth, van Donzel, and Einrich provide a seminal overview on the topic. Unfortunately, South Asia is not given the importance it deserves, despite the number of leading studies that have already been published. Furthermore, since 2002, several new works have been devoted to the issue of *ziyarat*.[9] Most of the time, they are anthropological works centered on a given *dargah*, or even multi-sited places, but they were in any case conceived as monographs. In the wake of our multidisciplinary approach, we thought of implementing less-explored approaches, especially those referring to the different categories of space-related issues.

The issue of space was the core approach of a book published in French by Amir-Moezzi (1996), *Lieux d'islam*. The collective volume addresses the issue of place (*lieu*) instead of space, under three different parts: religious and historical places, mystical places and cultural places, which include places from Africa to Java. The relation between place and space is nonetheless addressed in the first contribution authored by Jambet. He reminds the polarity of Islam which starts with the direction of the canonic prayer and is reinforced with the obligation of *hajj*, the canonic pilgrimage, to which should be added 'a flowering of secondary poles'. Framing on Aristotelian philosophy, Jambet states that the place is not the absolute end of the interpretation of the space (Amir-Moezzi 1996: 19–20). From the beginning of Islam, Muslim mystics have identified a number of places and spaces which are beyond the physical word.

Recently, Green provided a new approach regarding the issue of space. First, he spoke of space as territory, before introducing the dialectic between the territorial construction and the textual construction of sainthood (Green 2012: 33–4). For him, the shrine itself is like an embodiment of the saint, and as such, it plays a distinct and significant role in the process of sanctification. Then in his last book *Terrains of exchange*, Green refers to the concept of terrain. A terrain is 'conceived as a distinctive environment that lent shape – defining colour and flavor – to their religious product'. Drawing a parallel with the winegrower's concept of terroir (in French), he claims that the 'terrains of exchange. . . aim to capture the intersecting dimensions of "locality" and "globality" ' (Green 2014: 7). Furthermore, a terrain 'is a market of religious transactions' (Green 2014: 11).[10]

In our volume on devotional Islam, the way we wished to raise the issue of space and place is expressed in the three elements of the subtitle: shrines, journeys and wanderers. Drawing on de Certeau, the place is the order in which elements are arranged in their relations of coexistence. There is a space as soon as we take into account factors of direction, issues related to speed, and the time variable. Thus, the space is a 'practiced place', a place where different operations delimit spaces through the actions performed by historical subjects (Certeau 1990: 173–174). In this respect, the shrine is a main illustration of the dialectic between place and space.

Mainly known in South Asia as a *dargah*, a Persian-originated term meaning *threshold*, the Muslim shrine is also known through other words whose meaning and use vary according to time and regions, such as *mazar*. During the last phase of the Delhi sultanate, the place was better known as a *khanaqah*, which was the exact Persian equivalent of the Arabic word *zawiya*.[11] When Ibn Battutta (1304–1377) visited Sehwan Sharif in the mid-thirteenth century, he spoke of the *zawiya* where he stayed a few days. And after a few years, the epigraphic texts left by the Delhi sultan Firuz Shah Tughluq (1309–1388) in the same Sehwan Sharif spoke of it as a *khanqah*. But later, the *saint des saints* of the sacred places was shifted from the place where the Sufis lived to the place where a Sufi master was buried. Although most of the scholars interpreted this change as a decline of Sufism, it is more relevant to observe the spread of a new religiosity which was closely related to new social, political and economic conditions. Furthermore in the cultural sphere, singing mystical poetry was still a main part of the devotional practice.

The shrines under study will be analyzed through the multilevel spatial context in which they were built and where they grew up. In the field of place understood as a physical space, the urban environment was a key factor. The study of the interaction between the space of the shrine and the space of the city often plays a tremendous role in the fabric of the society. If the shrine was framed by the urban, in return the urban was also framed by the shrine. In this regard, a main contribution is Wolper's work on how Sufism transformed the urban space in Medieval Anatolia (Wolper 2003). Wolper's goal is to examine the role of dervish lodges, conceived as both buildings and institutions, in religious and cultural transformation. Throughout her study, she addressed the issue of both places and spaces. First, she examined how these buildings changed the hierarchy of spaces in Anatolian cities, and second, she addressed how the dervish lodges worked as places where different types of authority were mediated (Wolper 2003: 3). However, regarding South Asia, the lack of sources does not allow in many cases implementation of thorough studies in this matter, despite pioneer works here again.[12] Another lens through which the shrine is studied is as a place of social fabric.

As a matter of fact, it is also very common to claim that the shrine is a place where all the different categories of population, referring to creeds, social groups, castes and so on, are mixed and intermingled. Here, we turn back to the issue of popular religion. In using this expression, which is reminiscent of a number of cleavages expressed in Muslim societies, such as *khass-am* (elite-people) or *ashraf-ajlaf*,[13] we don't pretend there is no social distinction in the space of the shrine. Nor do we wish to challenge the Turnerian theory of the *communitas*, although it did not prevent social discriminations inside the shrine. We just want to state that the religiosity performed in the space of the shrine is shared by the many segments of the society, belonging to local elites, outsiders, discriminated categories like women, transgender, religious minorities, but also powerful statesmen, low middle classes, high middle classes, landowners, beggars, etc. It is in that sense that the religion of the shrine is popular. We also take the shrine as a place where many things are possible, despite the control taken by the state or by powerful lobbies. It means that the shrine as a sacred place and space is open to new social negotiations, and it is to some extent like a distorted mirror of the interwoven strata of local, regional and national society.

After the shrine, the second topic related to space is that of journey. First it implies the idea of displacement and movement. Rather than focusing on displacement as travel, we thought of it as a linkage between different spaces and places. The journey performer will of course start his journey from home, but sometimes, the journey to the *ziyarat* will include a number of steps before reaching it. Furthermore, the *ziyarat* itself can be made of different internal journeys. Finally, the journey can be a physical journey, but most of the time it is replicated in the symbolic level, in the spiritual realm. *Journey* is consequently not understood in the common meaning. It is a multidimensional term which can refer to different levels of reality, not only physical reality. It echoes the spiritual journey a Sufi is supposed to achieve for reaching the ultimate goal: the merging with God, the *fana fi'llah*.

On the other side, visiting the main shrines is on the agenda of many politicians. Contrary to what is sometimes claimed, the relation between the shrine and the politics is as old as Sufism. In South Asian context, it started as soon as in the thirteenth century, during the Delhi sultanate. We have already spoken of the attempt by Firuz Shah Tughluq to leave his mark on Lal Shahbaz Qalandar's shrine in Sehwan Sharif. It was a true political action, when one knows that he wanted to reduce the Sohrawardiyya influence on the State. As spiritual masters of many people, the State thus wanted to control the shrine's attendants but vice versa, the Sufis looked for the protection of the State. By protection, it means mainly the financial support of the prince and during the first Tughluq princes, the heads of the Sohrawardis obviously increased the wealth of the *tariqa*, as well as their personal wealth. And to some extent, the violence of the *qalandar*s towards them was but a protest against the collusion of the Sufi establishment with political power.

The third topic related to space is that of the wanderer. Despite what was suggested by the orientalists, and the homologies with Hindu tradition, the tradition of wandering *faqir*s has been attested in Sufism since the beginning. The wanderer is a figure of sainthood which has survived mainly in South Asia. It has almost disappeared from Turkey, but looks to be still alive also in Central Asia, especially in Chinese Central Asia. It is of course highly necessary to distinguish the wanderer from the traveler or from the pilgrim in other words. The wanderer, who is himself known under different denominations, is a renouncer: he has given up all what is related to the mundane and material world to wander from one tomb to another. Since they want to die in the mundane world, they live in the company of the dead. While the word *qalandar* was very common in the time of the Delhi sultanate, as an equivalent of the word *rend* from Persian poetry, the most spread could be today that of *malang*, whose origin is unknown.[14] Finally, there is a paradox when shrines were built to host the wanderers' tombs. As a matter of fact, these ascetics illustrated the vanity of life in adopting reverse values: they lived outside instead of having a house, a fixed place. Death was their environment since many were living in the graveyards, and they dressed like women with long hairs and jewels. The building of a tomb thus sounds like a scenario for capturing the wandering of the ascetic.

Beyond the focus on shrines and space, this volume addresses many other issues we do not explicitly express. The issue of sainthood can be framed in a single question: is there a specific kind of sainthood in the shrines? Once again, we don't pretend to propose an exhaustive answer. We rather focus on specific categories of saints for which it is most useful to have a look at the vocabulary. We find the Arabic-originated terms such as *walaya* or *wilaya*, two words which are also employed by the Shiites for the *imams*. This word is built on an Arabic root meaning closeness. The one who is close to God is the *wali* (pl. *awliya*). It thus doesn't refer to sanctity or to the sacred, as in the case of the Latin word *sanctus*, however, the same rooted word *sant* is used in Hinduism. Nonetheless, it is an interesting word since it can be understood as referring to the closeness of the buried Sufi to the pilgrim, and to the closeness between the buried Sufi and God. Consequently, the dead saint is an intercessor and a mediator, and the place where he lies is a bridge between the mundane world and the spiritual world.

While the cult usually develops from the grave of a dead saint, the dead saint's spiritual power or his charisma was transmitted to his descendants or, if he was not married, to the descendant of his successor. Following Weber, we can coin this type as hereditary charisma. For centuries, the heads (*murshid*s, *pir*s, *sajjada nashin*s) of the most important Sufi shrines have accumulated wealth. Thanks to the pilgrims' donations, they have acquired lands and became landowners, or *zamindar*s. They are often the backbone of a social class which can be compared with the gentry of England. The comparison is nevertheless only relevant in terms of wealth and of social dominant class. The main difference is indeed the religious role the *murshid*s play. Another distinct feature is the entanglement of the network of their followers with that of their clients. By clients, we mean the people who work for them, in cultivating their fields or in running their shops.

Another implicit issue is that of pilgrimage, a word used in a number of contributors' chapter titles in this book. Obviously, one would wonder why the word pilgrimage was not incorporated into this title. It is true that the old Latin word *pelegrinus*, or pilgrim, encompasses many aspects of the topics the contributions are dealing with, since it refers to mobility and circulation. Interestingly in French and in English, the word *pelegrinus* gave birth to two words, pèlerinage/

pilgrimage and pérégrination/peregrination. The first one was quickly given a spiritual or even religious meaning, while the second was more secular, related to leisure since the eighteenth century onwards. Furthermore, the field of pilgrimage studies is currently a field of its own which has already crossed many stages, following the evolution of the social sciences, as it was recently summarized by Dionigi Albera and John Eade (Albera and Eade 2015).

In the context of Islam, there is an ambiguity in the term *pilgrimage*, since it is used for the hajj and the umra, the lesser pilgrimage, the canonic visit to Mecca, which is one of the five pillars of Islam, and the visitation to the tombs of the saints. The polarization of the hajj as the only allowed pilgrimage is stronger than ever, although it doesn't deserve attention yet in South Asian Islam.[15] Other pilgrimages are underestimated, for example the visitation to Jerusalem, the third sacred city of the Muslims (Zarcone 2010). Also, there are the pilgrimages performed by the Shias to the *atabat*s and other places where the Ahl al-bayt are buried in Iran, Iraq and also Syria.[16] Beyond the many academic works devoted to the hajj and other Sufi-related pilgrimages, it is quite amazing to observe that few studies have been conducted on Shia sacred places.[17]

Nonetheless, the pilgrimage studies were started, and were dominated for a long time, by the Christian-centered works, and in this book we also want to argue that the pilgrimage is thus working most of the time as a paradigm, but a Christian paradigm. Thus the problem is that the reality we are facing in the field shows that what was coined as a pilgrimage in Christian-dominated context doesn't fit such sacred places in the South Asian environment. Better, using the word *pilgrimage* does catch but a very thin side of the reality observed in fieldwork. On the other side, all the words for *pilgrimages* obviously share a number of common features which can explain the success of the pilgrimage studies.

Furthermore, in focusing mainly on shrine and space, which can be also understood in a dialectic relation of fixed and mobility, the instrumentalization operated by a variety of institutions and actors, from the Nation-State level to the community or sect level, is more understandable. It allows one to locate the worship performed in a shrine in the double discourse of globalization and nationalism, since the visit paid to shrines is often a main tool in building identity. For example when the Hindus left Sindh in Pakistan for India, they did rebuild their shrines which were now out of reach in their new homeland. This is evidence of how rituals performed in shrines played a role in non-religious process.

Beyond the pilgrimage studies and to better frame the scope of the present volume, it is also necessary to revisit some ancient issues of social sciences at large, first of all being that of authority. The performance and display of authority is closely related to the construction of sainthood. Gaborieau and Zeghal have identified three poles in the religious authority of Islam: esoteric, exoteric and politic (Gaborieau and Zeghal 2004: 7). The authority in the abstract sense – distinguished from raw power, strength and violence – means the right to enforce obedience in the name of principle values shared by those subject to it. From this abstract sense derives a concrete sense: the individuals and institutions that embody this abstract authority and do its work. The three-level classification of authority nevertheless darkens the role played by mediation tools which are used for making it relevant to a variety of consumers. Also, there is the complex issue of legitimacy and finally, we can wonder whether magic, for example can be coined as esoteric or if it doesn't work as a distinct field of operation.

Two other main topics are to be briefly addressed: the relation between Sufism and saint worship or cultism, and the gender issue. The gender issue is related to the shrines: in the context of patriarchal societies, it is important to investigate the place of women and authority, knowing that the issue has not been addressed much yet. Paradoxically, the women are often depicted as being the main and best 'clients' of the so-called spiritual guides in shrines. This is often explained by the fact that women would be more vulnerable to emotion than men. Nevertheless, the issue of how women are able to build a legitimacy as a saint in a patriarchal society has rarely been addressed, except in some pioneering works (Abbas 2002; Pemberton 2010), as well as whether their practice of authority is different from the man's or not. Finally, there is also the issue of the 'third-sex' involvement in the shrines.[18] Although such figures were observed in other cultural contexts, the presence of the *hijras* looks like a typical feature of South Asian religiosity, beyond the religious belonging.

Regarding the religious affiliation, a common character of these shrines is to be a shared place where Muslims, as well as Hindus, Christians, Sikhs and others can pay a visit to a saint. Once again, such a situation has been observed in other cultural contexts, for example in the Mediterranean milieu, but it has always fascinated scholars, from the West as well as from the East. Despite numerous works, the topic still attracted them often (Bidgelow 2010). It can be explained by the contrast between the high violence perpetrated into intercommunal strife in India, and also intersectarian ones in Pakistan, and, on the other side, the peaceful visitations Muslims and Hindus can pay to the same shrine. Once again, it looks to be very volatile to propose a theory, and even to build some paradigm, so pregnant is the issue of locality in the making of religious harmony through the visitation of shrines. It means that this system is made possible through the building of narratives embedded in local reality. It is obviously a very complex matter and before being able to suggest categorization, many case studies will have to be implemented.

Furthermore, the issue of the relation between Sufism and saint worship was addressed at length by scholars. Mayeur-Jaouen has provided evidence that the issue is recent and in relation with the birth and quick spread of *islah*, or reform, in the late nineteenth-century Muslim world (Mayeur-Jaouen 2004: 203–11). However, almost since the beginning of Islam, ulamas condemned the veneration of the saints, be they Sufi or not. It doesn't mean they did condemn Sufism understood as a spiritual quest. Thus, they separated the cult, where the pilgrims bowed down facing the saint's tomb, which was to be addressed to Allah alone, and the spiritual path largely based of imitation of the life of the Prophet Muhammad. Beyond the issue of the saint as mediator, it is crucial to understand how spiritual authority could be entangled with political and social authority. In other words, how can it work in the twenty-first century? Finally, it is the main aim of this volume to stress on the crucial importance of locality and diversity. It doesn't mean that it is not possible to elaborate paradigms and pattern, but it seems that above all, the contributions highlight the plasticity of the cults as well as their capacity to fit a local culture, itself framed not following the religious frontlines, but rather to provide a harmonious system of social relations aimed at reproducing the domination of dominant classes.

For addressing the issue of spaces and places, the book is divided into two main parts. The first part focuses on authority and the figures of sainthood. The wandering ascetics, mainly known as *qalandar*s, were emblematic of the shrines of South Asia. But the figure of the *qalandar* was not static. Following the many upheavals like invasions, building and dislocation of empires that have shaped the Indian Subcontinent, the figure of the *qalandar* went through a number of modifications to adapt itself to the evolution of the society. In this respect, Alexandre Papas analyzes what he calls the illusions of anti-structure, borrowing on Turner's theory that was implemented by the Qalandari path. On another side, Mojan Membrano will highlight how the tradition of the *qalandar* was incorporated by a Kurdish community from Iran, the Ahl-e Haqq, with which the South Asian *qalandar*s were in touch.

Other contributions deal with the saints' charisma and the conflicting representations of sainthood. It thus deals with issues such as the construction and transmission of sainthood, and its relation with authority. Omar Kasmani addresses the issue of spiritual authority of the female fakirs in a town of Pakistan, Sehwan Sharif. Ute Falash deciphers how religious authority is negotiated at the shrine of Zinda Shah Madar in North India. Delphine Ortis studies the discourses which are implementing a normalization of holiness, and its relation with sainthood. The last contributor in the first part, Mikko Viitamäki, focuses on music in the famous Delhi shrine of Nizam al-Din Awliya. He addresses how music is a tool in the building of sainthood.

The second part is devoted to religious circulations and the making of the ritual spaces. This important issue is addressed by four contributors working on different contexts, geographical as well as religious. Muhammad Mubeen did a long-term fieldwork on the famous shrine of Farid al-Din Ganj-e Shakar in Pakpattan, in Pakistan. It allows him to decipher the many roles played by the Chishtis in the locality. The second contribution is the only one which does not focus on a Muslim shrine. Jürgen Schaflechner deals with the shrine of Hinglaj Devi, also known as Bibi Nani, in Baluchistan. It is an interesting place of worship in the Pakistan environment, since the Hindus have discouraged the Muslims to attend the shrine.

The third and fourth contributions are on pilgrimage politics and Sufi shrines policies. As we put earlier, the interrelation between political power and the shrines is as old as both are. Nonetheless, new trends have emerged in the last decades. The State policy in some cases was at least supported by Muslim intellectuals. The following chapter, authored by Mauro Valdinocci, examines how the Sufi discourse was framed to counter the 'new orthodoxy' wishing to exclude it from Islam. Finally, the last chapter by Alix Philippon focus on a case study of how Sufi shrines are politicized in Pakistan. It raises the issue of State policy on Sufism.

Notes

1 The issue of popular Islam is of course beyond the scope of this book. For a discussion, see Boivin 2009: 456–477.
2 By South Asia, we mean the northern part of the Indian Subcontinent, where Indo-Aryan languages are spoken. Although a paper is devoted to Hyderabad in Deccan, the spoken language of the involved communities is Urdu.
3 See for example Schimmel 1985.
4 They are most of the time places where something which is supposed to have belonged to the prophet is kept, from his body like his hair (Boivin 2015: 332), but mostly his footprints and/or sandals. On the footprints, see Hasan 1993 and Welch 1997. For Mayeur-Jaouen, the footpints of the Prophet in Sayyid al-Badawi's shrine in Tanta, Egypt, reinforce the believers' conviction that the visited place is a 'small hajj' (Mayeur-Jaouen 2004: 145).
5 In this respect, see for instance the collection of *madahun* and *munajatun* in Sindhi published by N.B. Baloch (1959).
6 See the book by Usha Sanyal which is titled *Devotional Islam in British India* (1996).
7 For the different topics and issues under study, such as *ziyarat*, *zawiya*, *khanaqa*, *wali*, *faqir* or *dargah*, the second edition of *Encyclopaedia of Islam* is a main reference, although it is mainly centering on the Middle East.
8 The literature related to the issue of pilgrimage is also quite huge, mainly based on a discussion of Victor Turner's paradigm of *communitas*. For a useful outlook, see Coleman and Eade 2004 and Albera and Eade 2015.
9 We don't intend to provide an analytic synthesis of the related literature. The most recent and important works are Werner and Basu 1998, Abbas 2002, Bellamy 2011, Benett and Ramsey 2012, Bidgelow 2010, and Pemberton 2010. In the field of Muslim pilgrimages, we also would like to point out that in this matter, as in many others, academic literature in French is highly neglected. See for example Chiffoleau and Madoeuf 2005, and Depret and Dye 2012.
10 It is beyond the scope of this introduction to introduce the 'sociology of religious economy' developed by Green, in which religious goods can be compared to any other goods.
11 On *zawiya*, see the seminal synthesis by Catherine Mayeur-Jaouen (Mayeur-Jaouen 2000).
12 See for example Eaton 1978 and Ernst 1992. These works are focusing on South India.
13 Although very simplistic, the cleavage between *ashraf* and *ajlaf* is much used in the context of South Asian Muslims. The *ashraf*s are supposed to be the descendants of external invaders, starting with the Arabs, Persians, Turks, Afghans and so on. They were said to be like an aristocracy. The *ajlaf*s are the descendants of the converts, mainly from Hinduism. Ideally, they were in the service of the formers.
14 It is to be noted that these figures of wandering Sufis are still underestimated by the second edition of the *Encyclopaedia of Islam*, since a few studies were published after it was completed in the early 2000s.
15 Among the few exceptions, see for example Metcalf 1990.
16 The 'thresholds', the Shia shrine cities of Iraq – Najaf, Karbala, Kaẓemayn, and Samarra – containing the tombs of six of the imams as well as secondary sites of pilgrimage.
17 In this respect, see the recent publication on Najaf (Tabbaa and Mervin 2014); on Mashhad, see Hakami 1989; on Qom, see Richard 1996. Little attention has been paid to Ali's relics, such as the *maula jo qadam* or footprints of Ali (Boivin 2015: 212).
18 The 'third-sex' is made of hijras, namely transgenders. They are given propitious qualities and use to roam around shrines. See in this volume Kasmani's contribution.

Bibliography

Abbas, Shemeem Burney. *The Female Voice in Sufi Ritual: Devotional Practices of Pakistan and India*. Austin: University of Texas Press, 2002.

Albera, D. and J. Eade (eds). *International Perspectives on Pilgrimage Studies: Itineraries, Gaps and Obstacles*. London: Routledge, 2015.

Amir-Moezzi, Mohammad Ali, *Lieux d'islam. Cultes et cultures de l'Afrique à Java*. Paris: Editions Autrement, 1996.

Baloch, Nabi Bakhsh. *Madāhūn ain munājātūn*. 2nd ed, Hyderabad: Sindhi Adabi Board, 2006.

Bearman, P.J., Bianquis, Th., Bosworth, C.E., van Donzel, E., and W.P. Einrich (eds). "Ziyarat." *The Encyclopaedia of Islam*. Vol. 11. Leiden: Brill, 2002.

Bellamy, Carla. *The Powerful Ephemeral: Everyday Healing in an Ambiguously Islamic Place*. Berkeley: University of California Press, 2011.

Benett, Clinton and Charles M. Ramsey (eds). *South Asian Sufis. Devotion, Deviation, and Destiny*. London: Continuum, 2012.

Bigelow, Anne. *Shared the Sacred. Practicing Pluralism in Muslim North India*. New York: Oxford University Press, 2010.

Boissevain, Katia and Michel Boivin. "The study of *ziyarat* in the Muslim World: from the Maghreb to South Asia", in D. Albera and J. Eade (eds), *New Itineraries and Pathways in Pilgrimage Studies*. London: Routledge, forthcoming.

Boivin, Michel,.*Historical Dictionary of the Sufi Culture of Sindh in Pakistan and in India*. Karachi: Oxford University Press, 2015.

Boivin, Michel. "Religion popolare e islamizziazzione nel mondo musulmano contemporano", in Roberto Tottoli (a cura di), *Islam III Le religioni e il mondo moderno*. Torino: Giulio Einaudi, 2009, pp. 456–477.

Certeau, Michel de. *L'invention du quotidien, 1. Arts de faire*. Paris: Gallimard, 1990.

Chiffoleau, Sylvia and Anna Madoeuf (dir.). *Les pèlerinages au Maghreb et au Moyen-Orient: espaces publics, espaces du public*. Beyrouth: Ifpo, 2005.

Coleman, Simon and John Eade (eds). *Reframing Pilgrimage. Cultures in Motion*. London and New York: Routledge, 2004.

Depret, Isabelle & Guillaume Dye (dir.). *Partage du sacré. Transferts, dévotions mixtes et rivalités interconfessionnelles*. Bruxelles: EME, 2012.

Eaton, Richard M. *Sufis of Bijapur 1300–1700: Social Roles of Sufis in Medieval India*. Princeton: Princeton University Press, 1978.

Ernst, Carl. *Eternal Garden: Mysticism, History, and Politics at a South Asian Sufi Centre*. Albany: SUNY Press, 1992.

Gaborieau, Marc and Malika Zeghal. "Autorités religieuses en islam", *Archives des Sciences Sociales en Religion*, 125, janvier-mars 2004, pp. 5–21.

Green, Nile. *Making Space. Sufis and Settlers in Early Modern India*. New Delhi: Oxford University Press, 2012.

Green, Nile. *Terrains of Exchange. Religious Economies of Global Islam*. London: Hurst and Company, 2014.

Hakami, Nasrine. *Pèlerinage de l'Imam Reza: étude socio-économique*. Tokyo: Institute for the Study of Languages and Cultures of Asia and Africa, 1989.

Hasan, Parveen. "The Footprint of the Prophet", *Muqarnas*, Vol. 10, Essays in Honor of Oleg Grabar (1993), pp. 335–343.

Mayeur-Jaouen, Catherine. *Histoire d'un pèlerinage légendaire en Islam. Le mouled de Tantâ du XIIIe siècle à nos jours*. Paris: Aubier, 2004.

Mayeur-Jaouen, Catherine,."Tombeau, mosquée et zawiya: la polarité des lieux saints musulmans", in André Vauchez (dir.), *Lieux sacrés, lieux de culte, sanctuaires. Approches terminologiques, méthodologiques, historiques et monographiques*. Rome: Ecole Française de Rome, 2000, pp. 133–147.

Metcalf, Barbara D. "The pilgrimage remembered: South Asian accounts of the hajj", in Dale F. Eickelman and James Piscatori (eds), *Muslim Traveller. Pilgrimage, migration, and the religious imagination*. London: Routledge, 1990, pp. 85–107.

Pemberton, Kelly. *Women Mystics and Sufi Shrines in India*. Columbia (South Carolina): University of South Carolina Press, 2010.

Richard, Yann. "Qom, un lieu sacré en Iran", in Amir-Moezzi, Mohammad Ali, *Lieux d'islam. Cultes et cultures de l'Afrique à Java*. Paris: Editions Autrement, 1996, pp. 60–69.

Sanyal, Usha. *Devotional Islam and Politics in British India. Ahmad Riza Khan Barelwi and his Movement, 1870–1920*. New Delhi: Yoda Presses, 2010 (2nd ed.).

Schimmel, Annemarie. *And Muhammad Is His Messenger. The Veneration of the Prophet in Islamic Piety*. Chapel Hill and London: The University of North Carolina Press, 1985.

Tabbaa Yasser & Sabrina Mervin. *Najaf The City of Wisdom. History, Heritage & Significance of the Holy City of the Shi'a*. Paris: UNESCO, 2014.

Welch, Anthony. "The Shrine of the Holy Footprint in Delhihi", *Muqarnas*, Vol. 14 (1997), pp. 166–178.

Werbner Pnina, Helene Basu (eds). *Embodying Charisma. Modernity, Locality and the Performance of Emotion in Sufi Cults*. London and New York: Routledge, 1998.

Wolper, Ethel Sara. *Cities and Saints. Sufism and the Transformation of Urban Space in Medieval Anatolia*. University Park: The Pennsylvania University Press, 2003.

Zarcone, Thierry. *Sufi Pilgrims from Central Asia and India in Jerusalem*. Kyoto: Centre for Islamic Area Studies, Kyoto University, 2010.

Part I

Authority and the figures of sainthood

2 Vagrancy and pilgrimage according to the Sufi qalandari path

The illusions of anti-structure

Alexandre Papas

Gâh sûfi gâh qalandar chist?
Chûn qalandar shudî qalandar bâsh.
Hamîd Qalandar, *Khayr al-Majâlis*

(Qalandar 2010 : 34)

If travelling is constantly praised in the Islamic tradition, wandering is not. From the hajj pilgrimage to the search for knowledge (*talab al-'ilm*), from the early emergence of the *rihla* literary genre to the late Reformist *safarnâmas*, travels not only involve discovering the world and raising questions about the self and the other, but reinforce faith and piety. Among Sufis, the itinerant practice is often associated with pious visits as well as initiatory journeys, such as gatherings of *tarîqa* members on specific occasions, meeting with spiritual masters, proselytizing missions and pilgrimages to holy places. Whether Mecca, Medina, Jerusalem or saints' shrines found in various locations, holy sites became major destinations for Sufi travellers. In her short discussion on the spiritual dimensions of travel in Islam, Annemarie Schimmel recalled that the travelling mystics perceived shrines as sources of divine grace, opening the doors of ecstatic paradise to their visitors. This is the case for Farîd al-Dîn Ganj-i Shakar's mausoleum in Paktpattan, known as the 'Paradise Gate' (*bihishtî darwâza*) (Schimmel 1994: 13).

Unlike travelling and its rules (Al-Hujwîrî 1911: 345–347), wandering has no specific destination, no proper end and tends to favour the journeying over the destination itself. Taking all these particularities into account, vagrancy seems to contradict the moral virtues or social benefits of the travels. In his *Risâlô*, the famous eighteenth-century Sindhi poet, Shâh 'Abd al-Latîf narrates the dangers of Sasui's vagrancy through the solitudes of Baluchistan as a perilous but salutary path, chanting, 'Only search and search, never find' (*durâng durâng ma lahâng*) (Schimmel 1994: 21–22). Such wanderings are not limited to mystical rhetoric. They correspond to real practices within a radical trend of Islamic mysticism which emerged as early as the eighth and ninth centuries through the figure of the *sâ'ih*, the vagabond saint. Finding his legitimacy in Quran 9:112 and its mention of 'Those who journey' (*sâ'ihûn*), against the canonical interpretation of this expression which endeavoured to obliterate the reference to the vagabond, mediaeval mystic exegetes understood the *sâ'ih* and his practice (*siyâha*) as a model of ascetic life based on renunciation and vagabondage (Touati 2000: 188–196). Extremely popular among the first generations of Sufis, in Baghdad as well as Khurasan 'schools', this model found its best promoters in the Sufi trend called Qalandarî, which first appeared in Iran in the eleventh century and developed 200 years later.

This chapter will be based on both classical texts, including poetry, and ethnographic data, collected either by myself or by ethnographers, in order to understand the practical dimensions of texts as well as the textual dimensions of practices. My purpose here is to restore the radical consistency of the pilgrimage according to the Qalandarî path, and to avoid two common pitfalls. While wandering pilgrims are often perceived by Orientalists, Muslim reformists or Sufi intellectuals as debauched tramps feigning devoutness and extreme spirituality, ethnologists and anthropologists tend to overextend the Qalandarî model of piety and to idealize any Muslim pilgrimage as a subversive spiritual act. It seems to me, as a historian, that the Qalandarî Sufi path lies between these two approaches: neither a falsification nor a synecdoche, it suggests that the Qalandarî pilgrimage is a rare reality.

Exemplary wanderers for Qalandarî pilgrims

Three prominent mediaeval masters are repeatedly quoted in Qalandarî sources as exemplary wanderers who underwent the great trials of spiritual vagabondage.

The first is Bâyazîd Bistâmî (d. 848/9 or 874/5) who is said to have 'left Bistâm and wandered in the Syrian Desert for thirty years. He practised asceticism and was constantly undergoing sleeplessness and hunger. He served 113 elders and learned something useful from each of them, among them Ja'far al-Sâdiq. (. . .) It is related that it took Bâyazîd twelve years to reach the Ka'ba. Every few steps, he would unroll his prayer rug and perform two *rak'ats* of prayer (. . .)' ('Attâr 1905: 136, 'Attâr 2009: 189–190). The hagiography presents the wanderings of Bistâmî as a long and slow pilgrimage during which he became a servant, an ascetic and a suffering mystic. Whereas the destination was ultimately the House of God in Mecca, like any hajj, the duration and the stopovers remained the most relevant features. On another occasion, Bistâmî chose a way station on the road to receive a revelation from God on his sanctity: 'One day I was sitting around, and it occurred to me, "Today I am the spiritual guide of our time and the eminent man of the age." When I thought this, I knew that I made a tremendous blunder. I got up and set off on the road to Khurasan. I took up residence in a way station and took an oath: "I will not get up from here until the Real most high sends someone to me to show to me" (. . .)' ('Attâr 1905: 141, 'Attâr 2009: 195). Throughout his life as a pilgrim, the Sufi looks everywhere for signs of God's reality, hoping to be rewarded for his piety. His quest, therefore, must avoid any easiness: 'One night I was in the desert and had wrapped my head in my robe. I had a nocturnal emission, and it was bitterly cold. I wanted to wash, but my self was lazy and said, "Wait until daybreak when the sun comes up. Wash then." When I saw my self's laziness, I realized that I was deferring my prayers. I broke the ice of my robe – it froze solid – until the air grew warm. I kept my self in this torment all winter. Before daybreak, I used to faint seventy times to punish it for its laziness' ('Attâr 1905: 144, 'Attâr 2009: 199). It was through the solitude of deserts that Bistâmî experienced both the physical and spiritual trials which could reinforce his devotion. And beyond devotion, he roamed the wilderness to find the divine kingdom, as is claimed in one of his theophanic locutions (*shath*, pl. *shatahât*): 'I crossed the deserts and I reached the steppes. I traversed the steppes and I attained the realm of the Unseen. I went through the realm of the Unseen and I arrived at the Sovereignty' (Bistâmî 1989: 124).

Lastly, in a chapter devoted to hajj, a well-known Sufi treatise mentions and then comments on an interesting saying of Bistâmî which actually undermines the usual conceptions of pilgrimage and sanctuary. He explains that far from a simple religious test or duty, pilgrimage is a trial of vision, not of strength, and that sanctuary is, in spite of appearances and beyond its physical aspect, an unlimited object of vision. ' "On my first pilgrimage I saw only the temple; the second time, I saw both the temple and the Lord of the temple; and the third time I saw the Lord alone." In short, where mortification is, there is no sanctuary: the sanctuary is where contemplation is. Unless the whole world is a man's trysting-place where he comes nigh unto God and a retired chamber where he enjoys intimacy with God, he is still a stranger to Divine love; but when he has vision the whole universe is his sanctuary' (Al-Hujwîrî 1911: 327). As a result, if pilgrimage consists of the acquisition of the vision of God, every movement, every motion should be a pilgrimage in so far as the world is a sanctuary, namely God's house, and therefore a place of pilgrimage. Rather than a theoretical account on pantheism, such conceptions provided Qalandars with a practical model of mystical life, in the name of which they devoted their existence to hallucinatory wanderings and elected sanctuaries, shrines and any holy sites as homes for their visions.

Although he was against extreme asceticism or spiritual excess, Junayd Baghdâdî (830–911) remained famous among vagrant mystics, primarily for his call for 'crossing the desert' which was expressed in a letter addressed to a disciple (Abû Nu'aym 1979: 259–260; Junayd 1983: 66–68):

'Do know, my friend, since you are asking me about this subject, that during the advance to the arrival there are wild desert stages (*mafâwiz muhlika*) and deadly spring sources, which should be crossed with a guide, traversed with perseverance, and with the use of a good mount. I shall mention only one of these dangerous stages, and I shall require you to set in your mind my description, to keep your attention on my directions, to listen carefully to what I am going to say, in order to understand my explanations properly. You should know that in front of you there is a perilous desert, if you are among those who are destined to go through. I leave you in God's care and I ask Him to protect you as the journey is highly risky and what you will see when you will walk is scary. Since the beginning, you will have to enter the large surface area without limit of *barzakh* (. . .) This is when there is no longer an access road for the one who is searching, no longer purpose for the one who is wandering, no longer salvation for the one who is running away (. . .)

Who will save you in this situation? Who will help you to escape the perils while you will be despairing of any release and sinking into the depths of this abyss? Be careful, be careful! How many men who set out on this venture have been swept along? How many presumptuous men have been knocked down as they lost their soul because of a deceptive illusion, hence run to their end? May God put us, you and I, among the few who avoided this, and may He not deprive us of what He has in store for these who have knowledge! Do know, my friend, that what I have just told you of this perilous desert, with a partial description, is just an allusion to the knowledge I will not tell you about. Anyway, to unveil this knowledge is impossible since the one who finds himself in this desert no longer exists (. . .)'.

Often perceived as a theoretician of sober spirituality, as opposed to Bâyazîd Bistâmî or Mansûr Hallâj, Junayd is sometimes carried away by his mystical enthusiasm to the extent that he uses a rhetoric of risk and danger which at once describes the trials of the body and the tribulations of the soul. In the above quotation, the Sufi explains the necessity to meander through the desolate lands in order to confront oneself with the desolation of the self. The initiatory journey forces one to spend time in the religious wilderness where there is no guide, no knowledge and no consciousness. Such are the teachings applied literally by Qalandarî practitioners who, distrustful of theosophical speculations or strictly symbolic interpretations, undertake real journeys, in the course of which they face the hardships of vagabondage, far from the comfort of armchair mysticism.

The third great tutelary figure for Qalandars is Mansûr Hallâj (857–922). The life of the famous martyr is renowned for what the *Kitâb al-'Uyûn* called 'his many wanderings (*siyâhât*)' (Massignon 1975: I, 225), which began in the early years of his spiritual training. Here again, the hajj pilgrimage was the occasion to experience a wandering, pious life. We learn that on his first visit to Mecca in 884–886, Hallâj ignored the rule of cleanliness and purity (*ihrâm*) for pilgrims; he stayed for a whole year in the *masjid al-harâm*, contenting himself with water and some bread, without moving except to perform the circumambulation (*tawâf*) (Massignon 1975: I, 148–149). Hallâj set off for Mecca again in 900–901, accomplishing a third hajj. In the meantime, he progressively became a wanderer. He kept a home at Tustar, and later in Baghdad, but he undertook many travels, walking with a stick in his hand, staying in mosques in towns and cities, using fortified inns (*ribât*) along the roads and meeting various people in religious places, markets or even in the streets, to whom he addressed provocative sermons. He went to Fars, Ahwaz, Khurasan, Transoxiana, Kashmir, Sistan, Sindh and perhaps East Turkestan (Massignon 1975: I, 178–183). As a sign of this evolution, even the physical appearance of Hallâj changed during his life. Having rejected the usual Sufi dress (*sûf*), he took the paraphernalia of religious vagabonds, holding a beggar's cup (*kashkûl*) and wearing dark blue rags (*muraqqa'a*) and an Indian covering (*fûta*) (Massignon 1975: I, 144–145). According to Louis Massignon, Hallâj's attitude is to be related to the exemptions (*rukhas*) that Sufis granted themselves. More precisely, he probably applied the *tark al-kasb* principle (also called *inkâr* or *tahrîm al-makâsib*), that is the right to renounce any occupation, to live in perpetual pilgrimage (*siyâha*) and beg (*su'âl*) (Massignon 1975: III, 241).

The life of Hallâj provides a vivid portrait of the holy vagabond to Qalandars, and not only explains how to reach spiritual states but what sort of men they have to be in order to follow this path. It might be interesting to note in passing that Hallâj's legacy is particularly important in Indian Sufism (Massignon 1975: II, 288–303). Various individuals such as Jalâl Bukhârî or Dârâ Shûkuh referred to the great wanderer when they established the confluence of Islam and Hinduism in a kind of mystical syncretism which will often be claimed, if not promoted, by Indian Qalandars. Sufi orders, like Shattâriyya, Naqshbandiyya and even Hallâjiyya, elaborated on the famous formula *Anâ'l-Haqq* and set up Hallâjian *dhikr* methods. Last but not least, Sufi music (*samâ'*) performed on Muslim shrines in India frequently invokes Hallâj's name or words.

To sum up this section devoted to the models of Qalandarî pilgrims, several points should be highlighted. Following the example of Bistâmî, Qalandars define their existence and presence on earth as a pilgrimage and an opportunity for mystical experiences. From Junayd, they learn how difficult, extreme and demanding this lifestyle is. Hallâj gives their 'school' a martyr to bemoan, a name to identify with and a saint to invoke. In the same way that wandering differs from travelling, vagabonds' pilgrimages – whether hajj or pious visits to shrines (*ziyâra*) – differ from both 'lay' believers' and Sufis' pilgrimages in that they are not limited in time and space, and involve specific conditions and practices. As we shall see in the next sections, these radical views are not only theoretical or poetical but correspond to real and historically attested forms of pilgrimage undertaken by past as well as present practitioners called Qalandars.

Poverty, vagrancy and piety

The famous eleventh century Hanbali Sufi, Khwâja 'Abd Allâh Ansârî, was one of the very few early mediaeval authors who wrote on Qalandars, and he provided quotations from Qalandarî masters who required their followers to be indifferent to common opinion as well as to general hostility towards them, and to definitively leave their home (Borûmand Sa'îd 1384/2005: 14). This call for a radical break meant the rejection of wife, children, home and work, that is to say of all the aspects of social life which would limit or contradict the spiritual path. In many *dîwâns* dealing with Qalandars, we also find various injunctions to renounce house, family, goods and any forms of domestic life. For instance, in the *Dîwân-i Awhadî Marâghah'î* (d. 1338), it is said: 'Qalandar once again, we've left behind all the cares of home / Love called us, and we took up the wayfarer's patched cloak.' In the *Dîwân-i Pîr Jamâl Ardistânî* (d. 1474), it is said: 'Wanderers and Qalandars are happy on the roads / Having no place no home, everywhere they are free.' The *Dîwân-i Amîr 'Alîshîr* (d. 1501) features the following scene: 'They saw a Qalandar considering poverty / One who has rejected his home and beings // They asked: where do you live dervish? / He answered: in my old rags' (Borûmand Sa'îd 1384/2005: 15). Following the examples of the great mystics mentioned above, Qalandars reacted against the material comfort and spiritual conformism of both common believers and institutionalized Sufis. Considering that the virtue of poverty (*faqr*) had been perverted, or at least neglected, by the latter, Qalandars brandished the *hadîth* saying: 'Poverty is my pride' (*al-faqr fakhrî*) to legitimize a conception of total poverty which refused all belongings but God (Papas 2010: 227–228, 235). As textual evidence, Muslim wanderers in India and Central Asia created their own literary genre called 'books of poverty' (*faqrnâma*) in which they describe their specific practices (shaving one's head and other hair, wearing the rags and the dervish hat, begging, etc.) and reaffirm their vow of poverty; they include, for instance, an explanation of the concept of *faqr* (the so-called stations of poverty) (Tortel 2009: 231–279).

To preserve their humble condition and to prevent themselves from returning to worldly life, Qalandars should remain itinerant. A condition of poverty, vagrancy is perceived as the second most important feature of the Qalandarî path, so much so that some Iranian scholars tend to favour, among the various etymologies of the word *qalandar*, the following hypothesis (Borûmand Sa'îd 1384/2005: 23–26): the name would come from the word *salandar* which became *kalandar* then *qalandar*. *Salandar* would mean vagabond, vagrant and wanderer, and would be composed of three Indo-European parts: prefix *sa* (out, outside) + stem *land* (land) + suffix *ar* (action) = getting out of the land. Interestingly, the word still exists in the dialects of Kermân and it is also the name of a tribe of nomads in Jîruft region (south of Iran), the Salandarîs. Thus, the etymology would attest that vagrancy is an essential part of the definition of the Qalandar. Whether this risky linguistic demonstration is accurate or not, it is clear that wandering is an ancient and founding Qalandarî practice. In fact, one of the earliest sources of the Qalandariyya, the hagiography of the famous mystic Jamâl al-Dîn Sâwî (thirteenth century), presents a discussion between Sâwî and his master, 'Uthmân Rûmî, dealing with travelling *and* wandering (Khâtib-i Fârisî 1999: 26–29, Borûmand Sa'îd 1384/2005: 19–20). We learn that, in *siyâha* and in 'the renunciation to the pleasure of stability' (*tark-i dhawq-i râhat*), dervishes obey God's command and Prophetic injunctions. Wandering should be considered the proper activity of humankind, epitomized by Abraham, Moses, Jacob, Joseph and Jesus, used by the conqueror, Alexander the Great and practised by the Prophet Muhammad himself during his *hijra*.[1] Far from the religious buildings which claim to honour God, on roads and in the humble places in this world, Qalandars seek visions and signs of the divine creation.

It is no coincidence that this apologia for vagabondage precedes Jamâl al-Dîn Sâwî's travels from Iran to Damascus. There he performed pilgrimages (*ziyâra*) on Prophets' and saints' shrines (*mazâr-i anbîyâ*, *mazâr-i awlîyâ*) and eventually met at the mausoleum of Zaynab (the daughter of Imâm Zayn al-'Âbidîn), a wanderer named Jalâl Darguzînî (Khâtib-i Fârisî 1999: 30–34, Karamustafa 2006: 40–41). This naked, silent ascetic who stayed in contemplative solitude (*khalwa*) became Jamâl al-Dîn's mentor, and initiated him to the Qalandarî path. Then, when Jamâl al-Dîn became a master himself, he attracted disciples from as far afield as Balkh who had left their homeland years before, wandering in graveyards (such as the *gûristân-i Bilâl Habashî*) or shrines, and had decided to live as Qalandars (Khâtib-i Fârisî 1999: 38–41). From the thirteenth century onwards, further generations of Sufis chose the itinerant lifestyle to endure the vicissitudes of this spiritual quest and discover the signs of God throughout the Muslim world. They described themselves: 'We are the recluses of the outskirts / Roaming the world from one end to the other', quoted by Amîr Husaynî (d. 1318); and: 'He crossed the entire surface of the globe / He saw all of its plains and mountains', quoted in the *Dîwân-i Shaykh Bahâ'î* (d. 1621) (Borûmand Sa'îd 1384/2005: 19–21). We see how wanderings are often linked to pious visits to shrines, involving a permanent pilgrimage which perceives the entire world – at least, the *dâr al-islâm* – as a network of holy places. According to the aforementioned Khwâja 'Abd Allâh Ansârî, the Qalandar performs a circumambulation (*tawâf*) around the world, begging for food and wisdom, living in 'dead places' (i.e. where people do not live) like sanctuaries, mosques, shrines and cemeteries in order to enjoy a spiritual death (Borûmand Sa'îd 1384/2005: 18). This radical concept of the pilgrimage, which echoes the conception of total poverty, extends the ritual of circumambulation around the Ka'ba, and by imitation around the holy tombs, to the scale of the globe. Another lesson we learn from Ansârî is the emphasis on death in pious life. Like other Sufis who, elaborating on the *hadîth* 'die before die', suggested annihilating oneself in *mors mystica* (Chodkiewicz 1998), wanderers acquired an intimacy with death through mortifications and contact with graves. Shrines became their living spaces.

Once more, these radical statements should not be reduced to figures of speech. Other examples throughout the mediaeval and modern periods confirm the existence of Qalandarî pilgrims who, indeed, experienced asceticism, covered considerable distances, spent time near graves and so on. Sources show, for instance, that they often travelled and lived in groups, called *jawqî qalandar*. We find this expression in, among others, an anecdote of the *Dîwân-i Shâh Da'î Shîrâzî*, a fifteenth-century text featuring a respected, lodge-established Sufi (*khânqâdâr*) who built a nice house. One afternoon, while the Sufi was having a meal, a group of Qalandars passed by and asked for charity. Among them was the famous Fakhr al-Dîn 'Irâqî (d. 1289) who presented a dramatic contrast from the established Sufi (Borûmand Sa'îd 1384/2005: 19). These groups could range from small parties (three or five people) to larger crowds; they were able to travel long distances. They could stop in towns and cities to beg and to attract people and encourage them to join their path. Although staying in towns represented a danger for the Qalandars' quest, wanderers entered cities, even huge ones, where they deliberately caught the attention of the throngs. In mediaeval India, in addition to the famous Haydarî groups wandering in the Awadh region, Simon Digby described groups of Muwallihs and Abdals in the Delhi Sultanate, on whom the hagiographical tradition mainly retained the ascetic antinomianism and violence (Rivzi 1978: 309–310, Digby 1984: 66–68, 80–81, 91–98).

Others were travelling alone, like the well-known Bektashi poet of the fourteenth century, Kaygusuz Abdal, who, after being appointed *khalîfa* by Abdal Musa, left his lodge in Elmalı (Southern Anatolia), reached Damietta in Egypt and stayed at the Qalandarî lodge named after Jamâl al-Dîn Sâwî. Then, Kaygusuz went to Hijaz, Damascus, Baghdad, Kufa, Najaf and Kerbela and finally returned to Elmalı. A second case is that of the sixteenth-century Qalandarî poet, Yetim Ali Çelebi, who decided to leave the Ottoman lands and set off for Arabia, Persia, Bukhara and Samarkand (Ocak 1999: 166–167). Interestingly, during the same period, another Turkish dervish told his story to Ogier Ghiselin de Busbecq, a Flemish diplomat in Istanbul: the anonymous traveller, who 'was one of that kind of sect whose devotion consists of wandering into the most distant countries, and in worshipping God in the loftiest mountains and in the wildest deserts', could reach China (Cathay) by using caravans along the 'Silk Road' (Yule 1866: 236–238). At the gates of China, in the early eighteenth century, a Sufi Qalandar named Muhammad Siddîq Zalîlî wandered for several years from shrine to shrine in the Tarim Basin. He described his peregrinations in a versified travelogue (*safarnâma*) (partly translated and commented on in Papas 2010: 139–209). Among the numerous references we find at the turn of the nineteenth and twentieth centuries, it is worth mentioning the account of a Polish explorer in the 1880s who noticed that numerous Qalandars lived in graveyards in the south oases of East Turkestan (Grabczewski 1885: 200, 212–213), while other explorers observed the presence of Qalandar *dîwânas* visiting various shrines in the same region (Stein 1907: 267, 412–413). As for nineteenth-century India, a fascinating case is Gulshâh's life, briefly recounted in Zayn al-'Âbidîn Shîrwânî's *Bustân al-siyâha*.[2] He was a Madârî Qalandar, wearing just a lungi and consuming *bang* and hashish, who travelled barefoot for thirty years in the Deccan, Sindh, Kashmir and Kabul (Afshârî & Mîr 'Âbidînî 1374/1995: 62). With regard to the present time, I would also mention the existence of isolated *majdhûbs* who roam the holy places of Cairo and the Delta, or Qalandar-like *ashiks* in Xinjiang who go from shrine to shrine at the time of religious festivals and receive alms for their prayers and songs.[3] In Haryana, India, Bû 'Alî Shâh Qalandar's *dargâh* at Panipat still contains a series of rooms for wandering fakirs (Srivastava 2009: 139). Lastly, in the early stages of their initiation, Pakistani and Afghan *malangs* must travel from one shrine to another, acting the command of God or their master (Ewing 1984: 359, Frembgen 2008: 97–98, 106). These are examples of peripatetic pilgrims who, unlike the large majority of pious visitors, strived to follow the Qalandarî path embodied in the practice of total poverty and perpetual pilgrimage. If we look more closely at the religious topography of Qalandars' itineraries, we find specific places which differ from shrines but remain linked to them.

Unholy places for wandering pilgrims

It is well known that the wandering pilgrimage of Qalandars is often described as *darbidar*, a 'door to door' journey, which literally means that dervishes go to shrines but also houses, bazaars and other places in order to beg or procure food, and that they figuratively attain thresholds between this world and the beyond. Besides shrines, Qalandarî wayfarers use various places which, according to texts, cover both literal and metaphoric meanings. As opposed to mausoleums, these sites are intentionally called by profane, irreligious and even blasphemous names.

A very frequent word of this kind is *kharâbât*, meaning 'ruins, wreckage' but also 'tavern, brothel'; 'slum' could also be an appropriate translation. It is sometimes associated with the word *maykhâna*, that is 'wine-cellar, tavern'. *Kharâbât* is used metaphorically (*majâzî*) in Sufi poetry, suggesting that the unlawful circles and places the Qalandar moves into are actually sites of devotion, even sacred places where mystical intoxication can be enjoyed. Many verses illustrate this point (Borûmand Sa'îd 1384/2005: 349–351, Frembgen 1998: 184–185). The *Dîwân-i Awhad al-Dîn Kirmânî* (d. 1238) talks of Qalandarî groups in these terms: 'They were the drunkards, the Qalandars, the lovers / They were the drunks, the idolaters, the fornicators // They were the regulars of the depths of brothels / They were the treacherous of the frocks.' The *Dîwân-i 'Abd al-'Alîshâh Kâshânî* (d. 1302) calls out: 'Hey you, the Qalandarî lout of the slum bazaars / You, the friend of taverns, the friend of slums // Promise me that we will sign a pact // To confide the two world affairs to the slum chief.' Lastly, the aforementioned *Mathnawî-yi Amîr Husaynî* relates: 'One night, I was sitting in this tavern / I was attending the Qalandars' drinking bout // In my palm, the bartender gave me your glass // So that my soul fell into your trap.' In all these distiches, the lexis of drunkenness and depravity should be interpreted in mystical terms. However, the metaphor does not mean that these places did not exist and that Qalandars did not use them. In fact, *kharâbât* were favourite destinations for wandering pilgrims seeking sex, alcohol and drugs, and yet they could also be used as inns on the pilgrimage routes. In his *Dîwân-i Asrârî*, a narrative lying between reality and imagination, Sîbak Fattâhî Nishâpûrî (fifteenth century) details the wanderings of a mystical drug addict who arrived in a city, visited the *mazâr* and its great mausoleum, and met Qalandars with whom he shared narcotics and enjoyed a party at the tavern (Kadkanî 1386/2007: 428–429). In the recent past, in Iran, bands of Khâksâr dervishes used to smoke their opium and hashish in houses which were specifically named *kharâbât* (Gramlich 1965: 76). This last word could also be interpreted as marginal spaces in religious topography, which is to say, in the wilderness of the margins and isolated places, in the mediaeval sense of Junayd's desert, as well as in the modern practice of, for example Qalandar *majdhûbs* like the Pakistani Mama Ji Sarkar (d. 1991). Sarkar lived for long periods 'in the wilderness surrounding the village', wandering 'around in the forests and hills of the Margalla mountains near Nurpur before settling in Rawalpindi' (Frembgen 1998: 142, 145).

If *kharâbât* remain poorly documented, *langars* are relatively well known to historians and ethnographers. Although the term itself is not impious, it is clearly profane and may provoke distrust, if not disgust. Originally meaning anchor, *langar* corresponds to a halt; a road station devoted to commensality, where religious vagabonds can rest and eat, but also share news and information and transmit oral messages, like those sent by masters to their disciples. We know, for example in fourteenth-century Iran, the codified *inshâ'* used by Shaykh Shihâb al-Dîn Qalandar and the reply sent by Mawlânâ Jalâl al-Dîn b. Husâm Harawî (Borûmand Sa'îd 1384/2005: 353–360). *Langars* can be attached to shrines, and they are open kitchens which distribute free meals to pilgrims. As early as the thirteenth century, in Konya, the *Manâqib al-'Ârifîn* (Aflâkî 1362/1983: 596) recalls that 'the day of the death of Jalâl al-Dîn Rûmî, seven bulls have been brought to the funerals. One of them has been sent to the *langar-i qalandarân* at the disposal of the gnostic, Abû Bakr Jawlaqî Nîksârî, to be sacrificed. The master ordered the sacrifice of the beast immediately in order to distribute the meat among the needy and the poor'. In Damietta, at the same time, the *langar* under the direction of Jamâl al-Dîn Sâwî and Pîr Balkhî was full of Qalandars and was used for seclusion (*khalwa*) as well as companionship (*suhba*) (Khâtib-i Fârisî 1999: 77–78). Various mediaeval sources, such as Hamîd Qalandar's *Khayr al-majâlis* and geographical records, give the names of free kitchens and their owners (*langardârân*) in India and Iran (Qalandar 2010: 141–142, Kadkanî 1386/2007: 199, 260–262). What strikes the historian is the persistent bad reputation of these inns throughout the fourteenth and fifteenth centuries. While Amîr Husaynî's *Qalandarnâma* describes a crowded *langar* in Khurasan used by Sufis and tramps, others claim that these places are run by depraved owners and packed with hashish smokers and wine drinkers. They even serve as dens for agitators, like the 300 Qalandars of Zangî 'Ajam who rebelled against the governor of Kerman region (Borûmand Sa'îd 1384/2005: 356). Worse, perhaps, than moral debauchery and political subversion, some *langars* are accused of heresy. Jâmî cites the case of Qâsim Trabîzî and his followers in Kharjard in Khurasan (Jâmî 1370/1991: 590–591). To refer to a contemporary case again, it is noteworthy that India and Pakistan seem to be the last regions where *langars* still exist. They consist of charitable kitchens attached to Sufi shrines or communities which distribute food to the poor, including groups of *bî shar'* fakirs (Werbner 1998, Gaborieau 2005: 546–548).

A last and no less ambivalent place of predilection for Qalandars which is heavily used on pilgrimage is the lodge called *qalandarkhâna, qalandar sarâ* or *takîya* (*-yi qalandarân*). Deprived of a home, Qalandars partly live in collective houses, where no family is admitted. They can be located in the vicinity of shrines or near them, like the Takîya Sharîf of Kâzimî Qalandars in Kakori, Uttar Pradesh today.[4] Historically, they seem to be ancient institutions, financed by religious leaders and followers, or alternatively by sultans or hakims. Along with the case of Jamâl al-Dîn Sawî's lodge in Cairo, the *zâwîya* of Shaykh Ibrâhîm al-Qalandarî in Jerusalem, near Mâmilâ cemetery is attested for the fourteenth century. A *qalandarkhâna* also existed at that time in Baghdad, close to the Tigris River. This last place had the infamous reputation of being a nest of alcoholics (Karamustafa 2006: 53–54, Kadkanî 1386/2007: 92, 272–273, 284–286). In Western Iran, under the Jalâyirids (1340–1411), the dervishes of the convent of Shihâb al-Dîn Qalandar were exempted from all obligations to the government for a plot of land in their possession (Inalcik 2006: 121–122). Later, in 1657–8, Shâh 'Abbâs II built a *takîya* for unruly Sufis in Isfahan (Borûmand Sa'îd 1384/2005: 361–364, 369–371). Despite this official support, *qalandarkhânas* were usually viewed with doubt and suspicion by the local population and visitors. An interesting testimony comes from the German naturalist Engelbert Kämpfer who crossed Persia in 1684–5. Visiting various *takîyas*, he described, quite negatively, the modest houses which were situated in out-of-the-way places, in city alleys where lazy beggars and ragged dervishes lived, benefiting from the low rent, and smoking their water pipes all day long (Kimpfir 1360/1981: 136–137). Earlier, in 1646, the French missionary Eugène Roger despised the Qalandars he met in the streets of Jerusalem, calling them 'fools, idiots, blind from birth'. Their bad reputation did not prevent the spread of *qalandarkhânas* along the routes of the hajj pilgrimage into the nineteenth century. They were found in Istanbul, Bursa, Damascus, Jerusalem and Cairo. For instance, in 1849, the Zâwîya al-hunûd in Jerusalem, run by a certain Shaykh, 'Abd Allâh Efendî, was named the 'Indian house for Qalandars' (*Hindî qalandarkhâna*). Another Indian *kalenderhane* existed in Bursa. In Istanbul (Eyüp neighbourhood), in the late nineteenth and early twentieth centuries, the dervish, Hafiz Mehmed Emin Efendi stayed at an Uzbek *kalenderhane*.[5] (Zarcone 2009: 24, 26, 33, 35, 101). In Central Asian cities like Bukhara, Samarkand and Tashkent, *qalandarkhânas* were highly organized and housed corporations of religious beggars (Olufsen 1911: 396–397, Papas 2010: 273–282).

Kharâbât, *langars* and lodges play a crucial role in the Qalandarî pilgrimage, not only as convenient places for the roving lifestyle, but also as paradoxical sites of spiritual initiation. Not reducible to simple, provocative metaphors hiding highly abstract concepts of love and transcendence, they could correspond to real practices of depravity and to an underclass, if not underworld, sociability. For the Qalandariyya, the path to sanctity and its shrines, which is the aim of Sufi pilgrimage, would pass by the crime, as if sacredness would stand in the depths of the profane, as if the divine himself would lie in the mire of the world. As much as the holy graves, these dens of iniquity were the landmarks of the Qalandarî pilgrimage roads. This does not mean, of course, that all the customers of gloomy brothels, dirty canteens and miserable inns were dervish pilgrims seeking revelation. I only suggest that, among them, there were some vagrant mystics. Whether they succeeded or not is a question that scholars have not been able to answer.

Conclusion

The lesson Qalandars taught to other pilgrims, as well as their observers, is more interesting than the issue of spiritual achievement. As we have seen from the beginning, wandering differs from travelling, and the wanderers' pilgrimage differs from the others' pilgrimage. While the former is perpetual, worldwide and paradoxical, even antithetic, the latter is temporary, circumscribed and consistent, perhaps synthetic (in the sense that both hajj and *ziyâra* are limited to holy places and presuppose moral conduct and purity of acts). Considering that the absolute end of pilgrimage does not justify any relative means, Qalandars reject conventional forms of Muslim pilgrimages and advocate radicalism in piety. The peregrinations of the vagabond challenge or question, rather than necessarily reverse, the usual categories of spiritual journeys – pure and impure, pious and impious, sacred and profane. Wanderers deliberately provoke the other pilgrims and announce that what they believe to be their most religious act is just not enough, that what they experience around the Ka'ba or at Sufi mausoleums is merely a play, a performance.

This announcement may find an echo among the anthropologists of Muslim pilgrimage, especially those who, often creative and inspiring for their colleagues dealing with other Muslim areas, work in South Asia and are influenced by Victor Turner's paradigm (Turner 1974: 166–230). Analysing pilgrimages, including the hajj, the British scholar highlighted a radical process in which social actors experienced an alternative reality to the structural routine and constraints of everyday life, a reality defined as liminality and *communitas*. While the first concept designates a transitory period between a given social structure and another order of things or relations, the second, which moves in liminality, names a sentiment of undifferentiated, equalitarian and existential relationships. Pilgrimage is this suspended time during which social actors leave the common stage to approach, through the sacred, their own absoluteness as creatures. This process involves a simplification of all community structures, a kind of flattening of hierarchies and inequalities – an anti-structure. As a result, Muslim pilgrimages, that is to say hajj and – South Asianists would add – pious visits to shrines, represent the anti-structural counterpoint to Muslim societies in that they present the opportunity to subvert the traditional mundane order and to create new communities living up to the Creator's expectations. The question implicitly raised by the Qalandarî case is whether this anti-structure really occurs in 'common' pilgrimage, whether, in other words, the experience of non-Qalandarî pilgrims would not be a comedy, a social convention. If it is restricted in time and space, if it is dedicated to institutionalized and conventional holy places, if other liminal *communitas* are possible outside the sacred journey, if it is not conducted according to the Qalandarî principles, then pilgrimage itself would fail, and the anti-structure would be just an illusion among many others. The effective pilgrimage, anti-structural and liberating, does not seem to occur very frequently.

Notes

1 In another source written in 1668–9 (quoted in Afshârî & Mîr 'Âbidînî 1374/1995: 112), *siyâha* is considered the second of the seven qualities of the dervish – along with patience (*sabr*), exile (*ghurbat*), etc. – and originates from the Prophet Khidr, while patience comes from Ayyûb, exile from Yahya and so on.
2 Shîrwânî (1779–1837) was a great Sufi traveller (belonging to the Ni'matullâhiyya, not a Qalandar) who spent several years in Afghanistan, India and the Middle East, where he met numerous shaykhs.
3 See figures 2.1 and 2. 2.
4 See figure 2.3.
5 See figure 2.4.

References

Abû, Nu'aym (1979) *Hilyat al-Awliyâ'wa Tabaqât al-Asfiyâ'*, vol. 10, Beirut: Dâr al-Kutub al-'Ilmiyya.
Aflâkî (1362/1983) *Manâqib al-'ârifîn*, ed. T. Yazıcı, vol. 2, Tehran: Dunyâ-yi Kitâb.
Afshârî, M., Mîr 'Âbidînî, A.T. (1374/1995) *Âyîn-i qalandarî: mushtamil bar chahâr risâla dar bâb-i qalandarî, khâksârî, firqa-yi 'ajam wa sukhanwarî*, Tehran: Farârawân.

'Attâr (1905) *Tadhkirat al-Awliyâ'*, ed. R.A. Nicholson, London and Leiden: Luzac and E.J. Brill.

'Attâr (2009) *Memorial of God's Friends. Lives and Sayings of Sufis*, transl. P. Losensky, Paulist Press: New York.

Bistâmî (1989) *Les dits de Bistami (shatahât)*, transl. A. Meddeb, Paris: Fayard.

Borûmand, Sa'îd (1384/2005) *Âyîn-i Qalandarân*, Kerman: Dânishgâh-i Shahîd Bâhunar.

Chodkiewicz, M. (1998) 'Les quatre morts du soufi', *Revue de l'histoire des religions*, 215 (1): 35–57.

Digby, S. (1984) 'Qalandars and Related Groups: Elements of Social Deviance in the Religious Life of the Delhi Sultanate of the Thirteenth and Fourteenth Centuries', in Y. Friedmann (ed.) *Islam in Asia*, vol. 1, pp. 60–108, Jerusalem: The Hebrew University.

Ewing, K. (1984) 'Malangs of the Punjab: Intoxication or Adab as the Path of God?' in B. Metcalf (ed.) *Moral Conduct and Authority. The Place of Adab in South Asian Islam*, pp. 357–371, Berkeley: University of California Press.

Frembgen, J.W. (1998) 'The *majzub* Mama Ji Sarkar: a friend of God moves from one house to another', in P. Werbner and H. Basu (eds) *Embodying Charisma. Modernity, Locality and the Performance of Emotion in Sufi Cults*, pp. 140–159, London: Routledge.

Frembgen, J.W. (2008) *Journey to God. Sufis and Dervishes in Islam*, transl. J. Ripken, Karachi: Oxford University Press.

Gaborieau, M. (2005) 'Un sanctuaire soufi en Inde: le *dargâh* de Nizamuddin à Delhi', *Revue de l'histoire des religions*, 4: 529–555.

Grabczewski, B. (1885) *Kaszgarja. Kraj i ludzie. Podróż do Azji środkowej*, Warsaw: Nakład Gebethnera i Wolffa.

Gramlich, R. (1965) *Die Schiitischen Derwischorden Persiens. I. Die Affiliationen*, Wiesbaden: Franz Steiner.

Al-Hujwîrî (1911) The Kashf al-Mahjûb. The Oldest Persian Treatise on Sufism, transl. R.A. Nicholson, Leiden-London: Brill-Luzac & Co.

Inalcik, H. (2006) 'Autonomous enclaves in Islamic states', in J. Pfeiffer and Sh.A. Quinn (eds) *History and Historiography of Post-Mongol Central Asia and the Middle East*, pp. 112–134, Wiesbaden: Otto Harrassowitz.

Jâmî (1370/1991) *Nafahât al-Uns min Hazarât al-Quds*, ed. M. 'Âbidî, Tehran: Intishârât-i Ittilâ'ât.

Junayd (1983) *Enseignement spirituel. Traités, lettres, oraisons et sentences*, transl. R. Deladrière, Paris: Sindbad.

Kadkanî, M.R.Sh. (1386/2007) *Qalandariyya dar Târîkh. Digardîsîhâ-yi yik îdi'ûlûjî*, Tehran: Sukhan.

Karamustafa, A. (2006) *God's Unruly Friends. Dervish Groups in the Islamic Middle Periods, 1200–1550*, Oxford: Oneworld.

Khatîb-i Fârisî (1999) *Manâkib-i Camâl al-Dîn Sâvî*, ed. T. Yazıcı, Istanbul: Türk Tarih Kurumu.

Kimpfir, E. (1360/1981) *Safarnâma-yi Kimpfir*, transl. Kaykawûs Jahândârî, Tehran: Shirkat-i Sihami-yi Intishârât-i Khwârazmî.

Massignon, L. (1975) *La Passion de Hallâj, martyr mystique de l'Islam*, 4 vols, Paris: Gallimard.

Ocak, A.Y. (1999) *Osmanlı İmparatorluğunda Marjinal Sufîlîk: Kalenderîler (XIV-XVII. Yüzyıllar)*, Istanbul: Türk Tarih Kurumu.

Olufsen, O. (1911) *The Emir of Bokhara and his Country*, London: William Heinemann.

Papas, A. (2010) *Mystiques et vagabonds en islam. Portraits de trois soufis qalandars*, Paris: Cerf.

Qalandar, M.H. (2010) *Khair-ul-Majalis (Malfoozat Hazrat Shaikh Naseer-ud-din Mahmood, Chiragh-i-Delhi)*, transl. I.H. Ansari & H.A. Siddiqi, Delhi: Idarah-i Adabiyat-i Delli.

Rivzi, S.A.A. (1978) *A History of Sufism in India*, vol. 1, New Delhi: Munshiram Manoharlal.

Schimmel, A. (1994) *Das Thema des Weges und der Reise im Islam*, Opladen: Westdeutscher Verlag.

Srivastava, K. (2009) *The Wandering Sufis. Qalandars and Their Path*, Bhopal: Indira Gandhi Rashtriya Manav Sangrahalaya.

Stein, M.A. (1907) *Ruins of Desert Cathay. Personal Narrative of Explorations in Central Asia and Westernmost China*, vol. 2, London: McMillan & Co.

Tortel, Ch. (2009) *L'Ascète et le bouffon. Qalandars, vrais et faux renonçants en islam*, Paris: Actes Sud.

Touati, H. (2000) *Islam et voyage au Moyen-Âge. Histoire et anthropologie d'une pratique*, Paris: Seuil.

Turner, V. (1974) *Dramas, Fields, and Metaphors. Symbolic Action in Human Society*, Ithaca: Cornell University Press.

Werbner, P. (1998) '*Langar*. Pilgrimage, sacred exchange and perpetual sacrifice in a Sufi saint's lodge', in P. Werbner and H. Basu (ed.), *Embodying Charisma. Modernity, Locality and the Performance of Emotion in Sufi Cults*, pp. 95–116, London: Routledge.

Yule, H. (1866) *Cathay and the Way Thither. Being a Collection of Medieval Notices of China*, vol. 1, London: Hakluyt Society.

Zarcone, Th. (2009) *Sufi Pilgrims from Central Asia and India in Jerusalem*, Kyoto: Center for Islamic Area Studies at Kyoto University.

Figure 2.1 An *ashik* at Imami Asim shrine in Xinjiang, 2006 (Lisa Ross and Alexandre Papas Archives)

Figure 2.2 A *majdhûb* at 'Abd Allâh b. Abî Jamrah shrine in Cairo, 2010 (Nathalie Clayer and Alexandre Papas Archives)

Figure 2.3 Qalandariyya Kâzimiyya shrine and lodge at Kakori, Uttar Pradesh, 2009 (Alexandre Papas Archives)

Figure 2.4 A former *qalandarkhâna/kalenderhane* in Istanbul, 2009 (Alexandre Papas Archives)

3 Qalandars and Ahl-e Haqq

Mojan Membrado

The term Qalandar has a large spectrum of meanings: from a wandering pilgrim, a mendicant and an ascetic, to an organized group of dervishes. As the Qalandarî tradition was inherently opposed to norms of any kind, its essential effects are best seen in other, more structured traditions that existed in the geographic area with which Qalandars had rich interactions.

The Ahl-e Haqq order, also known as Yârsân, is originally a Kurdish mystical tradition with multiple divisions which have their own specificity and identity. Because of the considerable range of doctrinal and practical diversity that is a natural outgrowth of their historical evolution and geographical dispersion, neither the Ahl-e Haqq communities nor the Qalandars can have their beliefs and practices fully represented by a single representative model. We can, however, see the essential beliefs and practices of the Qalandars reflected in the way the Ahl-e Haqq authors use the term Qalandar and Qalandarism in their writings.

The first part of this chapter presents several of the defining qualities of Qalandarism as a way of life, such as celibacy and detachment from the material world. It compares the approach of Ahl-e Haqq and Qalandars in regard to these features. Through excerpts from Ahl-e Haqq texts, we see, for example how some Ahl-e Haqq authors passionately advocate detachment from material concerns, an essential feature of the Qalandarî tradition, as well. The second part of this chapter presents Qalandarism as an organized tradition with some of the orders that grew out of it, including the *Khâksâri* order, demonstrating close relationships to a branch of the Ahl-e Haqq. Section one of the second part begins by discussing the historical changes leading to the emergence of the Qalandarî tradition and then identifies certain Sufi branches that emerged from it. One of the most prominent of these is the Iranian *Khâksârs*, in which some of its more spiritually advanced members became affiliated with a branch of Ahl-e Haqq. Section two focuses on the links which might be found between *Khâksâriyyeh* and the Ahl-e Haqq order, especially in regard to their rites and angelology.

The main primary and secondary sources for information on the Qalandarî tradition can be divided into two groups: those published in Iran, such as Mir'abedini & Afshari, *Â'yin-e Qalandarî* (1374/1995) Tehran; Moddaresi Chahardehi, *Khâksâr va Ahl-e Haqq* (1358/1979) Tehran; Monajjemi, *Mabâni-ye solûk dar selseleh Khâksâr Jalâli va tasavvof* (1379/2000) Tehran; Shafi'i Kadkani, *Qalandarî yyeh dar Târikh* (1386/2007) Tehran; Zarrinkoub, *Jostejoo dar Tasavvof-e Iran* (Vol. 1) (1357/1978) Tehran; and those published in academic publications in the West, such as R. Gramlich, *Die Schiitischen Derwischorden Persiens* (1965) Wiesbaden; the *Khâksâri* texts published by V. Ivanov in *The Truth-worshippers of Kurdistan* (1953) Brill; or G. Böwering's study on *Khâksâr* rituals in *Les voies d'Allah* (1996) Fayard.

The main source chosen to describe the Ahl-e Haqq tradition is the works of a twentieth-century Ahl-e Haqq master, Hâjj Ne'matollâh Jeyhûnâbâdi (d. 1920), who, in his writings, provides clear interpretations of the primary sacred sources of the Ahl-e Haqq tradition known as *kalâm*. He also gives detailed inside information on the Ahl-e Haqq rituals and teachings, while giving a clear picture of their inner universe and conflicts within the order. Since the tradition has largely been passed down orally, his mystical epic, *Haqq al-Haqâyeq* or *Shâhnâmeh Haqiqat*, written in Persian verse, was chosen because it is the first published written work presenting Ahl-e Haqq sacred history and beliefs from within. We will draw on one of his unpublished works, *Forqân al-Akhbâr*, as well for greater clarification of the relationship between the Ahl-e Haqq and certain Sufi brotherhoods. These sources help us to identify and understand the way that links between these groups are perceived by their members.

Qalandarism as a way of life

Etymology and historical overview of the term Qalandar

The term *Qalandar* has different meanings in different places and periods. Among its various etymologies, we find the word *salandar*, which has become *kalandar*, then *qalandar*. It means 'one who has no fixed abode' (*âvâreh, bi-khânemân*). According to Yazici (1978: 493–5), this term appears for the first time in a robâ'i of Baba Taher 'Oryan (eleventh century) and in a short treatise entitled *Kalandar-name* by the famous 'Abd Allâh Ansârî (d. 481/1088–9). It is derived from the Persian *Kalantar* or *Kalandar*, a name given to members of a class of dervishes that existed in the Muslim world, mainly in the thirteenth century. They differed from other Muslims due to their adherence to the doctrine of *Malâmatiyyeh*[1] and their non-conformist behaviour and lifestyle. According to Shafi'i Kadkani (2007: 37–49), two possibilities exist for the origin of the term Qalandar, and both express the idea that it was a location rather than a person.

The term Qalandar can refer to either a mystic detached from the world or an organized group. The organized group known as Qalandariyyeh existed in Iran in the thirteenth century (Karamustafa 2006: 56). Their presence has been recorded in the southwest Iranian town of Shahr-e Zur, the homeland of the Ahl-e Haqq, situated halfway between Mowsul and Hamadân, before the end of the thirteenth century (Karamustafa 2006: 57). Bâbâ Tâher (eleventh century), who according to

Ahl-e Haqq narratives is one of their masters, calls himself a Qalandar in a poem attributed to him:[2]

> I am a *rend* (cunning) whose name is Qalandar
> I have no home, no family, no anchor
> When day comes I turn around the world and when comes night, I put my head down on a brick

In his study on the life of some Qalandars found in hagiographical and historical sources, Papas (2010: 41, 58, 117) clearly pinpoints predominant features like vagrancy, material detachment and the challenging of norms which could best define the Qalandarî lifestyle.

The term Qalandar, the figure and its features in the Ahl-e Haqq sources

Alongside the informative primary and secondary Qalandarî sources generally used, it is beneficial to know how the Ahl-e Haqq authors refer to the term Qalandar and what the main features of a Qalandar are as reflected in the Ahl-e Haqq texts and oral tradition. The term Qalandar is often used in the Ahl-e Haqq sources as a title to designate a high-ranking companion. For example among the companions of the founder of the order and among the eponyms of consecrated families (*khândân*), one comes across names like 'Âli Qalandar, Zolnour Qalandar or Shâh Mohammad Qalandar. Although the dates when these figures lived and the basic historical information about them are often unknown, like many other prominent figures of Ahl-e Haqq, the traditional account in the Ahl-e Haqq hagiographical literature is worth studying. What matters is not the objective reality of such traditional accounts, but the fact that certain Ahl-e Haqq devotees believed in them and continued to perpetuate them because they convey something important about their beliefs.

The name Qalandar was used by 'Âli Qalandar, one of the closest companions of the founder of the Ahl-e Haqq order (Jeyhûnâbâdi 1984: 163). According to the Ahl-e Haqq accounts, the essence (soul) which animated 'Âli Qalandar's body was the same as John the Baptist's in Jesus Christ's era or Hosayn's, the grandson of the Prophet Mohammad. One of the functions of this essence is for its bearer to give his life for the Beloved in each period of human history. 'Âli Qalandar lived his life in celibacy and is a martyred saint. He is the namesake of one of the original branches of the Ahl-e Haqq order, the 'Âli Qalandarî consecrated family (*khândân*).[3]

Another example of this name appearing in a high-ranking Ahl-e Haqq is Zolnour Qalandar (see Jeyhûnâbâdi 1363: 298–300), who was the talented son of Khâtun-e Asmareh, the great granddaughter of Seyyed Abolwafâ, the founder of the Abolwafâi branch of the Ahl-e Haqq.[4] Many miracles and extraordinary deeds are attributed to Zolnour. He also lived in celibacy and had no descendants. However, another branch (*khândân*) of the Ahl-e Haqq order, the Zolnouri family, has been founded in his name.[5]

A third example is Shâh Mohammad Qalandar, also known as Mohammad Beyg or Seyyed Mohammad Nûrbakhsh.[6] He was a high-ranking Ahl-e Haqq figure (*Shâh Mehmân*, partial theophany). He first appeared in the Bakhtiyari region, and then emigrated to Lurestan. Unlike 'Âli Qalandar and Zolnour Qalandar who lived in celibacy, Mohammad Beyg had four sons. One of them, Âtash Bag, became his spiritual heir and the founder of the famous Âtash bagi branch of the Ahl-e Haqq.[7]

From the above examples, we can conclude that in the Ahl-e Haqq context, the term Qalandar was sometimes used as a title to designate certain high-ranking Ahl-e Haqq figures who manifest a high essence. It does not necessarily imply features like celibacy or vagrancy; some Ahl-e Haqq who are also Qalandars, like Mohammad Qalandar, have not been single or have not travelled. The principal feature among the Ahl-e Haqq Qalandars is detachment from the world.

The following excerpts written by an Ahl-e Haqq master accurately describe the Qalandarî attitude regarding the material world. This world is ephemeral in contrast to the other world which is eternal; focusing on the ephemeral is against Wisdom:

> O friend, know God for the world is ephemeral with no survival, it flows like a flood. Then good deeds and acts remain like a rock whereas the ephemeral is swept away like a thorn with the flood. Friends, gain weight like a rock by good deeds so that the flood cannot wash you away.
>
> (*Forqân al-Akhbâr*: A 23, B 19)

> Friends, listen to the advice of this least [the author] for he has no desire to be among the group of the worshippers of the ephemeral. Take refuge in God, God loves his creatures. [. . .] O believers, do not be attracted by the ephemeral world.
>
> (*Forqân al-Akhbâr*: A 28, B 25–26)

Detachment from the world that went beyond apparent material actions and what others might think of them was strongly encouraged by enlightened Ahl-e Haqq and Qalandar masters alike. The following section is an excerpt of Hâjj Ne'matollâh Jeyhûnâbâdi's poem in *The Book of the Kings of Truth* (Jeyhûnâbâdi 1363: 372–375), on the true nature of material concerns and the world.

Infidelity of the world[8]

I have reason to complain of this world that turns
Of the noise and the clamour that rises as it churns
Of its counter movements that deceive
And the shifting fluctuations we perceive
What can I say about this world, so crooked and bent
At times it appears lovely, at times beyond contempt [. . .]

No one here has seen the least stability
This world grants nothing but infidelity
Now it's the spring, now it's the fall
So it's always been, for one and all
Though the world constantly changes its hue
Shades of pain is all that it yields for you
Many have journeyed down this trodden lane
They lie beneath the earth, having lived in vain
And you, my heart, do not allow this world to catch you unaware
For it knows full well how to entrap you in its snare [. . .]
In the end, all that remains is a person's name
The memory of his beneficence or his ill fame
The benevolence of the good remains with them eternally
The malevolence of the bad will accompany them perpetually
O heart, devote yourself to beneficence with all your might
For it will deliver you here and in your eternal plight
Such goodness will endure in the people's memory
And in the other world bring you joy and prosperity

Traditionally, high spiritual ranks were usually achieved by those who could lead an ascetic life, those who had the strength to limit their needs for food, sleep and carnal instincts. In order to not leave their self-control in the hands of their basic nature, these persons subdued their natural instincts. Celibacy was one means of self-mortification. Moreover, celibacy was a way to reduce the attraction of the world because the commitment to family and making the efforts necessary to provide them with a comfortable and secure life could take such a dominant place in a man's life that he might even commit illegal acts to increase material gain for his family.

> Friends, pay attention to what you do, for in this ephemeral material world all efforts you make to gain something for your family in an unlawful manner are of no avail. [. . .] Get out of your heart the attachment to this world and to the descendants and children: be a lover of God. Plant [the seeds of] good deeds, for this is the way for salvation.
>
> (*Forqân al-Akhbâr*: A 30, B 28–29)

For the love of his family, the human being constantly wishes to extend his material position. In order to be responsive to the needs and the comfort of his family, one might sometimes have to resort to unlawful means to have sufficient income. This danger of being drawn into unlawful acts out of love for the family led writers to describe the love of family as a scourge or chains.

> The one who is wise spends everything he earns in the way of God. Happy is the person who in this world does not enter into material affairs and does not found a family. God be witness, spouse and children are all a scourge

> that causes damage to religion and faith. It is for the sake of the family that one commits unlawful and forbidden business. Straining a lot in the world is futile. Whatever excesses one commits struggling to raise his children in comfort is useless. On the day of the accounting none of them is there to help him. 'He has lost this world and hereafter' [Koran 22:11]. Except by the good deeds, there is no salvation [. . .].
>
> (*Forqân al-Akhbâr*: AB 34–35)

Celibacy therefore becomes important, not only to control one's carnal instincts, but also to prevent worldly greed. Despite this, celibacy was not the highest virtue for the Ahl-e Haqq as it was for the Qalandar; for the Ahle-e Haqq celibacy itself could become a kind of effort that the ego could take root in. They had to keep their eyes on their goal, which was to recognize the theophany and to follow him. According to the Ahl-e Haqq vision of the world, human history is composed of several cycles. In each cycle, God manifests himself in a human form to guide mankind. The Divine Essence can manifest Himself in any form He wishes; that is to say, God can choose to manifest in any man. But in general, He chooses to appear in the descendants of a pious and spiritually awakened man. For this reason, some Ahl-e Haqq ascetic masters who initially chose a life of self-mortification and celibacy, returned to live with their family in the hope of one day having a child who would be a theophany or the vessel of one of the essences in their angelology. We saw this in the cases of several Ahl-e Haqq Qalandars mentioned earlier.

Hâjj Ne'matollâh Jeyhûnâbâdi was one of these Ahl-e Haqq masters who turned away from celibacy after initially adopting it. He describes how he experienced a sudden spiritual awakening (*tajalli*; see Corbin 1972: 345) in 1900, following a near-fatal illness around the age of twenty-nine. The event drastically changed his attitude toward material preoccupations. He withdrew from all worldly affairs and led a life of ascetic austerity in seclusion in a small retreat (*riâzat-khâneh*) in the Kurdish village of Jeyhûnâbâd. In a year, twelve followers secretly gathered around him (Elahi 1981: 554, 556). During the second year of his retreat (1902), he decided to don the white habit of dervishes and no longer cut his hair and beard. Barefoot and in a state of fasting and asceticism, he undertook a voyage to the shrine of Soltân Eshâq (Sahâk, the founder of the Ahl-e Haqq order, see Minorsky 1987: 546). Then he stopped meeting with others and engaged in a complete retreat that lasted for two years. Subsequently, he emerged from his retreat to live with his family. In the following excerpt, he explains why he returned to his family.

> When I first became spiritually conscious I decided to leave two things
> In order to become detached from this world:
> Leaving my wife
> and isolating myself from any material concern
> Suddenly, in a dream,

the Spiritual King told me:
'Leave these immature thoughts Ne'matollâh,
withdraw this temptation
If you want to be happy in this world and in the hereafter
you should work hard during this life
Do not divorce your wife,
do not leave this world,
because God is with you in every situation
According to the Ahl-e Haqq tradition
the Demiurge King
Continues to appear in the human body throughout time
Wherever a seeker of the Truth could be found
He appears in the Truth seeker's family
making of him an accomplished father
Do keep your family as the family is a curtain over the mystery
The King of the Truth chooses to become the guest of a good family
So go now and build a home for the Truth
Gain the other world by making offerings and vows
Be busy night and day with praying,
Be lover of the Master as the moth
So that the King of the Truth appears in a human body in your home
You will then be illuminated by the divine light
and honoured in the both worlds'
When I heard this news from the Truth in my dream,
I applied all in awakening
I put into practice the order of the Truth,
I obeyed Him with praise and peace
So then the living essence of the Truth
appeared to me in the spiritual world as a sun
My heart became illuminated with the light of the Beloved,
I was intoxicated by the Eternal Friend as the moth.

(Jeyhûnâbâdi 1363: 396–397)

As we can see through the excerpts above, despite this divergence of lifestyle over whether to be celibate and have a family or not, the most common feature among all Ahl-e Haqq Qalandars was detachment from the world for the purpose of achieving their higher goal. What was important wasn't whether one was celibate or not, but how one used one's material life to achieve a spiritual goal.

Qalandarism as an organized tradition

Qalandarism could also be regarded as a collective and organized tradition. Despite their disorganized and decentralized appearance, the Qalandars formed a military mobile and underground order (Borumand Sa'id 2005: *passim*). They initiated those they considered fit to their cause. Animated by egalitarian aspirations, they fought injustice. They had their own secret language and signs. Even though these characteristics are affirmed by this author, it must be mentioned that they are not supported with references. However, there is no doubt that from a historical perspective, (Yazici: *op. cit.*), Qalandariyyeh was the name given to a movement whose origins can be traced to the period after the onset of *Malamatiyyeh*, in the ninth century. According to Karamustafa (2006: 55), the Qalandariyyeh order was formed in the thirteenth century, and it was strongly influenced by Buddhism.

One difference between Qalandars and *malâmatis* is their tendency to secrecy. In contrast to the *malâmatis*, Qalandars do not dissimulate their faith (*taqiyyeh, ketmân*); they prefer to provoke rejection in those around them to ensure that they are not bound by social custom. On this point, Qalandars diverge with Ahl-e Haqq followers, for whom being discreet about their faith has been a leitmotif for centuries.[9]

Qalandars as a group have been connected with other traditions. They probably influenced the popular religious movements, as van Bruinessen describes:

> Tendencies towards organization and settlement became apparent among the Qalandar from as early as the thirteenth century on in Asia Minor and Egypt as well as in India. They probably influenced and were gradually absorbed into the popular religious movements whose heirs we find among the Bektashis, the Alevis and the Ahl-e Haqq.
>
> (van Bruinessen 1991: 67)

We will first discuss the historical changes leading to the emergence of the Qalandarî tradition. Some Sufi branches claim to be of Qalandarî tradition, such as the Iranian *Khâksârs*. In this section, we will point out the links which might be found between Iranian Qalandars, e.g. *Khâksâri* dervishes and the Ahl-e Haqq order.

From Qalandars to Khâksârs

In *Nafahât al-Uns*, Jâmi, a Persian poet of the fifteenth century and one of the last great Sufi poets, considers Qalandariyyeh a branch of *Malâmatiyyeh* (Mir'abedini & Afshari 1374, 1995). However, Sohrawardi (1145–1234) sees a difference between Qalandars and *malâmatis* regarding concealment of their faith.

> The term *Qalandarî* [. . .] covers in its historical usage a wide range of dervish types. It was unknown in western Islam and loosely applied in the East to any wandering *faqir*, but it was also adopted by certain groups and even distinctive orders were formed, hence the problems of defining the term. To begin with the time of the formation of silsilas, Shihâb ad-din as-Suhrawardi writes: The term *qaladariyya* is applied to people so possessed by the intoxication of 'tranquility of heart' that they respect no custom or usage and reject the regular observances of society and mutual relationship. Traversing the arenas of 'tranquility of heart' they concern themselves little with ritual prayer and fasting except such as are obligatory (*farâ'id*). Neither do they concern

> themselves with those earthly pleasures which are allowed by the indulgence of divine law . . . the difference between the *Qalandarî* and the *malâmati* is that the *malâmati* strives to conceal his mode of life whilst the *Qalandarî* seeks to destroy accepted custom.
>
> (*Awârif*, pp. 56–7 translated and quoted in Trimingham 1998: 267)

Mir'abidini and Afshari (1374, 1995) conclude that there were two types of Qalandars. One group could be considered closer to the *malâmati*[10] tradition, the only difference being that the *malâmati* would hide their devotion, whereas the Qalandarî would externalize and even exploit it, going out of their way to incur blame. The second type of Qalandars was considered 'out of religion' by Sufis; historically, the majority of Iranian Qalandars were in this second group.

The organized Qalandars have been divided into several groups, some of which have still survive today. Mir'abedini and Afshari (1374, 1995) name several groups like *Jawâliqiyyeh, Heydariyyeh, Madâriyyeh, Naqshbandi Qalandars, Bektâshiyyeh, Noqtaviyyeh* and *Jalâliyyeh*. Here, we will study more closely the case of the *Jalâliyyeh* which is considered to be the origin of Iranian Qalandarism (Zarrinkoub 1357: 73). *Jalâliyyeh* was a group of Shi'ite Qalandars, disciples of Seyyed Jalâl Bokhârâi (1192–1291).[11] Seyyed Jalâl Bokhârâi was affiliated to the Indian *Sohravardiyyeh*. His grandson, Seyyed Jalâl ed-Din Hosayn (also known as *Makhdoom Jahâniyân*, 1308–84, Uchh), propagated Qalandarism among the disciples of his grandfather (Mir'abedini & Afshari: 1374, 1995). The centre of Indian *Jalâliyyeh* was the city of Uchh, near the tomb of Seyyed Jalâl Bokhârâii. *Jalâliyyeh* Qalandars, like *Jowlaqqiyyeh*, practised the '*châhâr zarb*'[12]: they shaved their heads and facial hair. They were wandering dervishes and beggars; they gave what they earned from begging to their spiritual master (*pîr*). *Jalâli* dervishes were the surviving Qalandars; they stood against the established religious practices and their actions aimed to demolish routine and habits (see Zarrinkoub 1357: 375 and his references). According to Zarrinkoub (1357: 373), Qalandariyyeh dervishes, known in the Indian Territory as *Jalâliyyeh* and *Jalâli* dervishes, were apparently the origin of the Iranian *Khâksâriyyeh* order.

The *Khâksâriyyeh* is composed of four sections (*silsila*):

1 *Jalâli (Abu Torâbi, Gholâm-'Ali Shâhi)*
2 *'Ajam*
3 *Ma'sum 'Ali Shâhi*
4 *Nûrâii*

As stated by Modarresi Chahardehi (1358: 3), in Iran today, only the *Jalâli Khâksârs* have an organization, and the other groups form minorities. The *Jalâli Khâksârs* – known as wanderer *Jalâli* dervishes during the *Qâjâr* era (1796–1925) – stem from Gholâm 'Ali Shâh Jalâli's path, also known as Gholâm 'Ali Shâh Hendi (Indian). There is no precise data on Gholâm 'Ali Shâh Hendi being the originator of the wanderer *Jalâli* dervishes and the *Khâksâri* order.[13] According to Zarrinkoub (1357: 376), Gholâm 'Ali Shâh would have been a *Jalâli* master of the early

Qajar era or the late *Zand* period (eighteenth century). It seems that he played a considerable role in the process of change which occurred among Indian *Jalâlis*, giving it a Shi'ite angle. Influenced by *Heydaris* and *Ahl-e Haqq*, the Iranian *Jalâlis* no longer follow the old Qalandarî tradition of Seyyed Jalâl. Apparently, this is the reason why *Khâksâris* attribute their origin to Seyyed Jalâl ed-Din Heydar, who is not a historical figure but a mysterious code name composed of these two well-known names: Seyyed Jalâl ed-Din Hosayn (Jalâl Sâni 1308–84) and his predecessor, Seyyed Qotb ed-Din Heydar 'Alavi (fourteenth century).[14] These two characters were both linked to Uchh, where Seyyed Jalâl's convent was located. This combined name for a fictional character reported by *Khâksâris* was intended to prove that their path had Shi'ite origins (Zarrinkoub 1357: 376).

Khâksâris have no literature of significance, and *Khâksâri* disciples were generally from the lower or illiterate social classes (Zarrinkoub 1357: 378). Contrary to other Sufi paths, *Khâksâris* are considered by the majority of their opponents as *bi-shar'*, or disrespectful of legal religious laws and without a registered Sufi genealogy (*silsila*).

II.2- Khâksâr and Ahl-e Haqq

In his study on the variants of the same myths and ideas in the Ahl-e Haqq, *Alevi* and some Indian traditions, van Bruinessen concludes:

> Religious lore of this kind, as well as various yogi-like practices such as walking on fire, were probably carried to the west by Qalandar-type vagrant dervishes. Especially during the thirteenth – fifteenth centuries, large numbers of these half-naked, mendicant dervishes, repositories of antinomian mysticism and popular religious and magical lore, roamed about the entire Islamic world, from India to the Maghrib. Their role in the formation of the Ahl-i Haqq, the Bektashi order and the various Alevi sects can hardly be overestimated. Although their numbers rapidly declined after 1500, they are still frequently mentioned as late as the seventeenth century, and they may have formed one of the major channels of communication between the various sects mentioned.
> (van Bruinessen 1995: 122)

The community commonly known as 'People of the Truth', *Ahl-e Haqq* is one of the most widely spread religious communities in Iran, both geographically and statistically. It is an esoteric order on the boundary of exoteric rationalistic Islam, and traces of pre-Islamic beliefs are found in their angelology and cosmogonic myths. This order is well established in Southern Kurdistan, but can also be found in other parts of Iran, Iraq, Caucasus, Turkey and Azerbaijan. Some research also mentions India, Pakistan and Afghanistan. No aspect of the Ahl-e Haqq community, including their beliefs and practices, can be presented in a single way as there are many sub-groups within this community with various and often contradictory beliefs and practices. This inherent variety creates a conflicting perception of the Ahl-e Haqq amongst outsiders and even within the Ahl-e Haqq followers themselves.

Ahl-e Haqq communities are divided into eleven branches. At the top of each branch, a family has the function of initiating the members (their lineages are called *seyyeds, pîrs*). By the time of Soltân Sahâk, founder of the order (thirteenth to fifteenth century), seven of these initiator consecrated families (*khândâns*) are considered to have been established, and the latest families are thought to have been formed sometime between the seventeenth and eighteenth centuries.

The Ahl-e Haqq communities have a non-pyramidal hierarchical structure. There are at least eleven sources of power and decision-making centres. This is the reason why the schism which occurred during the seventeenth and eighteenth centuries did not create a great problem, as it might well have done in the case of a pyramidal structure. In fact, the only outcome of this schism was that the number of *khândâns* increased, and the structure remained fundamentally unchanged. However, a non-pyramidal structure may have the disadvantage of creating gradual separation and independent development of its branches. The institution of initiation (*Sar-sepordan*) which creates not only a vertical loyalty but also a horizontal link between *khândâns* helps to prevent this problem. A vertical loyalty is present between the *khândâns* and their followers, and a horizontal loyalty is established between the *khândâns* initiated by one another. In this way, the roles and positions of the various families are recognized by others, and as a result, these branches are tied to one another (Hamzeh'ee 1990: 205–218).

In some cases, the horizontal loyalty links go beyond the boundaries of the Ahl-e Haqq order and tie other orders to this structure. This is the case of the *Khâksâri* order, related by horizontal loyalty links to the Ahl-e Haqq.[15] As previously mentioned, the *Khâksâri* order is divided into four branches. Modarresi Chahardehi (1358: 12, 106) affirms that all the *Khâksâr* branches (*Nûrâi, Ma'sûm, 'Ali Shâhi* and *Jalâli Khâksârs*) send their advanced disciples to be initiated by an Ahl-e Haqq *seyyed* from the *Ayâzi* family. The *Ayâzi* family quoted by Chahardehi is in fact the *Shâh Hayâsi* family, one of the last Ahl-e Haqq *khândâns*. *Khâksâri* dervishes consider Shâh Hayâs, the founder of this *khândân*, to be identical in essence[16] with Seyyed Jalâl the founder of their own order (Soltani 1381, 2002). When a *Khâksâri* dervish reaches the stage of guidance (*maqâm-e ershâd*)[17], he offers nutmeg, sugar, money and other offerings to a *Shâh Hayâsi* Ahl-e Haqq *seyyed* in the presence of his *Khâksâri* masters. This means that the advanced *Khâksâri* dervish observes the ritual of initiation (*sar sepordan*)[18] and becomes affiliated to the Ahl-e Haqq order at the instigation of his *Khâksâri* guides.

Beyond the loyalty links, and more generally, Zarrinkoub (1357: 377) states that the relationship between *Khâksâriyyeh* and the Ahl-e Haqq order is obvious. Regarding the cult of secrecy, *Khâksâris*, like Ahl-e Haqq, consider their beliefs a secret to be concealed from outsiders. They use similar technical expressions; for example the word *seyyed* is typically used to designate the lineage of the Prophet, however, in the Ahl-e Haqq context it designates the members of one of the Ahl-e Haqq families (*khândân*). In the excerpt below, the text of an *ijâzeh* (license) attributed to a *Khâksâri* master, we see how the technical sense of the word *seyyed*, as it is used by the Ahl-e Haqq, has influenced the *Khâksâri* literature to some extent.

> 'Can a *Khâksâri* be initiated by any *seyyed*?'
>
> According to the *fatwa* [legal opinion issued by a religious authority] of twelve[19] *Ahl-e Haqq* consecrated families (*khândân*), he cannot. The only person authorized to initiate him is an *Ahl-e Haqq seyyed*, meaning a descendant of one of the twelve *Ahl-e Haqq* families (*khândân*).
>
> (see Modarresi Chahardehi 1358: 47)

Khâksâris and Ahl-e Haqqs share a variety of similar habits and traditions. Generally, all Ahl-e Haqq men are traditionally obliged to wear 'sealed' (*mohr*) mustaches throughout their entire life. A 'sealed' mustache has never been cut, shaven or trimmed, especially on the upper lip area (*shâreb*); *Khâksâris*, like Ahl-e Haqqs, have 'sealed' (*mohr*) mustaches. The prohibition of marriage between a *pîr* and a follower is another common tradition in both orders. As a *pîr* is supposed to act like a father towards the lay members who have been initiated by his family, the Ahl-e Haqq *pîrs* are not allowed to marry the daughters of their disciples. Similarly, in different branches of *Khâksâriyyeh*, dervishes are not traditionally permitted to marry the daughter of their spiritual master nor his wife (after his death). Even though in practice, some infractions can be observed, these laws and opinions exist in both traditions.

Regarding the similar rites, among the *Khâksâri* ceremonies is the rite of the *qâpi* (Gate; see Monajjemi 1379: 1139–141) which symbolizes the passage of a dervish from one stage to the next. It is performed, for the first time, when a disciple is initiated into the *Khâksâri* order. Each *qâpi* belongs to a spiritual king (*Soltân*) and his four disciples.

> The first *qâpi* is the symbol of the stage of Knowledge (*Ma'refat*), the king of this *qâpi* is Shâh Khoshin and his four disciples are Hendûleh, Pirmard, Khodâdâd and Ahmad.
>
> The second *qâpi* represents the stage of Law (*Shari'at*), the king of this stage is Khâvandgâr which is another name for 'Ali. His four disciples are the forth, sixth, seventh and eighth Shi'ite imams.
>
> The third *qâpi* is the Path (*Tariqat*). Its king is Shâh Fazl Qalandar, and his disciples are Nassim, Tork (the son of Nassim), Mansûri and Mir Malang-e Zanjir Pâ ('Ali's name in this stage is Yahyâ Qalandar).
>
> The forth *qâpi* is the stage of Verity or Truth (*Haqiqat*). The king of this stage is Soltân Eshâq (the founder of the Ahl-e Haqq order) and his four disciples are Pîr Benyâmin, Dâwûd, Razbâr and Pîr Mûsi.
>
> (Modarresi Chahardehi: 114–115)

In Ahl-e Haqq traditions, the order of the stages is somehow different: Law (*Shari'at*), Path (*Tariqat*), Knowing (*Ma'refat*) and Truth (*Haqiqat*) (see Elahi 1354: 7–8). Nevertheless, all the kings named above and the majority of their disciples are well known figures in Ahl-e Haqq traditions as well. According to the Ahl-e Haqq texts, Khâvandegâr is the name of the deity in the pre-eternity era and Shâh Fazl is a partial theophany, anterior to Shâh Khoshin. In the excerpt above, the disciples of Shâh Khoshin were: Hendouleh, Khodâdâd, Pîr-e mard and Ahmad. Ahl-e Haqq texts make mention of Hendouleh and Khodâdâd, as well as other names such as Mâmâ Jalâleh, the mother of Shâh Khoshin, Bâbâ Faqih and others (Jeyhûnâbâdi 1363: 163; Elahi 1354: 32). Shâh Fazl's companions in the Ahl-e Haqq tradition are Nassimi, Zakariâ, Tork-e Sar Bor and Mansur-e Hallâj (Jeyhûnâbâdi 1363: 149; Elahi 1354: 30); the only name which differs from the excerpt above is Mir Malang-e Zanjir Pâ, substituted by Zakariâ in the Ahl-e Haqq texts. In the fourth *Khâksâri* stage (*qâpi* of *Haqiqat*), we notice the name of Soltân Eshâq (Sahâk), the founder of the Ahl-e Haqq order, and his four closest companions, called 'four *pîrs*' by the Ahl-e Haqq devotees. Through the comparison of the Ahl-e Haqq and *Khâksâri* traditions[20], we can deduce that the names of the *Khâksâri* saints, having reached the stage of Verity (*Haqiqat*), are almost the same as in the Ahl-e Haqq angelology.

Even though the basic historical information about these figures is often unknown, they nonetheless play an important role in the hagiographical literature of the Ahl-e Haqq and the *Khâksâr* orders. As we know, what matters is not the objective reality of such accounts, but the fact that certain devotees believe in them and continue to perpetuate them. Through the study of the Ahl-e Haqq literary production, we can conclude that the *Khâksâri* order is considered in the Ahl-e Haqq sources as a Shi'ite esoteric path (*tariqat*) and the link relating it to the Ahl-e Haqq is believed to be ancient. According to *Forqân al-Akhbâr* (p. A50), the three paths of Shi'ism are: the *Khâksâri* path which belongs to Soltân Mahmûd Pâteli and then to Seyyed Jalâl ed-Din Heydar; the '*Ajami* path which belongs to Habib 'Ajami known as Chehel gysoo;[21] and then the *Komeyli* and Sufi paths. The *Shâh Ne'matollâhi* order originates from the Sufi (*Naqshbandi*) path, then it has undergone Shi'ite influences and it also carries links to the Ahl-e Haqq order. The holy Ahl-e Haqq figures in Shâh Fazl's period[22] were either illustrious Sufis or *Khâksâr* dervishes who were initiated to the Ahl-e Haqq order in Shah Fazl's era (Jeyhûnâbâdi 1363: 149–148).

From the *Khâksâriyyeh* point of view, the Ahl-e Haqq order belongs to the stage of Verity (*Haqiqat*) which is the highest stage of religion (Modarresi Chahardehi: 144). They consider those who have not entered the *Khâksâri* order to be 'people of Law (S*hari'at*)', *Khâksâri* dervishes 'people of the Path (*Tariqat*)', those initiated by an Ahl-e Haqq master 'people of the Truth (*Haqiqat*)' and, when they attain knowledge of divine secrets, 'people of the Knowledge (*Ma'refat*)'.

The few examples above highlight the relationship and similarities between *Khâksâriyyeh* and the Ahl-e Haqq order pertaining to certain rites, habits, practices, expressions and angelological accounts. Additional examples can be provided for each point in a more detailed work. The Ahl-e Haqq studies thus far have mainly focused on the origins of the Ahl-e Haqq and reminiscence of the ancient religions in their beliefs. It is therefore also worth noting such concrete connections and similarities. Qalandarism was a strong element in the religious substratum from India to the Middle East. Its predominant features – vagrancy, material detachment and challenging of norms – have influenced certain inner attitudes towards spirituality over time. As a way of life, the essence of Qalandarism has survived in some ascetic circles of the Ahl-e Haqq order, principally through the aspect of material detachment. In the contemporary Iranian sphere, the *Khâksâriyyeh*, an organized tradition that stems from Qalandarism, is connected to a branch of the Ahl-e Haqq. The close relations between the Ahl-e Haqq and *Khâksâr* have encouraged a reciprocal influence testified by some common rites and angelological accounts. The relations were further strengthened by clear horizontal loyalty links between two organized structures. Given the historical evolution of the *Khâksâriyyeh* and its Indian background, it becomes easier to understand how certain Qalandarî-type literature and practices found their way into the Ahl-e Haqq traditions.

Notes

1 *Malâmâtiyyeh* is a name given to people who deliberately conceal their spiritual condition under an unpleasant guise. This is the principle of the path of blame, known as *talbis*, literally 'travesty' or the act of 'hiding the truth and manifesting it other than it is', see Amir-Moezzi (1995: 167–180).

2 مو آن رندم که نامم بی قلندر / نه خان دیرم نه مان دیرم نه لنگر / چو روج آیو بگردم گرد گیتی / چو شو آیو به خشتی وانهم سر

3 The 'Âli Qalandarî branch is the second *khândân* in the Ahl-e Haqq order, see Elahi (1354: 72).

4 The Abolwafâi branch (known also as the Khâmûshi branch) is the fourth *khândân* in the Ahl-e Haqq order, see Elahi (1354: 68, 72).

5 The Zolnouri branch is the eighth *khândân* in the Ahl-e Haqq order, see Elahi (1354: 72).

6 According to N.A. Elahi (1354:70), this Seyyed Mohammad Nûrbaksh is not the same as the historically renowned Seyyed Mohammad Nûrbaksh, see Trimingham (1998: 57).

7 The Âtash bagi branch is the ninth *khândân* of the Ahl-e Haqq order, see Elahi (1354: 72).

8 Translation from Persian into French by Leili Anvar; translation from French into English by Martin Hoffman. For the complete version see http://hadjnemat.com/works_extracts_en.php.

9 For more details on the importance of secrecy and the reasons for it in the Ahl-e Haqq order, see Mokri (1962: 384–385).

10 On the relationship between *Malâmatiyyeh* and Qalandarî yyeh, see Mir'abedini & Afshari (1374, 1995): on the relationship between *Malâmatiyyeh*, Sufism and *futuwwa*, see Zarrinkoub (1357: 335–357); on the relationship between Qalandars and *Khâksârs*, see Zarrinkoub (1357: 359–379). On the relation between Qalandars and '*ayyârs*, see Zarrinkoub (1357: 360); Mir'abedini & Afshari (1374, 1995); Borumand Sa'id (1384: 205). '*Ayyâr* is a Persian word which means *yâr*, friend. The cult of '*âyyars* (*â'in-e 'ayyâri*), according to certain authors, was an Iranian cult, deriving from the ancient cult *â'in-e Mehr*, see Natel Khanlari (1348, 1969).

11 See Trimingham (1998: Appendix; Suhrawardi Silsila p. 270).

12 The so-called 'four shaves' designates the shaving of head hair, eyebrows, moustache and beard which runs against the normative Islamic tradition. For a study on the 'four shaves', see Afshari 2005; on the significance of hair in the Islamic sacred sources and

in the general Sufi perspective, with a special focus on the Qalandars, see Ridgeon (2012: 233–264).

13 According to Modarresi Chahardehi (1358: 88), Karim Khan Zand (1705–1779, the ruler of Iran from 1749 until 1779) had a boy named Gholam ʻAli who was one of the masters of the *Khâksâr* order. His path was called Gholam ʻAli Shahi. He lived in Shiraz and his tomb is in a place near Kermanshah called Mand'ali.

14 According to Zarrinkoub (1357: 373), Qotb ed-Din Heydar Alavi is the person who met with Ibn Batuta (1304–1369) in Uchh in the tomb of Seyyed Jalâl ed-Din Bokhari and who gave him a *khirqa*. *Khirqa* literally means 'rag', a dervish's garment, which is a symbol of his vows of obedience to the rule of his order. This term is also used as an equivalent to *silsila* or *tariqa* (Trimingham 1998: 306).

15 Another example could be found in Edmonds (1969: 92) who mentions a loyalty link between the Ahl-e Haqq *pîrs* and the *Naqshbandi* Sufis of the Hawrâmân region. According to Nikitine (2002: 426) some branches of the *Ne'matollâhi* order are also linked to the Ahl-e Haqq.

16 On the doctrine of transmigration of the soul, see During 2005.

17 On the requirements of this stage, see Monajjemi (1379: 156).

18 For details on the ritual of initiation, see Elahi (1354: 60–64; 132–137); Hamzeh'ee (1990: 199–204).

19 On the number of the Ahl-e Haqq *khândâns* and the different lists from 1850 to our times, see M. Membrado, 'Consecrated families' in C. Mayeur-Jaouen & A. Papas (eds) *Family Portraits with Saints*, Klaus Schwarz Verlag, Berlin, 2014, pp. 238–235.

20 The names of the holy figures that were, according to *Khâksâri* tradition, in the stage of the Path (*tariqat*) are extracted from Modarresi Chahardehi (1358: 45). The names at the stage of Verity (*Haqiqat*) are from Elahi (1360: 670) and Jeyhûnâbâdi (1363: *passim*).

21 *Chehel gysoo* (forty tresses) is a name given in the '*Ajami* order to a person who attains the stage of guidance (*maqâm-e ershad*), see Modarresi Chahardehi (1358: 185).

22 According to the Ahl-e Haqq sources, Shâh Fazl-e Vali appears at the end of the third/ninth century, probably in India, see Elahi (1354: 30).

References

Afshari, M. (2005) 'Châr zarb (chahâr zarb)', in *Dâyerat al-Ma'âref-e Eslâmi*, vol. 11 (http://www.encyclopaediaislamica.com/madkhal2.php?sid=5357) (accessed 14 August 2012).

Amir-Moezzi, M.A. (1995) 'Scandale et liberté dans la spiritualité musulmane', in C. Baron and C. Doroszczuk (eds) *La sincérité – l'insolence du cœur*, Revue Autrement, Collection Morales, 18: 167–180.

Borûmand Saʻid, J. (1384/2005) *Â'in-e Qalandarân*, Kermân: Dâneshgâh-e Shahid Bâhonar.

Böwering, G. (1996) 'Règles et rituels soufis', in A. Popovic and G. Veinstein (eds) *Les Voies d'Allah. Les ordres mystiques dans le monde musulman des origines à aujourd'hui*, pp. 139–156, Paris: Fayard.

Corbin, H. (1972) *En Islam iranien: aspects spirituels et philosophiques. Les fidèles d'amour, shiʿisme et soufisme*, vol. 3, Paris: Gallimard.

During, J. (2005) 'Notes sur l'angélologie Ahl-e Haqq', in G. Veinstein (ed.) *Syncrétisme et hérésies dans l'Orient seljoukide et ottoman: XIV-XVIII Siècle*, pp. 129–153, Leiden: Peeters.

Edmonds, C.J. (1969) 'The Beliefs and Practices of the Ahl-i-Haqq of Iraq', *Iran. Journal of the British Institute of Persian Studies*, 7: 89–101.

Elahi, N.A. (1354/1975) *Borhân al-Haqq* (Third ed.) Tehran: Tahuri.
——— (1360/1981) *Âthâr al-Haqq* (Second ed.) vol. 1, Tehran: Tahuri.
Gramlich, R. (1965) *Die Schiitischen Derwischorden Persiens*, Wiesbaden: Steiner.
Ivanov, V. (1953) *The Truth-worshippers of Kurdistan; Ahl-i haqq texts edited in the original Persian and analysed by W. Ivanow*, Leiden: Brill.
Jeyhûnâbâdi, H.N. (1909) *Forqân al-Akhbâr*, unpublished manuscript.
——— (1363/1984) *Haqq al-Haqâyeq; Shâhnâmeh Haqiqat*, Tehran: Hoseyni.
Karamustafa, A. (2006) *God's Unruly Friends*, Oxford: Oneworld Publications.
Massignon, L. (1963) 'La "futuwwa" ou "pacte d'honneur" artisanal entre les travailleurs musulmans au Moyen Age', in *Opera Minora*, vol. 1, pp. 396–421, Beirut: Dâr al-Ma'âref.
Membrado, M. (2014) 'Ahl-i Haqq consecrated families (*khândân*)', in C. Mayeur-Jaouen and A. Papas (eds) *Family Portrait with Saints. Hagiography, Sanctity and Family in the Muslim World*, Berlin: Klaus Schwarz-Ehess.
Minorsky, V. (1987) 'Soltân Ishâq', in *First Encyclopaedia of Islam 1913–1936*, vol. 4, p. 546, Leiden: E.J. Brill.
Mir'abedini, A. and Afshari, M. (1374/1995) *Â'yin-e Qalandari*, Tehran: FarâRavân.
Modarresi Chahardehi, N. (1358/1979) *Khâksâr va Ahl-e Haqq*, Tehran: Eshrâqi.
Mokri, M. (1962) 'Le "secret indicible" et la "pierre noire" en Perse dans la tradition des Kurdes et des Lurs Fidèles de Vérité (Ahl-i Haqq)', *Journal Asiatique*, CCL (3): 369–433.
Monajjemi, H. (1379/2000) *Mabâni-ye Solûk dar Selseleh Khâksâr Jalâli va Tasavvof*, Tehran: Tâbân.
Natel Khanlari, P. (1348/1969) 'Â'in-e 'ayyâri', in *Majjaleh Sokhan*, 18: 19–26 19: 113–122.
Nikitine, B. (2002) 'Tâwûsiyya', in *Encyclopédie de l'Islam*, 2nd ed., vol. 10, p. 426, Leiden: Brill.
Papas, A. (2010) *Mystiques et vagabonds en islam*, Paris: Cerf.
Ridgeon, L. (2012) 'Shaggy or shaved? The Symbolism of Hair among Persian Qalandar Sufis', *Iran and the Caucasus*, 14: 233–264.
Shafi'i Kadkani, M.R. (1386/2007) *Qalandariyyeh dar Târikh*, Tehran: Sokhan.
Soltani, M.A. (1381/2002) *Târikh-e Khândân-hâ-ye Haqiqat*, Tehran: Sohâ.
Trimingham, S. (1998) *The Sufi Orders in Islam*, Oxford: Oxford University Press.
Van Bruinessen, M. (1991) 'Haji Bektash, Sultan Sahak, Shah Mina Sahib, and various avatars of a running wall', *Turcica*, 21–22: 55–69.
——— (1995) 'When Haji Bektash still bore the name of Sultan Sahak. Notes on the Ahl-i Haqq of the Guran district', in A. Popovic and G. Veinstein (eds) *Bektachiyya: études sur l'ordre mystique des Bektachis et les groupes relevant de Hadji Bektach*, pp. 117–138, Istanbul: Isis.
Yazici, T. (1978) 'Kalandar', in *Encyclopédie de l'Islam*, 2nd ed., vol. 4, p. 493, Leiden: Brill.
——— (1978) 'Kalandariyya', in *Encyclopédie de l'Islam*, 2nd ed., vol. 4, pp. 493–495, Leiden: Brill.
Zarrinkoub, 'A. (1357/1973) *Jostejoo dar Tasavvof-e Iran*, vol. 1, Tehran: Amir Kabir.

4 Women [un-]like women

The question of spiritual authority among female fakirs of Sehwan Sharīf[1]

Omar Kasmani

On a typically hot evening in July 2010 at the *dargāh* (*lit.* shrine) of La'l Shahbāz Qalandar in Sehwan, I came across a woman in her fifties dressed in black, her hands dyed with henna, and her fingers embellished with colourful rings. She referred to herself as '*ammā malangī new-Karachi wālī*' (*lit.* the ascetic mother from New Karachi). Chewing *pān* (betel-nut leaf), she said to me, 'I have been given so much that there is no one left between myself and the Qalandar. I do not believe in any fakirs and *malangs*, neither have I approached any,' then emphasizing her distinctiveness and pointing towards the tomb of the saint she added, 'after him, it is just me!' While she had stationed herself at the shrine of Abdullah Shah Ghazi in Karachi, she was a regular visitor at the shrine in Sehwan. More remarkable, and pertinent to this discussion, was her claim that she has received *fakīrī* through blood, i.e. her paternal uncle (*tāyā)* transmitted his *fakīrī* to her. This was already an unusual statement to make, as research suggests that most fakirs strive to become fakirs and do not inherit their charismatic roles as do sayyid hereditary *pīr*s of Sehwan; also, because women are traditionally excluded from lines and systems of patrilineal transmission or Sufi masters. When I inquired about her uncle's unusual decision to hand over *fakīrī* to her instead of a male member of the family, as would be the custom, her nephew interrupted our conversation. Then addressing me, he asked, 'Who delivered the last sermon after all?' Before I could even answer, he quickly repeated the question, adding, 'and whose sermon was it?' As he paused for what sounded like dramatic effect, I wondered if he had meant to speak of Muhammad and his last sermon. This was not the case. Referring to events in the aftermath of the Battle of Karbala (680 A.D.), he declared, 'It was Hussayn's sermon and *bībī* Zaynab delivered it'. More importantly, though, by evoking the example of Hussayn's sister, Zaynab, he had put to rest, in his mind and that of the listener, any suspicion regarding the validity of a woman's representative position. It is such negotiated and inventive employing of gender vis-à-vis the question of spiritual authorization amongst women fakirs at the *dargāh* of Sehwan that constitutes the central theme of this chapter.

Female spiritual masters, as Pechilis (2012) has argued, must innovate with what is available to them given their exclusion from the dominant tradition. Therefore, a prominent and also distinguishing trait of female masters 'is personal experience both in the sense of independent spiritual realization outside of initiation in a lineage (many female gurus are self-initiated), as well as a *pragmatic orientation* that relates experience of the world to spiritual knowledge' (2012: 114, my emphasis). In presenting the case of two women fakirs from Sehwan, I wish to illustrate how, contrary to their male counterparts' positions, such fakirs emphasize their femininity in order to validate their distinct positions as intercessors and spiritual healers. I will also reflect how, at the same time these individuals creatively dissociate themselves from a culturally circumscribed idea of womanhood thus distancing themselves not only from men but also from other women. I shall limit my discussion to a few meaningful instances where women fakirs inventively employ gender thus giving rise to a distinctly feminine imaginary of intercessory practice. However, first in order, is a brief historical review of the context in which this study is undertaken.

Sehwan: a place of confluence

Sehwan *Sharīf,*[2] as it is reverently known, is a pilgrimage town in Pakistan's Sindh province and home to the shrine of a thirteenth century antinomian mystic, Sayyid Uthmān Marwandī (d. 1274) better remembered as La'l Shahbāz Qalandar.[3] That Sindh attracted contemplative Sufis during the Middle Ages is widely known – a passage reopened with the Ghaznavid invasion around the turn of the first millennium. But Sehwan or Shivasthan (also Sivistan) as it was once known, had been a centre of Shiva pilgrimage long before the Sufis arrived in Sindh. According to Schimmel (1975), an exchange of ideas had already existed with its Hindu and mostly Buddhist population from the time of the early Arab conquests. The legendary mystic, Hallaj (d. 922) for example is believed to have travelled extensively to meet the sages of the region as early as 905. Over the next couple of hundred years, and especially with a rising threat of Mongol invading armies in lands beyond its western borders, Sindh was to host a new wave of scholars, mystics and theologians that travelled to and through its lands giving rise to a re-signification of its geography. Sufi itineraries, and points on those saintly journeys, would coincide with already existing sites of Shiva worship. It gives rise to new coordinates of charisma, adding new places of access to its sacred constellations like *dargāhs* and shrines, *khānqāhs* or Sufi lodges, sites of holy visitations and miraculous appearances. Sehwan is one such site of confluence.

Today, rising amidst Sehwan's otherwise ordinary skyline and arguably just where the ancient Shiva temple once stood, is a golden dome marking the burial place of the Qalandar.[4] Every evening, as its sun-washed glow turns dusky, the air fills with loud chants of '*mast qalandar*'; hundreds dance in trance-like motion, their bodies oriented toward the tomb of Sindh's most revered saint – his epithet, a popular reference across Pakistan, his *dargāh,* a sanctuary for the poor and distressed. Hindus, Muslims and Christians revere the saint, who some believe was a promised incarnation of a noble Hindu prince, or as legend has it, rose to the skies in the form of a falcon. Regardless, the history of the built mausoleum in Sehwan suggests that by the high period of the Mughal Empire, it may have already been a place of ritual significance. Given the paucity of sources, the history of pilgrimage to the site may not be easy to determine but it would be equally hard to override its present day appeal. Every year, in Sha'bān, the eighth month of the Muslim lunar calendar, over half a million pilgrims from across the country gather to celebrate the saint's annual fair and the ebb and flow of visitors is maintained throughout the year: pilgrims, tourists, devotees and fakirs.[5]

Its patron saint, La'l Shahbāz Qalandar commands, in popular South Asian memory, a distinct status: he is one amongst two and a half *qalandars* that make the local Sufi constellation.[6] Bū Alī Shāh Qalandar of Panipat (d. 1324) is his other male counterpart in South Asia, while Rāb'iah al-Baṣrī of Baghdad (d. 801), in lieu of being a woman, is considered just half a qalandar. With an antinomian mystic like the Qalandar at the centre of its imagination, and his historical accommodation in a continuum of Shivaite devotional heritage (Boivin 2008: 25), Sehwan remains an important point on the itineraries of the ascetically inclined and is a hotspot for those who wish to become fakirs: women and men, as well as *khadṛā* (or hijra) individuals.[7]

The case of women fakirs

The widely known status of Rāb'iah al-Baṣrī as a qalandar, albeit subordinate to her two male counterparts, stands as a significant index for women's aspirations for and access to positions of spiritual authority. Time and again, at the *dargāh* of Sehwan, I have come across women, some of whom are accomplished mediums, whereas others strive as they continue to reshape the ritual landscape, embodying the sacred as a lived reality (Basu and Werbner 1998). These are no ordinary visitors, for they do not come to make vows or seek common favours: sons, jobs or remedies to domestic problems and illnesses. Instead, they visit the shrine to establish and strengthen their contact with the mystic himself, La'l Shahbāz Qalandar – they are individuals who claim to have acquired intercessory positions and powers by virtue of their association with the saint and through the discipline of an ascetic life. More often than not, such women refer to themselves as fakirs, but occasionally they describe themselves as *pīrs*, especially in relation to their disciples (see also Callan 2008). These individuals are better referred to as *murshids* (spiritual guide, also *pīr*) for it conveys, to some extent, the function and capacities upon which such claims are made, i.e. to initiate disciples, to establish and mediate a contact between the saint and her followers, and to intercede on their behalf. Their pragmatic orientations require that such women act upon their inner calling, rely on visions and dreams as means of initiation, prefer individual propensity over genealogy, and thus make room for female practitioners alongside male heirs in Sehwan's landscape of charisma.[8] That said, women's increased access to spiritual careers, especially in the context of shrines cannot be fully appreciated without taking into account the role of nationalization of saints' places in Pakistan since the early 1960s.[9] The public administration of shrines, as has been argued, has gravely impacted the position of its traditional custodians, thus harnessing the role of sayyid groups and enabling in effect the participation of new publics, women and intersex persons in particular. Better road and rail networks have also meant that farflung shrines like Sehwan are more accessible to women than ever before. In gaining access to charismatic and power-filled sites like Sehwan, aspiring female fakirs were better placed to argue, establish and validate their spiritual careers, however, the obstacles they face are not only circumscribed in their gendered and embodied difference; fakir claims to charisma are fundamentally different to those of Sehwan's heriditary spiritual masters (Kasmani 2012).

It would not be an overstatement to suggest that the ritual landscape in Sehwan is marked by a contest of spiritual authority, especially amongst its various sayyid groups who seek disciples under the traditional system of *pīrī-murīdī*.[10] Fakirs, however, do not derive their positions from notions of descent or routinized charisma as the sayyids of Sehwan do. Instead, they 'become' *pīr*s and fakirs through a rigorous process of bodily and spiritual practices. This also means that their claims to charisma are less secure and more vulnerable than those of the sayyid groups. However, they articulate nonetheless a parallel system of spiritual exchange. In their positions as guides, they become important ritual agents around whom a collectivity of followers is organized.

To use the term fakir is not without its complexities. According to Ernst (1997: 4) it was first employed to exclusively refer to Hindu yogis and renunciants, and subsequently broadened to include Muslim ascetics informing its Mughal and later British usage in South Asia. To this day, it evokes an overestimated sense of renunciation and by extension, of death to the social world. However, the body of people who identify as fakirs today is at best a mixed bag of subjects and identities. The word fakir (from its Arabic root *faqr* or poverty) in its most common usage refers to (non-ascetic) beggars, and it is no surprise that many dress up in fakir garbs to earn a living at the *dargāh* and depend on the generosity of its visitors. But to do *fakīrī* for most of my interlocutors is to lead a life of ascetic poverty, discipline and contemplation. It accommodates the *malang* and the *majzūb*, the voluntary ascetic and the divinely attracted.[11] There are those who for one reason or another claim to have taken distance from the world, and those who continue to walk between worlds and a few who dedicate themselves to a life of itinerancy. It is a category broad enough to include holy mendicants, spiritual guides and charismatic healers: male aspirants who take a vow of celibacy and those who choose emasculation, giving up their male genitals in order to become *khaḍrā*-fakirs, women who renegotiate their familial ties and some who despite their spiritual goals continue to perform as wives and mothers. It is important to note that fakirs of this study do not fall into an established order, though there are some who adopt the *qalandarī* title as representative of their spiritual orientation to the saint of Sehwan. Unlike wandering fakirs, these individuals do not survive from the begging bowl. In fact, they ground themselves at the shrine of the saint and partake of the economy of the place as some fakirs are the sole breadwinners for their families. In return for performing rituals, blessing a thread, praying over substances, providing guidance on everyday matters and making vows on behalf of their followers, fakirs may not demand, but expect and often receive gifts and payments. And while these fakirs do not rely on notions of high descent and genealogy to validate their own claims, they nonetheless speak of their desires to transfer their *fakīrī* to a chosen offspring.

Although fakirs can be male- and female-bodied as well as *khadṛā* individuals and are found all across Sehwan residing and practising in many of its secondary shrines, fakir lodges, private homes and cemeteries, this discussion limits itself to fakirs at the *dargāh* and focuses primarily on gender as a means of spiritual authorization available to women fakirs of Sehwan. That the political and social structures are maintained and reproduced through individual acts and practices is demonstrated by an analysis of the ostensibly personal situations of two women fakirs. The aim is to highlight in the self-representations and practices of these individuals, an inventive imagination of gender. For if gender is grounded in the stylized repetition of acts through time (Butler 1990), the democratization of *pīrī-murīdī* harboured by a post-1960s public control of shrines in Pakistan, I suggest, highlights amongst its female subjects, the possibility of a different kind of repeating or a 'subversive repetition of that style' (Butler 1988: 271).

Moreover, the phenomenon of 'women as sites of divine agency' (Hollywood 2004) is significant with respect to Sehwan. Not only does it complicate the sayyid-centred model of *pīrī-murīdī*, it also supports the suggestion that spiritual authority and legitimacy can be sought beyond structures of lineage and gender, especially amongst non-sayyid female aspirants at the *dargāh*. In order to situate the practices of my interlocutors, in this case women *pīr*s and fakirs, I rely on personal accounts, life histories and especially arguments and discussions (Ewing 1997) so as to capture what is at stake in women fakirs' project of self-legitimization, as they creatively draw upon, while reshaping continuously, a culturally intelligible template of gender.

Finding amma: among men of the mosque

My first encounter with Amma was in the summer of 2009, when in the prayer space reserved for men, a woman dressed in black had reprimanded me for having dozed off in the 'presence' of the saint. Although meeting women at the *dargāh* is fairly unremarkable, Amma's everyday presence in this men's-only space was anything but ordinary. I did not think much of it though. Weeks later, during an exchange with a pilgrim, I met her again, this time in the role of a *murshid*, meaning Amma was his spiritual guide. And so began a journey through many conversations in and beyond the *dargāh*; Amma would speak of her life, her family, her spiritual distinction and her many followers both in and outside of Sehwan; I would listen eagerly. Amma – a term used for mother – is a middle-aged, Balochi-speaking woman from Jacobabad. She first came to visit the shrine about seventeen years ago and hasn't left since. She lives with her husband and three children in a rented house a few minutes' walk from the *dargāh* and spends her day sitting in a corner of the male prayer space, which also explains why most of her followers are male. *Fakīrī* is also her family's only source of income. 'He (the saint) chose me out of so many women here and gave me the guardianship of this mosque,' she told me. 'I am the first woman to have been given such a duty,' she added with an air of distinction.

Speaking of her *fakīrī*, Amma spoke of the first signs. She had started living in the verandah, a raised platform in the southern courtyard of the *dargāh* when she received her first *hāzirī* (*lit*. presence). This meant that during the evening *dhamāl*,[12] Amma would lose bodily composure and go into a trance-like state signaling the presence of a spirit given to her by the saint. This co-habiting spirit, which she refers to as *andar kā fakīr* (the fakir-within/inside) would initially communicate with her via her husband that is to say in moments when she would remain affected during *hāzirī*.[13] It was through this process, which lasted several months that a line of communication between Amma and the saint was finally established. Over time, the *hāzirīs* became less and less frequent suggesting she had learnt to master the *fakīr* within her. Such public performances of endurance and mastery in the *dargāh* courtyard can foster for the spirit-host, a spiritual reputation, an initial following and a somewhat stable means of income. Amma subsequently moved out of the *dargāh* to a rented house where her third child was born. One day, a woman walked up to her and gave her a set of black clothes, explaining how she had seen Amma in a dream in which the saint had instructed that these clothes be delivered to her. By then, Amma had come to the understanding that the saint had chosen her as his fakir. Over the course of time, through a series of similar signs, dreams and visitations, Amma was to assume the guardianship of the prayer space otherwise reserved for men.[14]

What had sparked my initial interest in Amma's story was her statement that once she passes away, her *pīrī-murīdī* would go to her children. And although the idea of transferring charisma through blood is part of the cultural template of the system of spiritual transmission of Sehwan, it was striking to notice a desire for genealogy beyond the sayyid-centred patriarchal model of spiritual authority. Amma had often reiterated this wish of hers, however, on one occasion, she had more to say: 'I will give my *fēz* (favour, grace), not to my son, but to my youngest daughter, Saira.' Not only is Saira special because she was born in Sehwan after the first signs of *fakīrī* were received, Amma had revealed to me that she had been signaled through a dream-vision in which the saint remarked, 'Your *fēz* will go to your youngest.' Expanding on this, Amma had told me, 'once I'm gone, I want people to come to my *āstānāh* (fakir dwelling). I will leave in a room, my belongings and my *fēz* and my youngest daughter, Saira.'

The first time I had brought up the issue of a woman's intercession with Amma, she had relied on the argument that she was chosen by the saint, and hence she is able to intercede between an ordinary pilgrim and the saint. Like other fakirs, she had mentioned dreams, visitations and signs that validated her spiritual achievements and her intercessory role. A year later, when I asked her the same question, she explained, to my interest, why her intercession was distinct and more effective than that of a man. She said, '*Awrat kī pīrī kā rutbā baṛā hē*' (the status of a woman's *pīrī* is great). Explaining this further, she used the word *bēchārī* (one who is helpless) to describe a woman. In other words, the subordinate status of a woman in society makes a woman helpless and unsupported. The saint, she explained to me, cannot refuse the plea of a woman fakir for he knows that in order to attain *fakīrī*, a woman, who by virtue of gender is socially vulnerable, must overcome more challenges than a man, especially with regard to family ties. Amma had in this instance turned a notion of vulnerability into a valuable trait. Relying on the same feminine power, Amma's husband brought up the concept of *niyāṇī* or little sister in Sindhi society. He told me that among Baloch and Sindhi people, the greatest conflicts can be resolved if one of the feuding parties can get a *niyāṇī* to intercede on their behalf. Hence, in his eyes, women were perfect instruments for intercession. In other words, Amma and her husband viewed her status as a woman not as hindrance but had instead employed femininity as a valuable characteristic to defend the distinct status of a female fakir.

Finding Zahida: among women of the courtyard

When I first became familiar with the women in the shrine's courtyard, a large part of my time was spent documenting personal narratives. These women often spoke of personal tragedies, illnesses, of afflictions and of possessions and evil spells, as literature on South Asian shrines has also attested (Bellamy 2011; Flueckiger 2006; Raj and Harman 2006). At the same time, my first few interactions led me to recognize another category of visitors: women, who, like Amma, were at the *dargāh* to attain, improve or maintain their spiritual ranks. These were women torn between family and the saint who often spoke of divided loyalties, of concerns of purity and menstruation, of their weak social status and the hardships of *fakīrī*, and not least, of their hard-earned spiritual ranks, which were fundamentally distinct to those of men. One such woman was forty-year old Zahida – she belonged to a Punjabi-speaking, middle-income family from Sargodha. A mother of eight, she was supported by her husband's income and had been visiting the shrine for almost seven years. A frequent visitor, she managed to spend almost half the year at the shrine. When in Sehwan, Zahida lived in the *dargāh* courtyard attracting regular exchanges with visiting women pilgrims. She also had a mentor whom she referred to as her *ustād* (*lit.* teacher, master). She had a following among women of the courtyard and had initiated disciples, almost all of whom were women she had met at the shrine, while some belonged to her native town and nearby villages.

Speaking of a special gift from the saint, she said, 'I have been given *dhamāl* like no other; it is just for me.' Referring to the aesthetics of her performance and the bodily control she is able to exercise during the daily ritual, she told me that even while she is completely absorbed in the performance, her *chādar* would never slip from her head. This ability to maintain propriety was unlike other women who in public perform the ritual bareheaded with their hair untied. On various occasions, Zahida had presented herself as being unlike the other women of the courtyard, and different from other female fakirs. However, she would not explicitly position herself against male fakirs. Defending her own choice to pursue *fakīrī*, she would sometimes use the often quoted example of Rāb'iah al-Basrī, the female mystic who is considered half a Qalandar. Months later, when I brought up the issue again, she had a more articulate response. In *fakīrī*, she explained, the path for men and women is the same. Quoting her own example she said, 'Had there been a difference, *murshid pāk* (a reference to the saint) wouldn't have made it work so far.' However, she added that just as men and women perform distinct roles in society, they do so on the path to *fakīrī* as well. The difference, she believed, comes from the manner and style with which the path is walked. For example she believed if purity is maintained, an accomplished female fakir can receive favours that no man, owing to his gender, could ever achieve. Stressing once again the importance of being a woman, and referring to the limitations of a male fakir, she hinted at the possibility of being chosen by the saint as his spiritual wife. This also explains to some measure why the saint doesn't like his female fakirs to have any conjugal ties with their husbands. Interestingly, Amma had also confirmed that in order to sustain her fakir work she has had to suspend her sexual relations with her husband for many years.

Earlier, the same evening, after *dhamāl*, I had come across Zahida while she exchanged notes with her *ustād* in the shrine courtyard. Once their consultation was over, I put the question of women's *fakīrī* to the *ustād*. He was categorical in his response, 'They are incapacitated to undertake such a thing,' he said. As I looked towards Zahida, she sat composed with just a smirk on her face. He quoted the example of Adam's expulsion from heaven and Eve's role therein. In short, despite counselling Zahida, he was of the opinion that women must not tread this path. Only after he left, had Zahida started to reflect on the exchange. Being a man, her *ustād* was incapable of understanding the operations of a woman, she argued. I was eager to discover how she interpreted the Adam and Eve story. According to Zahida, Adam was led to the forbidden fruit, not by Eve, but by God's will. The central reason for God to create the human race was His desire to be known, she explained. Hence, for Zahida, Eve not only facilitated the creation of this human society, she is the very instrument through which God's desire comes to be fulfilled.

This is not the first time that Zahida had relied on an interpretation that is distinctly her own. Not only had she validated her position vis-à-vis male fakirs, on a number of occasions she defended her unique position among women of the *dargāh* courtyard. 'People recognize me to a great extent . . . ones who have the sight, those who understand this, then if I walk two steps, they, to quite an extent, recognize me . . . that this person is walking with a purpose or is very close to Laʿl Sā'īn (the saint).' Similarly, she did not see herself as an ordinary householder woman and hence the norms of purdah, she had reminded me, that other women were bound to follow did not apply to her in the same measure. She mentioned a recurring dream as way of explaining her choice to spend extended amounts of time at the *dargāh* beyond the privacy of a home. In this dream she is repeatedly shown the *burqa'*, the customary garment that some purdah-observing women wear to cover their silhouettes in public. Although Zahida covered her head with a *chādar*, she chose not to adopt the full *burqa'*, despite the persisting dream. Later, in another dream, which as Zahida understood was connected to the previous ones, the archangel Gabriel appears but only to spit on her face. This upset her deeply and compelled her to share the dream with other women of the courtyard.

The women saw the reprimanding angel as a strict and unambiguous order to accept the *burqa'*, but cognizant of her distinct status as a fakir, Zahida wasn't convinced. After much reflection, Zahida had finally interpreted the recurring dream as progress in her fakir status; the image of the *burqa'* was in fact a sign for her to finally take distance from the public of the *dargāh* and thus an invitation to establish her own private space beyond the shrine premises.[15]

On *doing* gender differently: women fakirs of Sehwan

It may be argued that my interlocutors stress their femininity in ways that reaffirm the culturally prescribed idea of the feminine, in a manner of *doing* or reiterating gender in Butlerian terms and in this case, also to distinguish themselves from their male counterparts. However, there are instances where these women demonstrate a different kind of repetition, or perhaps a different way of *doing* gender. Time and again, Zahida has distinguished herself from *ghar kī awrat* or the householder woman. As a fakir, she is able to circumvent social and religious obligations; for example duties of a mother and wife and regulations for maintaining purdah, which she believes are necessary for ordinary householder women, thus articulating for herself a different template of *doing* gender.

Similarly, Amma distinguishes herself, not only from men as can be seen in previous instances, but like Zahida, from other women as well. She reaffirms the cultural notion that unlike men, women are impure. But referring to menstruation in her case, she had told me, 'After my third child, I sat outside the *darbār* (*lit.* saint's court), as I was *nāpāk* (*lit.* impure; unclean); I begged La'l to rid me of this monthly cycle of impurity. What kind of *fakīrī* would that be, if one had to stay away from him (the saint) for a week every month?' Also, that even though she appears to be like a woman, she isn't one in the 'real' sense. 'I am no longer like other women,' she said in our first meeting; then pointing towards me she added, 'I am just like yourself.' Intrigued, I put the question to a male fakir, who had on one occasion described women as 'impure, dirty and foul smelling'. I explained to him how, by ridding themselves of menstruation, women fakirs strived to validate their spiritual careers. After a day of thinking and contacting his spiritual sources, he reluctantly conceded that even though a woman's *fakīrī* is valid, it is greatly inferior to that of men; and that if women were able to rid themselves of this cycle of impurity, 'they would at best be like the *khadṛā*, but not like men'. In sharp contrast to this however, one of Amma's followers, in explaining his choice for a female murshid had remarked how male fakirs were no different to women, for in their vow of celibacy, they were reduced to leading passive, women-like lives. That said, it is important to consider that Amma's claim to *fakīrī* rests on what she calls *andar kā fakīr* or the fakir-within, the spirit that establishes communication between the saint and herself. According to her, the interceding fakir is always male, and although the spirit is able to make female appearances on her behalf in the dreams of pilgrims and disciples, it nonetheless complicates any assessment of female agency and intercession with regard to her capacities as a fakir. However, Amma is able to recover her weak social status in the strength of a *niyāṇī* while in the case of Zahida, the imagination of the saint as a male figure allows fakirs like her to be in positions of privilege vis-à-vis male fakirs.

In short, unlike their male counterparts, these women did not view gender as an unassailable hindrance in their desire to attain spiritual ranks. Moreover, as much as the *doing* of *fakīrī* for these individuals complicates the differences between a male and a female fakir and allows room for the subversion of gender regimes through, asceticism, service and devotion, it must not be read as an index to gender equality in an everyday sense. It is therefore important that we consider the ways in which figures of authority like Amma and Zahida are invested in the project of articulating a distinctly gendered space of *fakīrī*, which stems from their understanding of themselves as being differently bodied and differently orientated, on the one hand from men, and on the other hand from the householder woman.

Women fakirs in Sehwan *do* gender in that they reiterate a cultural template of femininity: they stress that their familial and maternal ties are a hindrance and consider their 'leaking'[16] bodies inferior to the secure bodily imaginaries of men (Longhurst 2001; Lamb 2005). Establishing that they no longer menstruate and are hence unlike other women, or the assumption that the presence of a male spirit in female-bodied fakirs complicates what it means to be a woman in the full sense re-affirms the male operative norm of *fakīrī*. Such departures from femininities do not preclude the idea that women's spiritual careers are argued and validated in its embodiment of maternal and therefore femininely nurturing characteristics so much so, femininity is employed as the distinctive character of women fakirs, as well as its validating feature. So much so, a male murshid may also be occasionally referred to as *amma* or mother by his disciples as a way to acknowledge his nurturing role. However, women fakirs' sexual and reproductive characteristics are considered both an asset and a threat and must therefore be managed. Cycles of menstruation are seen as real and physical hindrances to their engagement with saintly persons and places, and hence their unordinary presence in public spaces and interactions requires a sexual neutralization, which comes to be achieved through addressing them in familial terms.

As much as female-bodied fakirs actively adopt the post-sexual authority of mothers and espouse the gendered notion that women make for better listeners, guides and intercessors, they equally embrace and reassert their sexualities by refusing conjugal rights of their husbands in favor of belonging to the saint (Pechilis 2012; Flueckiger 2006; Ramaswamy 1996). A heterosexually imagined framework of Sufi devotion (Malamud 1996) makes it easier for women fakirs to take on subservient roles who unlike their male counterparts need not additionally feminize themselves in relation to a male saint (see also Abbas 2002).

In representing themselves in their spiritual orientations and in fakir corporeal terms, female fakirs were thus establishing a double distinction. Despite Amma's statement, 'I am like yourself,' and while hinging on a culturally defined axis of female-male difference of gendered, embodied and spatial performances, this distinction is aimed less at *I am like a man* and more at *I am not like a woman*. This paradigm, I contend, is constructed in the interactive space of a cultural vocabulary, which regards women as impure, lacking control and incapable of being on a par with men. These are notions of womanhood these women espouse and attempt to address in their *doing* of *fakīrī* – a *doing* not independent from a *becoming* in a way that renders gender performative and its boundaries negotiable. In the cases discussed, the realignment of meanings is, in my opinion, an outcome of women's inventive accommodation as well as distinction of their femininity, and in that sense, a direct response to the critique offered to their social prospects and spiritual aspirations.

Conclusion

Ethnographies of gender and religion in the context of Islam in South Asia tend to portray female religiosity within women-only spheres (Ruffle, 2011; Ahmad 2009; Ahmed, 2006; D'Souza, 2004; Hegland, 1998). Seldom do women of these accounts enjoy an influence over a male in public, and neither do they, unlike the fakirs of this chapter, take up roles of spiritual authority that are customarily reserved for men[17]. Not just that, only a handful of works that deal with Sufi topics have placed gender and sexuality at the centre of their inquiries or devoted their studies to the female and the feminine within Islamic streams of mysticism (Elias 2008; Kugle 2007; Abbas 2002; Malamud 1996; Hoffman-Ladd 1992 Shepherd 1985). That women mystics remain invisible, if not unrecorded, in historical accounts is largely a function of hagiographic transvestism (Pemberton 2010). In other words, women's spiritual feats could not be described without risking disclosures of their persons, meaning that all too often the accomplishments of Sufi women have been attributed to and predicated upon an overcoming of their feminine and therefore base natures. Their persons have been described as men in the disguise of women, or for that matter rare women, who achieve the status of a man. Even today, women fakirs in Pakistan preempt, in the eyes of the shrine public, the questionable character of their bodies and the validity of their public roles and practices. Despite this however, to explain performances of gender among women fakirs in the vocabulary of masculinization, an undoing of their femininities, or for that matter ritual transvestism would be to miss the point of women's labor of gender towards articulating a distinctly feminine space of spiritual authority and intercessory practice.

The doing and undoing of gender in the case of female fakirs, I argue, is a bodily device of accommodation; performances, which give the female fakir body a sense of self-mastery and control. Just as charisma gets embodied in ascetic practices involving the body (Werbner 2003), the gendered dimension of its 'technologies' can hardly be overemphasized, be it a case of imagining or expressing oneself in the feminine, cultivating gentle masculinities or the honing of pious selves (Shepherd 1985, Metcalf 1998, Abbas 2002, Mahmood 2005). Also because performances and identifications of gender cannot not be taken as porous, interchangeable at will and desirably fluid even when they 'involve some degree of movement (not free flowing but very scripted) between bodies, desires, transgressions and conformities' (Halberstam 1998: 147). More importantly, doing gender differently does not imply its undoing, more so because the corporeal, spatial and discursive performances of women fakirs are orientated not toward their desires to become masculine or men-like but constitute in its stead their efforts for fakir-becoming and thus women unlike other women. In other words, it is important to consider how the *doing* of gender amongst fakirs is not independent of doing *fakīrī*, or in other words, the shaping of a desired gendered and bodily disposition is geared towards its social recognition as a fakir body.

In Amma's efforts to stop menstruation, in Zahida's imagination of the gifted bodily performance of *dhamāl* and in the saint's instruction for these women to suspend their conjugal relations with their spouses, there is a gradual signification of an enduring body-in-control acquired through a routine of instructions and prescriptions, duly marked by corporeal barriers and accesses. If an inventive and strategic doing of gender is indeed a means of spiritual authorization available to women fakirs of Sehwan *Sharīf*, such validation of non-male careers of charisma must come with social recognition of embodied difference not only of that between men and women but also between women.

Notes

1 Initial data for this paper was collected in Sehwan over three research stays of different durations, including work with the French Study Group on Sindh (MIFS), adding up to eight weeks of preliminary fieldwork between July 2009 and July 2010. Subsequently long-term fieldwork was carried out lasting nine months between 2011 and 2012. The study draws on the researcher's M.A. project (Aga Khan University, 2009) as well as his doctoral project (2015) supervised at the Berlin Graduate School of Muslim Cultures and Societies and Institute of Social and Cultural Anthropology, Freie Universitaet, Berlin. I would like to thank Prof. Hansjoerg Dilger for his dedicated supervision of the project and members of the MIFS, in particular, Michel Boivin, Delphine Ortis and Remy Delage who have greatly contributed to my understanding of Sehwan through discussions in the field and in personal conversations.

2 Sehwan *Sharīf* is located 280 km north of Karachi in the administrative jurisdiction of Jamshoro district. According to the last Census Population record, it had a population of 48,000 inhabitants in 1998.

3 The saint is believed to be a direct descendant of 'Alī through Ja'far al-Sādiq. Born in Marwand, near Tabriz in present day Iran, Qalandar is known to have travelled through various parts of Sindh and north India before finally settling down in Sehwan. Some scholars refer to his Isma'īlī descent, while others describe him as an intoxicated mystic who identified with the spiritual lineage of Hallaj. According to Shivaite genealogy, the saint is believed to be Raja Bhartharī, an ascetic known to be a prototype of renunciation particularly among his Hindu followers (Boivin 2011: 19).

4 The site of the shrine corresponds to Schimmel's (1975) description of an old Shiva sanctuary on the west bank of the lower Indus. On the relation of Sufi centres and Shaivite cults, see Boivin (2008) 'Shivaite Cults and Sufi Centres: A Reappraisal of the Medieval Legacy in Sindh' in M. Boivin (ed.) *Sindh though History and Representations. French Contributions to Sindhi Studies*, Karachi: Oxford University Press, pp. 22–41. See also, Syed (1969) 'Urs je Moq'i te Pesh Kayal Khutbo', *Dum Mast Qalandar Magazine*, ed. 3, July 2012, pp. 5–6.

5 According to the last Census Record of 1998, it is estimated that 30,000 visitors arrive in Sehwan every weekend. For an account of the pilgrimage, see Frembgen (2011)

6 For more on Qalandars, see Karamustafa (1994) *God's Unruly Friends: Dervish Groups in the Islamic Later Middle Period, 1200–1550*, Salt Lake City: University of Utah Press. Also, see MIFS Newsletter no. 5 2010–1, pp. 2–4.

7 *Khadṛo* (pl. *khadṛā, khadṛan*) refers to intersex persons, emasculated individuals, as well as transvestites; also called *khusṛā, hijṛā, khwājāh-sarā* or people of the 'third sex'. For more on the subject see: Reddy (2005) *With Respect to Sex: Negotiating Hijra Identity in South Asia*, London: University of Chicago Press; Nanda (1998) *Neither Man nor Woman: The Hijras of India*, London: Wadsworth Publishing.

8 For more on the role of dreams and visions in spiritual initiation and shrine visitations, see Ewing (1990), Green (2003) and Mittermaier (2008)

9 For more on this subject, see Malik (1990) 'Waqf in Pakistan: Change in Traditional Institutions', *Die Welt des Islams*, 30 Nr. 1/4, pp. 63–97.

10 Refers to a system of spiritual guidance and intercession exercised through the relation of master and disciple. For more, see Pinto (2006) *Piri-muridi Relationship: A Study of the Nizamuddin Dargah*, New Delhi: Manohar. For more on contesting authority in Sehwan, see Boivin (2003) 'Reflections on La'l Shahbaz Qalandar and the Management of his Spiritual Authority in Sehwan Sharif', *Journal of the Pakistan Historical Society*, LI(4), pp. 41–74. For importance of the figure of the *pīr* in Sindhi society, see Ansari (1992) *Sufi Saints and State Power: The* pīrs *of Sind, 1843–1947*, Cambridge: Cambridge University Press.

11 While fakirs are individuals who adopt a life of mendicancy or ascetic poverty, *majzūb*s are those enraptured by divine madness or ecstasy, sometimes also referred to as *mastān*.

12 A kind of ecstatic ritual performance accompanied by music. Every evening in Sehwan, immediately after sunset, men and women gather in the *dargāh* courtyard to perform *dhamāl*. Men are on their feet, while most women sit and perform the ritual as their heads sway in circular trance-like motions. In the case of women, it is commonly associated with possession. It is believed that the possessing spirit makes its 'presence' manifest during the ritual, hence it is referred to as *hāzirī*. On the aesthetics of *dhamāl*, see Frembgen (2012) 'Dhamal and the Performing Body: Trance Dance in the Devotional Sufi Practice of Pakistan', *Journal of Sufi Studies*, 1(2012) 77–113 and Wolf K. (2006) The poetics of 'Sufi' practice: Drumming, dancing and complex agency at Madho Lāl Husain (and beyond), *American Ethnologist*, 33: 246–268.

13 It is important to note here that fakirs make a distinction between the disabling experience of oridinary spirit possession and the enabling character of fakir spirits that act as bridges to the saint.

14 For more on the subject of dreams and saintly space, see Mittermaier, A. (2008) '(Re) Imagining Space: Dreams and Saint Shrines in Egypt', in G. Stauth and S. Schielke (eds) *Dimensions of Locality: Muslim Saints, their Place and Space*, pp. 47–66, London: Transaction Publishers.

15 A more detailed account of Zahida's trajectory as a fakir is discussed in the researcher's doctoral dissertation; see Kasmani (2015)

16 Drawing on feminist theory, Longhurst (2001) illustrates the social construction of bodies and their relationship to public space, especially with regard to women who are considered to have fluid and insecure bodily boundaries, liable to seep and leak due to menstrual blood and breast milk.

17 While studies of female saints and ascetics within South Asia's Hindu and Buddhist traditions are relevant to this discussion (see DeNapoli 2014; Salgado 2013, Ramaswamy 1996, Ramanujan 1982), their emphasis on word-renunciation does not always correspond to the socially entangled character of fakir lived realities as evidenced in Sehwan.

References

Abbas, S. (2002) *The Female Voice in Sufi Ritual: Devotional Practices of Pakistan and India*, Austin: University of Texas Press.

Ahmad, S. (2009) *Transforming Faith: The Story of Al-Huda and Islamic Revivalism Among Urban Pakistani Women*. New York: Syracuse University Press.

Ahmed, A (2006) *Sorrow and Joy among Muslim Women: The Pukhtuns of Northern Pakistan*. Cambridge: University of Cambridge Press.

Ansari, S. (1992) *Sufi Saints and State Power: The* pīrs *of Sind, 1843–1947*, Cambridge: Cambridge University Press.

Bellamy, C. (2011) *The Powerful Ephemeral: Everyday Healing in an Ambiguously Islamic Place*. Berkeley: University of California Press.

Boivin, M. (2003) 'Reflections on La'l Shahbaz Qalandar and the Management of his Spiritual Authority in Sehwan Sharif', *Journal of the Pakistan Historical Society*, LI (4): 41–74.

——— (2008) 'Shivaite Cults and Sufi Centres: A Reappraisal of the Medieval Legacy in Sindh' in M. Boivin (ed.) *Sindh though History and Representations. French Contributions to Sindhi Studies*, Karachi: Oxford University Press, pp. 22–41.

——— (2011) *Artefacts of Devotion: A Sufi Repertoire of the Qalandariyya in Sehwan Sharif, Sindh, Pakistan*, Karachi: Oxford University Press.

Butler, J. (1988) 'Performative Acts and Gender Constitution: An Essay in Phenomenology and Feminist Theory', *Theatre Journal*, 40 (4): 519–31.

Butler, J. (1990) *Gender Trouble*, Reprint, London: Routledge, 2008.

Callan, A. (2008) Female Saints and the Practice of Islam in Sylhet, Bangladesh, *American Ethnologist*, 35 (3), pp. 396–412.

DeNapoli, A. (2014) *Real Sadhus Sing to God: Gender Asceticism, and Vernacular Religion in Rajhastan*. New York: Oxford.

D'Souza, D. (2004) 'Devotional Practices among Shia Women in South India', in I. Ahmed and H. Reifeld (eds) *Lived Islam in South Asia: Adaptation, Accommodation and Conflict*, pp. 187–208, Delhi: Social Science Press.

Elias, J. (2008) 'Female and Feminine in Islamic Mysticism' in L. Ridgeon *Sufism: Critical Concepts in Islamic Studies*, Volume II: Hermeneutics and Doctrines, Oxon: Routledge, pp. 298–315.

Ernst, C. (1997) *The Shambhala Guide to Sufism*. Boston: Shambhala Publications.

Ewing, K. (1990) 'The Dream of Spiritual Initiation and the Organization of Self: Representations among Pakistani Sufis', *American Ethnologist*, 17: 56–74.

——— (1997) *Arguing Sainthood: Modernity, Psychoanalysis and Islam*, Duke University Press.

Frembgen, J. (2011) *At the Shrine of the Red Sufi: Five Days and Nights on Pilgrimage in Pakistan*, Karachi: Oxford University Press.

——— (2012) 'Dhamal and the Performing Body: Trance Dance in the Devotional Sufi Practice of Pakistan', *Journal of Sufi Studies*, 1 (1): 77–113.

Flueckiger, J. (2006) *In Amma's Healing Room: Gender and Vernacular Islam in South India*, Bloomington: Indiana University Press.

Green, N. (2003) 'The Religious and Cultural Roles of Dreams and Visions in Islam', *Journal of the Royal Asiatic Society*, Third Series, 13 (3), pp. 287–313.

Halberstam, J. (1998) *Female Masculinity*, London: Duke University Press.

Hegland, M. (1998) 'The Power Paradox in Muslim Women's Majales: North-West Pakistani Mourning Rituals as Sites of Contestation over Religious Politics, Ethnicity, and Gender', *Signs*, 23 (2): 391–428.

Hoffman-Ladd, V. (1992) 'Mysticism and Sexuality in Sufi Thought and Life', *Mystics Quarterly*, 18 (3), pp. 82–93.

Hollywood, A. (2004) 'Gender, Agency, and the Divine in Religious Historiography', *The Journal of Religion*, 84 (4): 514–528.

Karamustafa, A. (1994) *God's Unruly Friends: Dervish Groups in the Islamic Later Middle Period, 1200–1550*, Salt Lake City: University of Utah Press.

Kasmani, O. (2009) *De-centering Devotion: The Complex Subject of Sehwan Sharīf*, unpublished M.A. Thesis, London: Aga Khan University (International) in the United Kingdom.
——— (2012) 'Of Difference and Discontinuity: Gender and Embodiment among Fakirs of Sehwan Sharif', *Oriente Moderno* XCII (2), pp. 439–457.
——— (2015) *Of f the Lines: Fakir Orientations of Gender, Body and Space in Sehwan Sharīf, Pakistan*. Ph.D. Thesis (unpublished). Berlin: Freie Universität, Department of Political and Social Sciences (Anthropology).
Kugle, S. (2007) *Sufis and Saints' Bodies: Mysticism, Corporeality, and Sacred Power in Islam*, Chapel Hill: The University of North Carolina Press.
Lamb, S. (2005) 'The Politics of Dirt and Gender: Bodily Techniques in Bengali India' in A. Masquelier (ed.) *Dress, Undress, and Difference: Critical Perspectives on the Body's Surface*. Bloomington: Indiana University Press, pp. 213–232.
Longhurst, R. (2001) *Bodies: Exploring Fluid Boundaries*, London: Routledge.
Mahmood, S. (2005) *Politics of Piety: Islamic Revival and the Feminist Subject*, Oxfordshire: Princeton University Press.
Malamud, M. (1996) 'Gender and Spiritual Self-Fashioning: The Master-Disciple Relationship in Classical Sufism', *Journal of the American Academy of Religion*, 64 (1), pp. 89–117.
Malik, J. (1990) 'Waqf in Pakistan: Change in Traditional Institutions', *Die Welt des Islams*, 30, 1(4), pp. 63–97.
Metcalf, B. (1998) 'Women and Men in a Contemporary Pietist Movement: The Case of the Tablighi Jama'at', in P. Jeffery (ed.) *Appropriating Gender: Women's Activism and Politicized Religion in South Asia*, pp. 107–121, New York: Routledge.
Mittermaier, A. (2008) '(Re)Imagining Space: Dreams and Saint Shrines in Egypt', in G. Stauth and S. Schielke (eds) *Dimensions of Locality: Muslim Saints, their Place and Space*, pp. 47–66, London: Transaction Publishers.
——— (2011) *Dreams That Matter: Egyptian Landscapes of the Imagination*, Berkeley: University of California Press.
Pinto, D. (2006) *Piri-Muridi Relationship: A Study of the Nizamuddin Dargah*. Delhi: Manohar.
Pechilis, K. (2012) 'The Female Guru: Guru, Gender and the Path of Personal Experience' in J. Copeman & A. Ikegame (eds.) *The Guru in South Asia: New Interdisciplinary Perspectives*, London: Routledge, p. 113–132.
Pemberton, K. (2010) *Women Mystics and Sufi Shrines in India*. Columbia: University of South Carolina Press.
Raj, S., Harman, W. (eds) (2006) *Dealing with Deities: The Ritual Vow in South Asia*, State University of New York Press.
Ramanujan, A. (1982) 'On Women Saints' in J. Hawley and D. Wulff (eds.) *The Divine Consort: Radha and the Goddesses of India*, Berkeley: Graduate Theological Union, pp. 316–324.
Ramaswamy, V. (1996) *Divinity and Deviance: Women in Virasaivism*. Delhi: Oxford University Press.
Ruffle, K. (2011) *Gender, Sainthood, and Everyday Practice in South Asian Shi'ism*. Chapel Hill: University of North Carolina Press.
Salgado, N. (2013) *Buddhist Nuns and Gendered Practice: In Search of the Female Renunciant*. New York: Oxford University Press.
Schimmel, A. (1975) *Mystical Dimensions of Islam*, Chapel Hill, NC: University of North Carolina Press.

Sehwani, N. (no date) 'Sehwan je Melay jo Tārīkhī Manzar', *Paighām-e-Qalandar*.
Shepherd, K. (1985) *A Sufi Matriarch: Hazrat Babajan*, Cambridge: Anthropographia Publications.
Werbner, P. and Basu, H. (eds) (1998) *Embodying Charisma: Modernity, Locality and the Performance of Emotion in Sufi Cults*, London: Routledge.
Werbner, P. (2003) *Pilgrims of Love: The Anthropology of a Global Sufi Cult*, London: Hurst & Co.
Wolf, R. (2006) 'The poetics of "Sufi" practice: Drumming, Dancing, and Complex Agency at Madho Lāl Husain (and beyond)', *American Ethnologist*, 33: 246–268.

5 Negotiating religious authority at a shrine inhabited by a living saint

The dargāh of 'Zinda' Shāh Madār

Ute Falasch

The following paper aims at discussing aspects of religious authority in Sufism as they are negotiated and expressed in the context of perceptions of the sacred character of a saint and his worship by focusing on the shrine (*dargāh*) of Badī' al-Dīn Shāh Madār (d. 1434) in Makanpur, a village in Uttar Pradesh, India.[1] The shrine's history as a sacred place extends back for more than 500 hundred years, and it is a major centre of pilgrimage in the region. The saint's title is often complemented with the epithet "*zinda*" (alive) that can be attributed in South Asia to Sufi saints to refer to *baraka*, the beneficent power, that God bestows on prophets and saints, and that is understood to be permanently present at the shrine. In this sense, it draws upon the concept of the "*walī*", the friend of God in Sufism, a status that is ascribed to mystics of a high spiritual state and charismatic characteristics. Existing in close proximity to God, the *walī* lives in the divine sphere eternally. However, in the context of shrine worship, the notion of "*zinda*" is open to interpretation and can also have a literal signification, as is the case with Shāh Madār. Legends speak of perceptions of the saint virtually residing in his tomb, and the inherent spiritual powers these perceptions imply are one of the factors to which the shrine of Shāh Madār owes its attraction as a centre of pilgrimage.

Sufi shrines achieve their significance through their ability to draw relevance to various realms of society, such as the religious, ritual, cultural, social or political spheres. Numerous studies have been attributed to their historical and current importance, their complex roles as sacred landmarks, their function as charitable institutions or the space they provide for religious discourses on questions of belief, values and proper Islamic behaviour. It has been pointed out that it is primarily the capability of the shrines to provide an arena for a multitude of perceptions and interpretations that are brought to them by different groups, and to permit the coexistence of these perceptions, from which they draw their meaning (Van der Veer 1992: 545–6).

By mainly focusing on the proprietors and caretakers of the *dargāh* in Makanpur, I would like to discuss the implications of the notion that the saint is alive for the religious authority at the shrine, their self-perceptions, the practical management, as well as the organization of rituals. I would further ask if this concept of "*walī*" is crucial for understanding the space the saint is given within the negotiation of the authority, which in turn results in the space the shrine provides for the perceptions of all other groups. It can be argued that the voice of the saint is added as an autonomous stream of discourse, with the consequence that among the competing discourses, none dominates. This allows more flexibility and hence it is extremely successful, as it allows different religious concepts to coexist.

Becoming a saint

Shāh Madār, a Sufi of Syrian origin and founder of the Madāriyya brotherhood, is certainly an enigmatic saintly figure. As with many Sufis of the mediaeval period, reliable biographic data about him are rare. However, they contain some basic information about his life and thoughts. Born in Aleppo, he travelled widely through the Middle East and India, where he met, for instance, his contemporary Sayyid Ashraf Jahāngīr al-Simnānī (d. 1405 or 1435) with whom he performed the *ḥajj*, the pilgrimage to Mecca. Al-Simnānī states that Badīʿ al-Dīn was an Uwaysī, which indicates that he received his spiritual initiation directly from the Prophet Muḥammad. A second chain of spiritual authority (*silsila*) links Badīʿ al-Dīn via his teacher Ṭayfūr Shāmī to Abū Yazīd al-Bisṭāmī (d. 875) and Abū Bakr al-Ṣiddīq (d. 634). The saint is said to have had an extensive knowledge of rare sciences such as alchemy, and he was also an advocate of the doctrine of *waḥdat al-wujūd*, 'the oneness of being', a term commonly associated with the teaching of the great Sufi Ibn al-ʿArabī (d. 1240). During his travels through India, he stayed for some years in Jaunpur, and a letter he wrote during this period explains the special position of the friends of God (*Awliyāʾ*) with respect to God and presents gnosis (*maʿrifa*) as superior to exoteric knowledge (Falasch 2009: 144–7).

Within the hagiographic tradition of the Madāriyya brotherhood, a multitude of legends have been built around his person over the course of time. Until the end of the nineteenth century they were, for the most part, passed on orally. The absence of written sources up to this point is largely due to the fact that most of his followers came from the lower social strata. However, some fragments of information found their way into Sufi biographies from the Mughal period, which agree that Badīʿ al-Dīn had attained a very high spiritual status. Yet some of the legends seem to have puzzled authors, such as the allegation of the saint's age of several hundred years. On the one hand, legends about the miraculous or superhuman powers of a saint are an intrinsic part of hagiographic traditions. Even though there have always been different opinions among Islamic scholars about the capability of the *walī* to actually perform a miracle, and some doubt it; in general, they are perceived as a gift of God and proof of the proximity of the Sufi to the divine (Gramlich 1987: 16–20). On the other hand, in the case of Shāh Madār, there is an obvious imbalance between accounts of these abilities in comparison to accounts of his biography, mystical methods and concepts, which define the characteristics of a spiritual teacher. This has contributed to his classification as a 'semi-legendary' saint (Rizvi 1986).

The emergence of the sacred place

In the hagiographic tradition, the origin and important topographic features of Makanpur are connected with Shāh Madār, as he is said to have chosen this remote area in the wilderness for himself and his followers as a place of settlement, having travelled widely in India and the Ḥijāz. Makanpur lies some 5 kilometres off the road between Delhi and Kanpur, south of the River Isan, a tributary of the Ganga, in a purely agricultural area. Situated more than 60 kilometres from Kanpur, and more than 100 kilometres from Lucknow, it is rather distant from the urban centres of the region. The name of the town is supposedly derived from a spiritual successor (*khalīfa*) of Shāh Madār, Makan Khān, in whose name a land grant was made in 1429 by Ibrāhīm Shāh Sharqī (d. 1440) of Jaunpur, the ruler at that time of the Sharqī kingdom, of which Makanpur was a part. Popular legends also mention a demon called Makan Deo as the namesake; he lived in the jungle there, terrorising the local people by killing them and drinking their blood, and could only be expelled by the saint (Nevill 1909: 303). In another version, Makan Khān was the former demon, who changed his name after accepting Islam and becoming a follower of Shāh Madār. Legends also speak about a cursed lake nearby, from which strange voices were constantly heard, calling '*yā ʿazīz, yā ʿazīz*'. When the saint placed his foot on the water, the lake immediately became dry, and he announced that this would be the location for his residence, where his tomb would be built later. As there was no other source of water, his followers soon became thirsty. Yet the saint gave his stick to his successor Jamāl al-Dīn Jaman Jatī and ordered him to draw it over the earth at a certain spot. This resulted in the emergence of the River Isan, and the issue of the water supply for the future settlement was resolved.

These legends can be interpreted in two different ways. On the one hand, they suggest that Makanpur was a new establishment, and it was not built on a former settlement or holy place. This is supported by archaeological traces that are found in a neighbouring village but not in Makanpur (Nevill 1909: 303). Bearing in mind that Sultan Ibrāhīm Sharqī of Jaunpur was an opponent of the Sultans in Delhi, the legends seem to speak of the cultivation of land sanctioned by the ruler through a land grant in order to promote the settlement of loyal subjects in a region that was a constant subject of dispute between the two Sultanates, comparable to the processes of settlement and Islamization that Eaton has described in Bengal (Eaton 1993), though in Makanpur the scale is much smaller. On the other hand, the reference to a local demon that had to be expelled or converted, and a lake that was drained may be interpreted as indicating that the region has been inhabited since ancient times and was part of the realm of different Indian dynasties. The nearby Qannauj was an important centre of Hindu and Buddhist culture in the mediaeval ages and became the capital of king Harsha's empire in the early seventh century. However, after Maḥmūd of Ghazna destroyed Qannauj in 1018, the city quickly lost its importance. Muḥammad of Ghūr conquered this part of northern India in 1194 (Pletcher 2011: 93–105), and Muḥammad Tughluq left it devastated in 1325 after fighting rebellious Rājpūt clans (Pande 1989: 24).

Considering these facts, the actual circumstances met by the saint and his followers have to be left open to question.

The remoteness of Makanpur does not seem to have reduced the importance of the *dargāh* as a major place of pilgrimage in India since its formation. Its strategic location, close to the Grand Trunk Road, has certainly been conducive to this. During the Mughal period, the saint's annual commemorative celebration (*ʿurs*) was, besides that of Muʿīn al-Dīn Chishtī in Ajmer, the biggest festival in India. People would gather in different places and march in processions to the shrine, accompanied by an even greater number of *malang*, the *faqīr*s of the Madāriyya, carrying standards and black flags. Francisco Pelsaert, merchant of the Dutch East India Company in Agra, reports in his *Remonstrantie* about a gathering of a vast number of people in Sikandra in 1626, who travelled in groups for more than 200 kilometres to distant Makanpur, protected by the *malang* and their standards (Pelsaert 2001: 69–70). Several *wakālat-nāma*s (letters of authorization) issued during the eighteenth century show that the shrine's catchment area went as far as Awadh and beyond (Perti 1992: 145–6; 181; 191; 193; 195–6; 205; 231). In the 1830s, the number of pilgrims was given as 1 million, and the fair (*melā*) that was held during the *ʿurs* lasted for seventeen days (Mrs. Mīr Ḥasan ʿAlī 1917: 372). However, the handling of the immense amount of pilgrims by the caretakers at the shrine seems to have been beset with difficulties, as can be seen in a warrant (*parwāna*) dating from 1681. ʿInāyat Khān, head of the caretakers, and responsible for the observance of the *sharīʿa*, is informing the ruler, then Awrangzīb (d. 1707) about the behaviour of the pilgrims. Many of them are said to indulge in intoxication and other unlawful activities. Moreover, they neither offer prayers nor observe the fast, and they even misappropriate the offerings (*naḍr*). Consequently, there was a request for a supply of horse and foot soldiers to restrain the pilgrims from committing such acts (Perti 1992: 45–6). Concerning the payment of the *naḍr*, a solution appears to have been found by introducing *wakālat-nāma*s that ask pilgrims to only give the offering through named caretakers at the *dargāh*. Nonetheless, in the eyes of Muslim reformers, Makanpur remained an ambiguous place. Shāh Walī Allāh, the influential Muslim thinker and *ḥadīth* scholar of the eighteenth century, for instance, regarded Shāh Madār's shrine, along with that of Ghāzī Miyān in Bahraich, as fitting examples for his criticism of the behaviour of craftsmen, who, in his opinion, neglected the ritual prayers, visited the shrines mentioned above and followed other superstitious practices (Rizvi 1980: 313).

Even though later reformers criticised certain practices in connection with the veneration of the shrines of saints, the prominence of the *dargāh* remained unaffected and this is reflected by the continued dedication to it by a number of rulers immediately after the death of Shāh Madār. The tomb of the saint was built by a son of Sultan Ibrāhīm Shāh Sharqī of Jaunpur. The saint had stayed in Jaunpur for some years and was highly revered by the Sultan. The tomb is a domed, closed structure, which is almost 10 square metres. There are perforated windows on all sides, and a small door to the south beneath the window, which only permits a bowed entrance. The tomb stands in a courtyard enclosed by a high wall, which has been designated as a *harām sharīf*. Two gates point to the west and to the south, and there is a small door to the east, named after Jaman Jatī, a successor of Shāh Madār. Later rulers such as *Ḥ*usayn Shāh Sharqī (d. 1500), Shīr Shāh Sūr (d. 1545), Akbar (d. 1605), Shāh Jahān (d. 1666), and Awrangzīb contributed to the *dargāh,* either by adding further buildings to the complex or donating land grants (Fanṣūrī 1905: 165–191). Awrangzīb's Friday Mosque is a particularly important feature of the shrine, and he improved the road connection to the town as he ordered a bridge to be built over the River Isan. He came to Makanpur in the year 1659, while marching against his brother Shāh Shūjā' to enforce his claim to the throne. His visit is also remembered because of a poem composed by Shiva Paṅdit, a poet in his entourage, which aims at highlighting the superiority of Makanpur in comparison to other places of pilgrimage in India (Cunningham 1994: 102–7). When Farrukh-siyar (d. 1719), grandson of the Mughal ruler Bahādur Shāh, visited Makanpur in 1712, he had a similar claim to the throne to that of his predecessor; he was with his troops on the way from Patna to Delhi after the death of Bahādur (Irvine 1991: 225–6).

The *Dargāh* in Makanpur today

With approximately 8,000 inhabitants, Makanpur is quite a large village today. The majority of the population is Muslim. Most of them claim their descent from Shāh Madār through his three nephews, Abū Muḥammad Arghūn, Abu l-Ḥasan Ṭayfūr and Abū Turāb Fanṣūr, who are said to have accompanied their uncle to India and become his successors. As the saint is supposed to descend from the Prophet Muḥammad, these families are *sayyid*s. Besides their family names, they also call themselves 'Ḥalabī', referring to Aleppo, the birthplace of Shāh Madār, or 'Madārī', which indicates that they belong to the Madāriyya, though the latter may be used by all members of the brotherhood. Besides the descendants of the saint, a few Muslim families who do not belong to this group live there, among them two *shīa* families. One third of the population are Hindus of different castes.

Pilgrims can reach Makanpur by public transport, either by bus from Bilhaur or horse *tonga* from the nearby Araul train station; there is no direct connection to bigger cities. From the bus stop at the entrance of the village, the road passes through the 'profane' part consisting of shops, a vegetable market and the secondary school. It then heads alongside the huge fair ground, bypassing the inner town towards the 'sacred' area with the shrine complex to the right. The *dargāh* is the most prominent feature in Makanpur and comprises several parts. There are two dominant gates through which one enters the main courtyard with three huge cauldrons (*deg*). Most of the rituals during the *'urs* are performed here. One side is occupied by the Friday Mosque, and on the other side there are two further courtyards that contain a smaller mosque, the tomb of Abū Muḥammad Arghūn, eldest nephew of Shāh Madār and a little museum in which gifts to the tomb are kept, such as precious cloths (*cādar*s) and the prayer carpet the saint is said to have brought from Iraq. Adjoining them is the last courtyard with the saint's tomb, designated as *harām sharīf.* In the past years, the walls, floor and the tomb itself have been resurfaced with marble, giving a graceful impression. Other recent contributions have been a large pilgrim's lodge and a new building of the *madrasa*, both situated outside of the shrine complex.

The two most important festivals in Makanpur are the *'urs* of Shāh Madār, with its main days on the sixteen and seventeen Jumādā I and the fair during *basant pancmī*, the Hindu spring festival. While the *'urs* certainly centres on the *dargāh*, Makanpur also hosts a huge agricultural fair with a cattle and camel market that lasts for eighteen days. During this fair, distinct rituals are performed at the shrine by Hindus. Nowadays, approximately 100,000 pilgrims are coming to Makanpur for each festival (Pande 1989: 385), which is a decline, assuming that estimations from the Mughal period are correct. However, it is still a considerable number when compared to other Sufi *'urs* festivals in India. While pilgrims tend to visit the shrine on the occasions of the festivals or regular rituals, the number of visitors on 'normal' days does not reach more than fifty, and they leave Makanpur the same day. Most of the people coming are farmers or from the lower social strata, a trend, that, as far as the historical sources permit us to conclude, has been dominant in the past as well. Being a shrine that primarily attracts this type of clientele, on the one hand means that the income is, by and large, sufficient for its upkeep, while the facilities provided for the pilgrims are rather basic. However, in 2012, the first hotel near the shrine opened. On the other hand, it seems that pilgrims are capable of coping with the existing poor infrastructure. The low degree of development in the areas of water and electricity supply is problematic though during the festivals. Throughout the *'urs*, people in the village rent out all available space to visitors. Still, most people either sleep in and around the shrine or bring their own tents and turn the fair ground into a huge camping site. There is no shrine kitchen serving free food (*langar*) to pilgrims; the provision of food to the needy is organized by individuals who can afford it – people from Makanpur, *murīd* or well-to-do worshippers of Shāh Madār.

Managing the *Dargāh*

The perception that beneficial power is present at a shrine is essential and a precondition for pilgrims to visit a sacred place. In this concept there is often no differentiation between the shrine and the persona of the saint, as Eaton, for instance, has shown before. Even though the donations are usually given to the *khādim*s, the symbolic contract as an expression of the exchange of gifts or donations against the fulfilling of a desire or spiritual experience is concluded between the pilgrim and the saint alone (Eaton 1982: 45). With regard to the authoritative body at the shrine of Shāh Madār, the question arises as to how the spiritual authority at a sacred place position themselves in relation to the living saint; in which ways do they exercise authority, and how do they perceive it with respect to the saint and to the different groups that come to the shrine. In their discussion of religious authority in Islam, Krämer and Schmidtke have – with reference to Max Weber – pointed out its relational and contingent aspects as it is an attribute that is not fixed, but is based on recognition and acquiescence. As there is no church or ordained clergy in Sunni Islam, each individual believer who has at least a minimum level of literacy and the required training is permitted to deal with Quranic exegesis (*tafsīr*) and to study *ḥadīth*, the reports on the sayings, deeds and practices of Muḥammad as the main sources of moral guidance, and act on this base as a religious authority. The authors highlight the different approaches of the *ʿulama*, the class of religious experts, and the Sufis with respect to the methods of gaining knowledge. There is a preference for the transmission through a teacher over the study of books in all fields of study; however, religious scholars draw their expertise from acquired knowledge through trained skills, while within Sufism there is also the possibility of gaining access to God or truth not only, or not at all, through textual knowledge but also, or exclusively, through spiritual experience, which may manifest itself in the charismatic *shaykh* (Krämer and Schmidtke 2006: 2–9).

In Makanpur, forms of religious authority are exercised in different contexts by using various methods, though, chiefly by the same experts. First, the administration of the *dargāh* of Shāh Madār is in the hands of the saint's descendants as they are the proprietors of the shrine.[2] In this role, they are responsible for its maintenance, practical management, the organization of the festivals and the supervision of the rituals. There are a number of duties at the shrine that are performed in a ritualized manner, which have been assigned to different families and are passed on to the next generation. The final balance of the income of the *dargāh* is shared evenly by all Ḥalabīs, but this is a minor amount. Second, the descendants of Shāh Madār are the leaders of the Madāriyya Sufi brotherhood. Badīʿ al-Dīn had a large following; the number of his spiritual successors is given as 1,442. Most of today's successors trace their lineage to the saint through the three most prominent, denoting the affiliation to their branch by the additional names *ʿāshiqān* (lovers), *dīwāngān* (madmen) or *ṭālibān* (students), which describe the spiritual characteristic of the respective successor. Between the descendants of the nephews of the saint, the master-disciple tradition (*pīr-i murīdī*) is preserved as well, and these *pīr*s constitute the fourth branch within the brotherhood, the *khādimān*. Traditionally, the eldest descendant of the *khādimān* is appointed as *takht-i nashīn* for the entire brotherhood, and primarily performs, as the head of the Madāriyya, prescribed ritual tasks. While he does not exercise spiritual authority over the other *pīr*s in Makanpur who act as *sajjāda nashīn* for their respective circles of *murīd*, he may exercise authority over the *malang* of the Madāriyya. The *malang* are a significant group within the brotherhood who are present in all four branches. They have a special status as they – following the example of Shāh Madār – live as wandering mendicants without family ties and are therefore believed to have a close spiritual relation to the saint. They are easily recognisable because of their black clothes, the black turbans wrapped around their uncut hair and the standards which they carry with them. *Malang* usually have a fixed abode, from which they undertake their travels. This is often located at a tomb or a *yādgāh* of Shāh Madār. The *takht-i nashīn* is entitled to send a *malang* to a certain place and provide him with instruction about his religious duties there. Finally, as *pīr*s, the *khādimān* guide their *murīd* on the path of spiritual growth by transmitting the teachings of Shāh Madār that include instructions about proper Islamic behaviour, spiritual exercises such as certain spoken and silent forms of *dhikr*, self-scrutiny and self-contemplation, and, of equal importance, support in situations of personal crisis. As Sunni Muslims, they follow the Ḥanafī school of law. However, they disagree with the reformist schools like the Deobandīs or Barelwīs[3] that have been founded in India in the nineteenth century, but in contrast, they emphasise their own tradition of transmitting knowledge about Islamic codes of conduct and normativeness which qualifies them as religious experts. The local *madrasa* mainly initiates students from Uttar Pradesh and Bihar. For several years it has received governmental acknowledgment. As their corpus of teachings is traced back to the founder Shāh Madār, it is considered an authentic tradition and is consequently regarded as more legitimate than that of the schools that were initiated later.

Despite the various implementations of religious authority at the *dargāh*, the *pīr*s face a challenge; the saint did not pass his charismatic qualities which he gained because of his status as a friend of God on to his nephews. As proprietors and caretakers of the *dargāh*, *pīr*s emphasise that they don't possess special or miraculous powers; they are certainly not living saints. The power to work miracles (*karāma*) that was granted to Shāh Madār stays on with him at the shrine. Because of this, their position as heads of the shrine and the brotherhood is at once legitimized and constricted. This fact is most noticeable by their outer appearance, which speaks of understatement as they don't distinguish themselves through their dress from other Muslim inhabitants of Makanpur in their daily routines. Hence, the competence they inherited is directed to ritual duties and organizational tasks, while their status as a *pīr* is acquired by passing through the entire spiritual training like all the other *murīd* in the Madāriyya, for which a basic standard of literacy in Urdu and knowledge of textual sources is required; some *pīr*s also have a command of fundamental Arabic. Every grown-up male member of this group who received the necessary training is, in principle, entitled to initiate *murīd*. Still, the number of full-time *pīr*s is limited; often men have to take up jobs to make a living, although they might still initiate disciples.

Creating narratives, organizing the ritual

The *pīr*s in Makanpur act on two levels with regard to the charismatic characteristics of the saint; first, as managers of the *dargāh* by constantly maintaining and reinforcing the saint's spiritual qualities through handing down, devising and adapting narratives that constitute the hagiographic tradition of Shāh Madār, and by performing distinct rituals that are carried out by them only. In this way, they guarantee the continuance of the spiritual magnetism of the shrine as well as their own legitimization as spiritual teachers in the *silsila* of Shāh Madār. Second, concerning their own activity as *pīr*s, a certain distance is kept from the vicinity of the shrine; thus, *pīr*s do not interfere in the power the saint exercises there with their own spiritual authority in a spatial sense.

One of the most apparent features of the narrative corpus about Shāh Madār is his extremely long life span. In the seventeenth century it was reported to be 125 years. Yet, over the centuries and with the growing number of legends surrounding the saint, his year of birth was continuously backdated, and today he is said to have lived for 596 years. This perception serves different purposes presented by *pīr*s of the Madāriyya. First, it places Shāh Madār at the top of the universe of the Sufis of South Asia. Generally, Muʿīn al-Dīn Chishtī is regarded as the first Sufi who came to India, while Shāh Madār probably arrived in the fourteenth century, when other Sufi brotherhoods had already established themselves. Nevertheless, in the tradition of the Madāriyya, Shāh Madār is the elder and the first to be present and he is consequently regarded as the *quṭb*, the pole of the Sufi universe. Furthermore, the spiritual genealogy of the saint can be established by this means. The spiritual genealogy is a fundamental concept within all Sufi brotherhoods as it unites the disciples with a *shaykh*, following his distinct method or path, and in this way, they become part of a spiritual family, often over great distances. The chain of transmission links the *shaykh* to one of the first great Sufis, who in turn establishes the link to the Prophet Muḥammad (Karamustafa 2007: 116). With reference to the importance of the gaining of knowledge through a teacher and face-to-face instruction in Islam, it is through this chain that the spiritual authority of a *pīr* receives validity and acknowledgment. The early links are not derogatory to this concept in any way; they are explained as spiritual links, as is the case with Bāyazīd Ṭayfūr al-Bisṭāmī. In the narratives about the spiritual training of Shāh Madār however, the gap in the dates of his life becomes irrelevant as the saint was able to meet al-Bisṭāmī in person because of his great age.

In the same way that the saint had the ability to move back in time, he promised his followers to be present in the future whenever they might call on him for help. This is the root of the saint's title '*zinda*', meaning alive. The views about how this 'being alive' has to be perceived are numerous and range from explanations that are set within mystical concepts about characteristics of the *walī* to popular ideas that the saint in his tomb is not actually dead, but continues to live there. In this sense, the notion prevails that the power of the saint is living and immediately present, and not somewhere distant with God, a fact which is metaphorically reflected by the multitude of legends about him. Typical examples are legends stating that his face displayed the beauty of God to such an extent that people involuntarily prostrated themselves before him, which is why he always covered his face with a veil. His clothes are said to have always been immaculate and he is believed to have lived in a state completely free of needs.

The ritual practice at the shrine of Badīʿ al-Dīn draws closely on these crucial features of the hagiographic tradition about the saint, some parts of which have been transmitted for several centuries. The tomb is organized in a way that creates a distance between the body of the saint and the people who visit the shrine. First of all, the *harām sharīf* is subjected to certain restrictions; for instance, women may not enter. This is not unusual, as women are not permitted in many shrines in South Asia, but generally they may enter the inner courtyards that contain the tomb. As open fires and food are prohibited as well, typical routines of the pilgrimage business with families that spend time at a tomb are not witnessed here; they are asked to go to the outer courtyards. Moreover, the tomb remains closed most of the time and can only be entered by members of the descendants of the saint through a small door in the south. This door is only opened at certain times for the changing of the *cādar*s and for the tomb to be washed twice a year.

The explanations given for these measures refer to essential characteristics of the saintly legends. The mission of Shāh Madār as a Sufi in India started in Mecca where he received orders from the Prophet Muḥammad to proceed to India and preach Islam there. He opted for the sea route and was shipwrecked. As the sole survivor, he was stranded in a deserted place, where he was awarded by an angel with clothes that would always remain immaculate and food that would prevent him from ever becoming hungry again. Therefore, it is said that he fasted for the rest of his life, which is the reason for the prohibition of food in the inner courtyard. Women are not allowed to enter because he is said to have been able to look through objects and clothes, which is why their approach is considered inappropriate. Additionally, they are in danger of feeling a terrible pain as if they were being burned alive, which might even cause death. The same applies for visitors in a drunken state. Stories about such incidents date back to the nineteenth century (Mrs. Mīr Ḥasan ʿAlī 1917: 373–5). As it is said about the saint that he always covered his face with a veil, nobody should see him uncovered, even when he died. He ordered that only water should be brought into his hut, and that the door should remain closed as the *ghusl*, the ritual washing of the body, would be performed by angels. When the door was opened later for the funeral prayers, his body was already washed and dressed in a shroud. This has consequences for the ritual at the tomb. During the monthly changing of the *cādar*s, the *khādimān* have to be careful to only remove the old cloths after the new ones are properly placed on the sarcophagus, as it should not remain uncovered. The washing of the tomb however has to be carried out blindfolded, because here the *cādar*s have to be removed.

Keeping a distance

The first impression for a visitor coming to the *dargāh* in Makanpur is that there is nobody who acts as a religious authority. One encounters, however, a few *khudām*, the servants at the shrine. It is their duty to show visitors around, give some basic information about the saint and explain the rules that have to be observed for men and women. They also provide assistance in reciting the *fātiḥa*, the opening verse of the Qur'ān, making free prayers (*duʿa*) or taking a vow, and they receive the offerings of the pilgrims. The position of a *khādim* is handed down within the same families since the *dargāh* was founded, and their main task is to take care of the daily routine, such as cleaning and serving visitors. They are paid from the income of the *dargāh*. *Pīr*s in Makanpur don't interfere with their manner of carrying out the duties, even though there seems to be a disapproval of the aggressive way pilgrims are asked for money.

The most obvious aspect of the spatial distance *pīr*s keep from the *dargāh* is the fact that they do not teach in its immediate vicinity, not even in Makanpur; instead they follow the habit of visiting their disciples and staying in their respective places of residence for some months every year. Each *pīr* from Makanpur has a number of *murīd* in a certain place. Their networks reach from Bengal to Rajasthan, Gujarat and Maharashtra, and Karnataka and Hyderabad in the South. *Murīd* would call on their *pīr* to come and stay with them, and subsequently would donate money to their master according to their abilities or provide for his expenses during visits. On rare occasions, a disciple would come to Makanpur, mostly with a special wish or in times of stress.

One might ask why the *khādimān* do not display their status as religious authority at the shrine more effectively. It could be presumed that this is largely due to mutual distrust and thinking in categories of rivalry that can be detected between *pīr*s, and which prevents them from presenting their approach to spirituality and subsequently attracting more disciples. I was told that the allocation of income and the assignment of duties have been the cause of disputes in the past, but they are settled now. This is certainly not exclusive to Makanpur; conflicts about succession or competition for resources at shrines, especially when it comes with status and prestige, have been well documented. Concerning the practice of keeping a distance from the shrine, I would however argue in another direction. As shown above, the *dargāh* has enjoyed an immense power of attraction for centuries, which is, in the perception of the families of the descendants, due to the spiritual power of the saint alone and should not be interfered with. Furthermore, concerning the propagation and interpretation of the qualities of Shāh Madār in the form of narratives, *pīr*s cooperate successfully and are able to rapidly spread their consent on certain issues through the entire Madāriyya network. The attitude of the families of the descendants towards the saint can be characterised by closeness and respect that is similar to the attitude towards an elderly member of a family. In my opinion, their approach to the *dargāh* resembles the role of a guest in the house of the saint, rather than that of a landlord. Visits are incorporated in the daily routines. However, they have fixed timings for men and women. Women come to the *dargāh* in the early morning or after dark, sweeping the floor and cleaning the holders for the *agarbattī*. In the morning they pray the *fajr*-prayer in the little mosque adjoining the *harām sharīf*. Men visit the *dargāh* after the *maghrib*-prayer and on Fridays after the *ṣalāt al-jamāʿa*, entering the *harām sharīf*, performing a circumambulation around the tomb and speaking a *duʿā'*. These visits would not be extended longer than necessary.

Visiting the shrine

The *dargāh* clearly serves as the resort for the pilgrims, Hindus and Muslims, who are welcomed with their wishes, perceptions and beliefs. The saint's *karāma* is not focused on a special field, such as healing for instance. Visitors come to the shrine with various desires that are concerned with all spheres of life, such as the wish for a proper marriage partner, a child, cases of financial distress, illnesses or those believed to be affected by possession by a ghost; others seek spiritual gain and fulfilment, while many just come to ask for blessings without a distinct wish. As indicated above, the *khādimān* perform rituals at the shrine that are their sole responsibility, but with regard to the ritual practice of different groups that perceive themselves as connected to Shāh Madār, they merely stay in the background, being either the supervisors of the rituals or even stay away completely having given their consent. I would like to highlight this fact with a few examples.

Murīd, though usually being visited by their *pīr* in their places of residence, are not only encouraged to express their spiritual experiences, for instance in the form of the compilation of eulogies (*naʿt*) to the saint, but also to take part in the organization of the ritual practices of commemoration and praise of the Prophet Muḥammad and the *Awliyāʾ*. In the path of the Madāriyya, music is not permitted. Ceremonies which are held on Thursday nights, on the day of the death of the saint each month, during *basant pancmī*, and, most significantly, during the *ʿurs*, have their focus on the recitation of *manāqib* and *naʿt* and are often planned and carried out by *murīd*. Still, the number of disciples that are coming to Makanpur, especially during the *ʿurs*, is limited. Principally, successors join their masters during the festival. For one thing, they could not all be accommodated; also, *murīd* organize the *ʿurs* celebrations at their respective places of residence. However, this is not the case for those who are appointed successors, and are awarded with the permission to initiate *murīd* and teach themselves (*ijāzat*). On the night of the final day, an announcement ceremony is held, in which the names of those *murīd* who have been awarded with a *khilāfat-nāma*, together with the name of their *pīr* and their place of residence are read out over the loudspeaker from the festival tent, which is situated on a wall overlooking the *harām sharīf* with the tomb, thus, presenting the new successors to the people and to the saint, sacralising their status.

The main ritual, which attracts the highest number of pilgrims during the *ʿurs* is the *dhammāl* performed by the *malang*. The entire ritual consists of two phases. During the first, the *malang* enter the *harām sharīf* and remain there for about an hour. Here they are largely undisturbed by the public. The audience gathers in the main courtyard of the *dargāh*, occupying all the available space and waiting patiently, but in a highly excited state, for the *malang's* return. Inside the inner courtyard the *malang* divide into four groups according to their membership of the four branches of the Madāriyya, each assembling in one corner of the courtyard. There they recite the *fātiḥa* and pray a number of *duʿāʾs*. Afterwards, they perform a circumambulation around the tomb three times anti-clockwise at a fast pace. They remain inside the *harām sharīf* throughout the *maghrib* prayer. They don't offer *namāz*, but after the prayer, they take a bow before the tomb of Shāh Madār. While the *malang* are inside the *harām sharīf*, the *takht-i nashīn*, the head of the Madāriyya brotherhood, enters the main courtyard carrying a frond and is seated on a throne dressed in a royal cloak and turban in the style of the Mughals. He joins the *malang* in the inner court for some time, but is seated on the throne again, before the *malang* finally enter the main courtyard. Here they assemble in front of the throne and start with the *dhammāl*, for which they loosen their turbans which hold their uncut hair. Then they jump from one foot to the other, two jumps per foot subsequently, forming a loose circle. The rhythm is given by calling the invocations '*ya ḥayyūm, ya qayyūm*' which could be translated as 'O the ever living, the ever existing' in relation to the names of Allāh, as well as '*dam madār, beṛā pār*', which could be translated in the sense 'with the help of the breath of Madār', and is the most prominent exclamation of the Madāriyya. The visitors join the *malang* by shouting the second part of the verses respectively. This performance doesn't take longer than thirty minutes, and after that the *malang* quickly proceed to their camp and, once the excitement has died down, the people leave the *dargāh* too.

As the most prominent ritual performed only once a year during the *ʿurs* of Shāh Madār to which successors, disciples and thousands of devotees are coming from all over India, the *dhammāl* represents an impressive and unique experience for all visitors. Actually, it is the only ritual during the *ʿurs* in which all groups of the Madāriyya may participate. Though intentions, expectations and feelings vary with each visitor, and many may come just for the excitement, disciples convey that, besides the feelings of joy and excitement, the attendance of the ritual arouses a strong emotional sensation of love and the notion of a positive effect, and with it, a deeper comprehension of Sufism. On the visitors' behalf, the *malang* pray at the tomb and therefore people wait patiently for their return. During the following *dhammāl* and the shouting of '*dam madār, berá pār*', the *malang* transmit the emotion of closeness to the saint to all followers of Shāh Madār, and through this, the spiritual bond with the saint, who helps remove all kinds of problems, is renewed. In that sense, thoughts of gratefulness are introduced into the emotional spectra experienced during the ritual, which results in feelings of pride and honour to be part of a big, esteemed Sufi brotherhood that consists of rich and poor, and anyone who seeks help from the shrine of Shāh Madār.

During the *melā* at *basant pancmī*, the *dargāh* is a centre of attraction too. While the rites of recitation mentioned above are mainly held at night, the shrine becomes a ritual space for Hindus during the day. Hindus are present at the *dargāh* for all ceremonies, but during this time it is reserved for them exclusively to perform the *cūdākaraṅa*, or *muṅdan* ceremony in the main courtyard of the *dargāh*. It is the eighth of the sixteen Hindu sacraments, in which a child receives his or her first haircut and it should take place at the end of the first year or before the conclusion of the third year. Most of these Hindus had come to the saint before to ask for help in having children. Now they are returning as parents with their children, and it is seen as unmistakable evidence for the living *karāma* of the saint. For this ritual, the presence of Brahmins is necessary to give guidance so that the respective Sanskrit formulas are conducted and recited correctly. The *khādimān* have an agreement with the Hindu priests and explain the propriety of this ritual by referring to Shāh Madār, who did not differentiate in his love and help for all children of God regardless of their creed.

Conclusion

Crucial for the understanding of the self-perception of the religious authority at the *dargāh* is the concept of the saint as a friend of God. I would like to argue, that, based on this concept, the notion of the possibility of an all-encompassing control of the sacred by human religious agents and the ability to define all its qualities and organize it into a canon of normative forms of dogma and ritual is rejected to a certain extent, though the parameters of the Islamic normativeness are acknowledged and respected. Instead, the sacred is ascribed to an independent and intangible existence that is beyond comprehension and control. Hence, the organization and management of the *dargāh* is carried out by a constant recourse to the saint. He is perceived as a part of the town; he is at the top of the hierarchy. In this sense, the series of statements of the saint as perceived and transmitted by the caretakers can be regarded as a separate stream of discourse that influences the actual management of the shrine. This has a consequence – in Makanpur there is a less pronounced hierarchy among the descendants of the saint. The power structure is not centralized in the sense that there is no leading family that dominates the ritual or is at the top of the hierarchy at the shrine; this is the saint. His opinion has to be taken into account when organizing the ritual. The duty of the *pīr*s is the transmission of his tradition without the intention of stepping into his shoes by gaining a saintly position themselves. Therefore, their position as a religious authority is interpreted along several lines. As *pīr*s, the *khādimān* constitute religious authorities for their *murīd*, sanctioned by their training as teachers in the path of the Madāriyya. However, while managing the shrine, a constant reference to the saint is needed that reinforces both the legitimization of the caretakers and his attraction for pilgrims. This non-dominant approach to the *dargāh*, which accepts different ritual practices at the shrine as expressions of worship that are intended and permitted by Shāh Madār himself, allows, in my opinion, religious concepts of the various visitors and pilgrims not just to coexist, but to even complement each other. Various interpretations of the spiritual qualities of the saint, as well as those of ritual practices, add to the perceptions of all other groups coming to the shrine. Thus, the *dhammāl* of the *malang* provides the experience of a present and immediate spiritual connection between the saint and his adherents for all pilgrims. The ritual practices of the Hindus support the comprehension of the friend of God as supporter of all humans regardless of their creed and the presenting of the successors at the *dargāh* proves the unbroken chain of transmission of knowledge to Shāh Madār. In this way the possibility of identifying themselves as a community of worshippers who benefit from the *baraka* of Shāh Madār is constantly approved.

Finally, I would like to present an outlook of the possible changes in the management of the *dargāh* in the future. In the last few years one can detect an increasing awareness among some *pīr*s in Makanpur that the apparent lack of an institutionalized and visible spiritual authority has consequences that are not always regarded as beneficial. There are two most important aspects that are drawn upon. First, the oral tradition of transmitting the knowledge about the saint. It is not stringent and leads to the possibility of incorporating a huge number of legends. It is not so much the fact that in the folk tradition such legends exist, as that the *pīr*s are aware that they fulfil the needs of the people believing in them. However, the lack of a unified corpus of information, set within the frame of an acknowledged Sufi tradition in South Asia propagated by the *pīr*s as a counterweight to them, is perceived as possibly repelling potential disciples with a higher education. Second, the absence of trained contact persons at the *dargāh* is seen as a demerit that might have the same consequences. Accordingly, initial attempts have been undertaken to resolve the first matter by collecting sources about the saint and publishing books, organizing conferences, establishing an interactive website and sending future *pīrs* to institutions of Islamic learning, such as the Azhar University in Cairo. However, the aim so far is not to alter the story, but to balance it differently. In my opinion, it might be interesting in future studies to see if those attempts will be successful, with the consequence of building an institutionalized authority that is visible at the *dargāh* and that controls and propagates the teachings of the saint to the 'outside world', particularly to Muslims interested in Sufism and other Sufi brotherhoods, and, entering the realm of speculation, if, at the same time, as a result the space the saint occupies is so greatly reduced that he might even lose his title '*zinda*'.

Notes

1 The paper is based on field research conducted in Makanpur between October 2001 and May 2002 and in May 2009.
2 The property of Islamic institutions, such as mosques, religious schools and shrines, are often religious endowments (*waqf*) under the control of state administration, represented by Muslim *waqf*-Boards.
3 The categorical rejection of the teachings of the Barelwī school of thought by Madārīs has its root in a theological dispute about the sound chain of transmission of knowledge within the Madāriyya (Dhū l-Fiqār ʿAlī Waqārī Madārī 1986).

Bibliography

Amīr Ḥasan Madārī Fanṣūrī 1905. *Tadhkirat al-muttaqīn, Vol. 2*. Kanpur: no publisher.

Coleman S. 2002 'Do you believe in pilgrimage? Communitas, contestation and beyond', *Anthropological Theory*, 2 (3): 355–68.

Cunningham A. 1994. *Report of a tour in Central Provinces and Lower Gangetic Doab in 1881–82. Vol. XVII*. Delhi: Rahul Publishing House.

Dhū l-Fiqār ʿAlī Waqārī Madārī 1986. *Sayf-i Madār*. Bombay: no publisher.

Eaton R. M. 1982 'Court of man, court of God, *Contributions to Asian Studies*, 17: 44–61.

Eaton R. M. 1993. *The rise of Islam and the Bengal frontier, 1204–1760*. Berkeley: University of California Press.

Falasch U. 2009 'Badīʿ al-Dīn', *EI3*, 3: 144–7.

Gramlich R. 1987. *Die Wunder der Freunde Gottes. Theologien und Erscheinungsformen des islamischen Heiligenwunders*. Wiesbaden: Franz Steiner Verlag.

Irvine W. 1991 [1921/1922]. *Later Mughals, Vols. 1 and 2*. New Delhi: Mehra Offset Press.

Karamustafa A. T. 2007. *Sufism: the formative period*. Berkeley: University of California Press.

Krämer G., Schmidtke S. (eds) 2006. *Speaking for Islam: religious authorities in Muslim societies*. Leiden: Brill.

Mir Hasan Ali, Ms. *Observations on the Mussulmauns of India*. Ed. by W. Crooke. London 1917 [1832].

Nevill H. R. (ed.) 1909. *Cawnpore: A Gazetteer, being Volume XIX of the District Gazetteers of the United Provinces of Agra and Oudh*. Allahabad.

Pande, K. N. (ed.) 1989. *Uttar Pradesh District Gazetteers*. Roorkee: Government Photo-Litho Press.

Pelsaert F. 2001 [1925]. Jahangir's India. The Remonstrantie of Francisco Pelsaert. Transl. by W. H. Moreland and P. Geyl. New Delhi: Low Price Publications.

Perti R. K. (ed.) 1992. *Descriptive List of Acquired Documents (1356–1790 A.D.), Vol. 3*. New Delhi: National Archive.

Pletcher K. (ed.) 2011. The history of India. New York: Britannica Educational Publishing.

Rizvi S. A. A. 1980. *Shāh Walī-Allāh and his times: a study of 18th century Islām, politics and society in India*. Canberra: Ma'rifat Publishing House.

Rizvi S. A. A. 1986. *History of Sufism in India, Vol. I: Early Sufism and its history in India to A.D. 1600*. New Delhi: Manohar.

Van der Veer P. 1992 'Playing or Praying: A Sufi saints day in Surat', *The Journal of Asian Studies*, 51 (3): 545–64.

6 How discourses and rituals construct figures of holiness

The example of the Indo-Muslim Martyr Ghāzī Miyān (Uttar Pradesh, North India)

Delphine Ortis

How do figures of holiness originate? What perpetuates them? This article is premised on the idea that in South Asia, like everywhere else, it is the discourses and the rituals that bring them to life. Discourses and rituals are the two tools of the saints' making. The studies on saints favour oral legend second to discourses, to the detriment of rituals, of festival cycles.[1] The life of the saint, his or her biography, is always the foundation in the elaboration of the saint's construction or definition. This article proposes another point of view by also taking ritual into account for the understanding of devotional Islam, for at least two reasons.

First, the ritual is also a tool of the fabrication of the saints, especially because it is what gives a material reality to the saint, at least the saint's grave, because the ritual needs a medium, and it is the grave that gives the saint a physical everyday life by actively animating his or her shrine, through the cult. In this way, the ritual constructs the saint as a living being. It also produces meaning and norms defining the figures of holiness. Second, in an conscious way or not, the hagiography reminds researchers of history, a domain in which they are surely knowledgeable. But this kind of multiple narratives circulate and is subject to various influences – foreign, learned and popular – independent of the saint's life. It is produced by different actors such as outsiders, members of the elite, or well-to-do people. The narrative presents a mixture of features connected to general and local themes; it is under the vagaries of time, subject to modifications, in order to answer the movements of history and requests of the political contexts. My case study will show how all these aspects are entangled. On the contrary, the ritual proposes a local configuration which is more stable, because as Hocart (1950: 51–52) wrote 'it [the rite] is a social quest' and the social life is lived rather than consciously represented.[2]

The issue which will be considered here is the status of the discourse in relation to that of the ritual in the elaboration of a figure of holiness. Which kind of relations occur between discourses and rituals? The ritual equally produces some norms characterizing the saint; do these come in support of, or in contradiction to, the discourses? Does the ritual play a role in the making of discourses itself?

These questions will be developed through the example of an Indo-Muslim 'martyr' (*shahīd*), Ghāzī Miyān. He has the unusual status of being the subject of many discourses of local actors who are either devout or antagonistic towards his worship. These discourses are very different in their form, in their context of utterance and are contradictory in their aims.[3] First, these multiple voices create a complex and ambiguous personality for Ghāzī Miyān, which is nevertheless always defined by his heroism.[4] Second, all of them give evidence of the great renown of this martyr in North India, even if it is necessary to face the fact that he is not historically confirmed. Third, the cult shows his wide veneration among the Muslim as well as the Hindu population, without discourses allow us to report it and to grasp the raison. Some discourses are even totally contradicting with the rituals. These three aspects justify the calling into question of the discourse's predominance over the ritual, at least for this specific case.

To do that, a portrait of Ghāzī Miyān, sketched in broad outline, will identify the place of the discourse for this specific figure of holiness. Then, three discourses collected by me[5] will be presented in three different sections and analysed to accentuate the image which each of them gives of Ghāzī Miyān. I will also examine how each of these narratives interprets the major event of the festive calendar of Ghāzī Miyān, the 'Fair of May-June' (*jeth melā*), celebrating his marriage with a young woman named Zohra Bībī. These three discourses are the legend of the 'servants' (*khuddām*, sing. *khādim*) of his 'shrine' (*dargāh*) at Bahraich, a hagiography composed in the seventeenth century by a professional hagiographer, and the ballads sung by a musicians' sub-caste, the Dafālī. Finally, the hagiography and ballads presenting the strongest contrasts will be reconsidered to discuss the opportunity for researchers to use the data that is at their disposal.

The portrait of Ghāzī Miyān

Sayyed Sālār Mas'ūd Ghāzī, alias Ghāzī Miyān, is the oldest Muslim saint (eleventh century) and the most popular in northern India. His 'sanctuary' (*dargāh sharīf*), housing his mortal remains, is situated in the north of the town Bahraich (Uttar Pradesh). The place and the cult are attested since the thirteenth century. To this day, they attract millions of Indians, native to northern India and Nepal, who come to seek the protection and the benefactions which he dispenses on the world, by displaying a limitless thaumaturgy.

For a long time, Ghāzī Miyān has been the hero of various narratives. Retaining only the founding elements, his life can be summarised and interpreted as follows. He is the archetype of the young hero of noble and martial origin, blessed with gifts of beauty and youth. He spends his short existence travelling in northern India, coming to the assistance of Hindu peasants that were oppressed by bad Hindu kings. By attempting to defend the people of Bahraich, suffering under the cruelty of the despotic king, Suhal Deo, he becomes a martyr in 1033 at age nineteen, on the edge of maturity, yet still a virgin and a bachelor. His bodily remains are buried in a tank consecrated to the worship of the Sun god (*sūrajkund*) in the jungle that surrounds Bahraich.

The three discourses elaborated their own versions from this scheme by taking two major characteristics of Ghāzī Miyān into account: the devotion of his followers and his historic authenticity. These determine the intention of each of the analysed discourses, and more generally, reveal the place of discourse in the construction of this holy figure.

Unexpected devotees

At first, the confessions of the devotees appears inconsistent with the type of holiness attached to the figure of Ghāzī Miyān. It is specifically by fighting the Hindus that Ghāzī Miyān acquired the quality of a martyr. It seems surprising that a large number of his victims – the Hindus themselves – should join the cult of their aggressor. Nevertheless, this association is at the heart of the religious practices.

The language of the propitiatory visit (*ziyārāt-darshan* for the visit or vision; *sīnī-prasād* for the offering of food) combines a double religious vocabulary, revealing that the participation of Hindus in the cult of this Muslim martyr is a basic element, which is supported by the gloss of the agents of worship. They explain these expressions with the fact that they are polyglot (*ziyārāt* and *sīnī* being Urdu, while *darshan* and *prasād* are Hindi words). Nevertheless, each of these terms expresses a different aspect of the devotional practice: the pilgrimage for *ziyārāt* and the exchange of a glance with the divinity for *darshan*; and the leftovers of food sacrificed to the gods for *prasād* and a specific dish for *sīnī*. Apart from the differences, these expressions underline the common aim of the acts accomplished in this shrine by Indians, regardless of their religion: on the one hand meeting and feeding Ghāzī Miyān to receive his favours, while on the other, gaining protection and healing by consuming and sharing the rest. Here, the differences seem reducible to or consubstantial with the assertion of a state of coexistence between Muslims and Hindus in their local practice. This association between Muslims and Hindus in fulfilling the needs for the worship of Ghāzī Miyān is also imperative in the cycle of the festivals.

The association of Hindus to the sainthood of a Muslim martyr makes him enigmatic; it is, in my opinion, the main reason for the development of different discourses. These tend to bring consistency, making the hero coherent despite his cult or, inversely, making the cult coherent despite its hero. As this article will show, this search for consistency, which sustains the three discourses, goes hand in hand with the second characteristic of Ghāzī Miyān: his failing of historicity.

A doubtful historicity

There is no proof that Ghāzī Miyān existed, even if the discourses attempt to claim a historical basis, in particular by linking him to historic persons, notably to Mahmud Ghaznavi, who is always presented as his maternal uncle. Nevertheless, Ghāzī Miyān is totally absent from chronicles of this dynasty, and the historians agree that there is no relationship between the two men. Moreover, there is a gap of two centuries between the date of the epic events of Ghāzī Miyān (his martyrdom being fixed to the 14 *Rajab* 1033) and the Muslim conquest of the Bahraich region in the thirteenth century.[6] Ghāzī Miyān makes his first appearance in history towards the end of the thirteenth century.[7] From the fourteenth century onwards, he is mentioned in some historical chronicles, which report the propitiatory visits of the Sultans of Delhi to his shrine.[8]

It is necessary to consciously not historicise Ghāzī Miyān,[9] because as Lingat (1989: 19) wrote in his work on the Buddhist kingship of Ashoka: 'to make history with legend is always spoiled by arbitrariness and subjectivity. [. . .] The underlying ideology is more important than the factual contents.' We thus leave it to the historians to untangle the history and the legend, the true from the false. Amin (2005: 265) attempted this by trying to identify, in the legend of Ghāzī Miyān, the image of the Turkish conquest of North India around 1000–1200, basing on the premise that historically the martyr has existed without, for all that, consider him contemporary to the period of his legendary exploits. But Amin did not manage to go beyond the two main statements recurrent in all the studies on this character: 'Ghāzī Miyān is officially absent in the history while his popularity is huge' (*ibid.* 270). However, the history, the legends and the worship give contradictory images of him. Even if in the discourses, as Dermenghem (1981: 18) underlines, the 'conceptual connections are expressed in language of history [. . .] the life of a saint is itself a rather extraordinary creation, transcending in a sense the history and the life which it tends to inform and to transform'. The mystery of Ghāzī Miyān does not reside in the history of the Muslims in India, but in the representation the local society made of this episode of its history.

In this singular configuration, where the lack of historicity combines with the ambiguity of a hero whose reality is above all a ritual one, the status of the discourse seems to give, retrospectively, legitimacy to the fulfilment of a worship which always appears primary. It is in the sense that Ghāzī Miyān is, for me, mainly a ritual figure, i.e. a figure of holiness defined through the ritual practices. Without any tangible biographical elements, the discourses could embroider the theme of the young hero as they pleased, according to the needs of the epoch and the social groups addressed, to give him as a character, the attributes which reflect their ideas and values. Let us consider which ideologies underlie the three discourses and which heroic figure each of them constructs from the ritual figure of Ghāzī Miyān. To best illustrate the point of view adopted here, I will consider the speakers and their audience, as well as the themes developed by narratives.

A local legend: from the jungle of Bahraich at the Muslim Conquest

The legend, named itihās (story) by the servants of the dargāh, is orally told to the pilgrims (Muslim and Hindu) who request it from them during the propitiatory visit. Unlike most of the Indian Muslim shrines, these servants are not the descendants of Ghāzī Miyān or his relatives but of his servants who accompanied him on his journey across India. Their discourse dedicates an episode to describing their origin and establishing and legitimising their functions, that is, the principle of 'duty' (*khidmat*, *sevā*) and its 'hereditary transmission' (*silsilā*).

As the only survivors of the caravan of the young hero, the servants would have established the first 'community' (*qaum*) or 'caste' (*jāti*) in the village where

Ghāzī Miyān's mortal remains were buried. Settled close to the tank (transformed into a grave to serve their master), these first inhabitants of the jungle of Bahraich would have cut it back and then cultivated it, so that their descendants could bloom and immortalise the duty of the daily and festive rituals. In short, they humanised the jungle and altered it to become part of the civilised world. Still today, the majority of them live next to the shrine, keeping up the practice of both activities fixed by the legend: ritual duty and farming.

The narrative of the servants gives Ghāzī Miyān the image of a young, skilful warrior and fervent Muslim who aspires to renunciation. He declines the thrones offered to him to be able to fight against the 'violence' (*zulum*), exercised against the oppressed populations – each time Hindu farmers – which he meets while he is crossing India. Ghāzī Miyān acquires his martyr status during one of these battles, when he is killed by the bad and treacherous Hindu king of Bahraich, Suhal Deo. From then onwards, he is characterised by his devotees as the one who is never dead but always living, and as the one who masters an area over which extends his worship, this area is called the 'locality of the bābā' (*bābā ke yahān*). The first thaumaturgical act mentioned in the legend is accomplished on behalf of the Hindu local population, predominantly in favour of sterile women and lepers. The legend concludes with the institution of the most important festival (the 'Fair of May-June', *jeth melā*), representing Ghāzī Miyān's marriage with Zohra Bībī, qualified as the greatest of his 'miracles' (*karāmāt*).

This discourse relates a journey of fulfilment, shaping a ritual figure from that of the conquering hero. It takes root in the institution of the shrine to which it gives its cohesion.

The shrine: an idealised reflection of the local society

The legend diachronically unwinds the space of the shrine which is conceived as a military camp and is reminiscent of the narrative depicting the class of the warriors. All of the protagonists met by Ghāzī Miyān during his life in this narrative are buried there beside him. Collectively called his 'court' (*darbar*)[10], they are saluted during the propitiatory visit. The legend demonstrates the configuration of the shrine and its spatial organisation, just as the shrine embodies the legend, inscribing physically in the ground the episodes of the life and martyrdom of its hero.

The protagonists affirm that this hero is not an isolated being, but that he is composed by relations based on interdependence. The relationships are instituted by the legend, which essentially expresses them in the language of kinship (affinity, sibling relationship and milk kinship) and of relations of service (servants and soldiers). Through these relations, the discourse evokes the organisation of the shrine, in which his devotees say Ghāzī Miyān reigns as a 'master of the house' (*jajman*) over a 'royal court' (*darbar*). The organisation of this shrine is based on the *jajmani* system, which hereditarily binds the martyr to several families belonging to various specialists' castes (including the servants). This *jajmani* system is the one which traditionally organises the local society of Bahraich. This shrine is also a *waqf*, of which Ghāzī Miyān is the owner.

The legend does not stop with the heroic figure of Ghāzī Miyān; it also constructs him as a ritual figure. It defines two versions of Ghāzī Miyān, appearing in a different guise when he is alive than when he is dead. In life, he is a young, single warrior at the head of a caravan; after his martyrdom, he becomes a married master of the house and thaumaturge at the head of the court of Bahraich. By describing in detail the martyr's capacity to accomplish miracles, the legend gives an account of his recognition as a local power (cf. the 'locality of the bābā') and of the festive calendar (the *'urs* celebrating his martyrdom and three other festivals marking the various stages of his marriage). It thus affirms that only the cult perfects Ghāzī Miyān and particularly the representation of his wedding with the young woman Zohra Bībī, like we now see it.

Love: source of power

The legend tells that Ghāzī Miyān meets the blind Zohra Bībī while crossing North India, at the well of the village of Rudauli. The young and handsome hero is thirsty and asks her for water. She lets him know that she is blind and therefore cannot serve him. He restores her eyesight, and she is then able to offer him some water to drink; they look at each other and immediately fall in love. But they depart in different directions. Some years later, following Ghāzī Miyān's martyrdom, the young woman dreams that he is calling her to come to him. Thus, she makes her way to Bahraich, accompanied by her two brothers and settles at the grave of Ghāzī Miyān. She lives on the floor near the grave, which she cleans with her long, thick hair. There, she has another dream: she is dressed as a 'bride' (*dulhan*), sitting next to Ghāzī Miyān who is dressed as a 'bridegroom' (*dulha*). She informs her relatives of her dream and asks them to send her the dowry for her upcoming marriage. Her parents answer favourably and travel to Bahraich in a wedding procession. Meanwhile, Zohra Bībī had joined Ghāzī Miyān. The inhabitants of her village decide to repeat this procession to Bahraich every year.

In this discourse, the theme of love is well detailed in its various modalities. Interpreted from the outset as love at first sight, a phenomenon which in Indian epic literature is known as the catalyst of this feeling, it gains a sexual connotation in the small gestures performed by Zohra Bībī on the grave of Ghāzī Miyān, and finally culminates in marriage. The celebration of this 'marriage' (*shādī byāh*) is performed during the 'Fair of May-June', the most important feast in terms of ritual significance, organisation and the number of pilgrims it attracts. The majority of these pilgrims are Hindus. Without going into detail here (Ortis, 2008: 124–225), several aspects clearly show that the different ritual sequences are based on the marriage ritual as it is performed in Bahraich by Muslim and Hindu inhabitants. The ritual comes also within the framework of local society. What is important here to grasp is the function of this marriage in the legend, as well as the process for constructing holiness.

In the summary of the legend, we saw that the servants attach importance to this marriage. They recognize this episode as a formative event of the martyr's life. In what ways does the marriage transform the martyr into a saint? By linking

Ghāzī Miyān with a feminine partner, this marriage completes and perfects the martyrdom work and gives to the martyr his permanent feature. From this point of view, this new being is shaped on the Hindu royal couple which is itself the ideal of the common couple. It's during the festival of 'Spring Fifth' (*Basant Panchmi*) that it appears clearly that Ghāzī Miyān is treated as a royal figure, this corroborates the configuration of his *dargāh*; these facts are confirmed by the gloss of the agents of his shrine. The Hindu king intrinsically needs a feminine principal to be effective in the world. In describing the marriage as the greatest miracle of Ghāzī Miyān, the servants also develop this idea. Their discourses interpret the 'Fair of May-June' as a real marriage which produces a miraculous healing of the lepers, that is the most valued of the thaumaturgical powers of this saint. The marriage acts on his powers, activates them and makes them more effective. His thaumaturgical powers are illustrated by a women's song collected by Gaborieau (1975: 311) in Nepal. Here are a few translated verses:

> "*We* [devotes] *shall obtain a palace;*
> *We shall obtain the object of our desire.*
> *You* [Ghāzī Miyān] *gave sons to those doesn't have.*
> *You gave the wealth to the underprivileged persons.*
> *You gave clothes to those were naked.*
> *You gave a body to the lepers*".

I will come back to these ideas further. Let us pursue for the moment the analysis of the legend.

From the shrine of Bahraich to the Muslim history

To characterise its hero and give itself a chronological frame, the legend refers to the Muslim history of North India, and shapes Ghāzī Miyān in the vein of the first Muslim conquerors by associating him with the military exploits of Mahmud of Ghazni, notably in the overthrow of the temple of Somnath, facilitated by his sole presence. The feats of arms of Ghāzī Miyān situate him in the State of Uttar Pradesh, between Delhi and the north of Bihar: the graves of his companions, as well as his cenotaphs and reliquaries mark the stages of his headway into India. In each of these places, the small graves demarcate the northern border between the urbanised and forested spaces, thus placing the conquest of the territory under the sign of humanisation and civilisation, through the establishment of an institution in charge of these shrines. These graves partly delimit the extent of the area where Ghāzī Miyān is powerful. However, the association with Mahmud of Ghaznavi is not achieved, since it is the brother of Ghāzī Miyān's nursemaid who becomes the 'maternal uncle' (*mamu*) in Bahraich, and replaces Mahmud of Ghaznavi, who was certainly too prestigious and too terrible to be buried in this obscure corner of Uttar Pradesh.

In addition, the martyrdom of this 'victorious conqueror' (*ghāzī*) is compared with the greatest of Muslim martyrdoms: that of the grandson of the Prophet

Husain in Karbala.[11] Ghāzī Miyān is considered the greatest martyr after Husain, and the district of Bahraich, locally perceived as a vast covered cemetery, is deemed a second Karbala. But, in this legend, it is the Hindu functions of warriors and kings in society which really establish the motives of the martyrdom of Ghāzī Miyān, namely how to expand and define the kingdom's territory by war and marriage (Ghāzī Miyān achieves both by the ritual) and how to defend the social order from forces working to destroy it (it is in this fight that he becomes a martyr). Muslims and Hindus recognise the existence of a category of singular beings (named *vīra* by the latter): human beings that are transformed into a kind of deity by sacrificing themselves in war.

Eventually, this discourse aims at giving the image of a coherent whole of the shrine, where the ritual and heroic figures of Ghāzī Miyān are in harmony. Both are projected in an idealised society, echoing the local society that is brought together by worship. In the legend, the heroic and ritual figures of Ghāzī Miyān are embellished according to criteria defined by a universe of shared Islamic and Hindu values. It can be situated midway between the two following discourses, and proposes a rather convincing synthesis of the two most contradictory facets of the character: the victorious Muslim conqueror and the saint of the Hindus.

The hagiography: a late jihadist reconstruction of Ghāzī Miyān's life

The only written trace of the life of Ghāzī Miyān is an example of Arab-Persian literature: a hagiography. *The Mirror of Mas'ūd* (*Mir'āt-i Mas'ūdī*, Mas'ūd alias Ghāzī Miyān), written in Persian at the beginning of the seventeenth century under the reign of the Mughal emperor Jahangir, thus appearing six centuries after Ghāzī Miyān's martyrdom. His author, the hagiographer 'Abd al Rahman Chishti, a native of Uttar Pradesh, was an eminent Sufi shaykh of the Chishtiyya brotherhood. This point is important, considering that one of the principal saints of this order, Nizam ud-Din, determined the standards of the Persian hagiography. Chishti's work, initially intended for the literate Muslim elite, was popularised in the vernacular languages (Urdu and Hindi) in the nineteenth century. A pamphlet found on the market of Bahraich gives a summary of the book. This pamphlet is an adapted version of *The Mirror of Mas'ūd*, entitled 'History of Mas'ūd' (A'ina-e Mas'udi), and written by Akbar Merathi (1938) in common Urdu. It was commanded by the administration of the shrine at the end of the 1930s.

The pamphlet, constructed in two parts, shows a dichotomy in the character of Sayyed Sālār Mas'ūd Ghāzī. In the first part, he is depicted as an emblematic figure of Islam's victory over the non-believers. He grows up as a pious and virtuous Muslim, pure of body and spirit, and excelling in all the arts. In 1034, at the age of sixteen, he leads a crusade into the central plain of the Ganges and the conquest of territories is the result of his efforts alone. His enemies, the Hindu kings, appear with perfidious characteristics. But Mas'ūd turns out to be more cunning and thwarts all their projects. In the second part, taking place on the site of his future martyrdom, the literary style changes into a more conciliatory tone.

Reaching the Oudh, beyond Doab, he appears in the guise of a peaceful huntsman and land-clearer, who proposes to the Hindu kings of the region to share the virgin jungle of Bahraich in which he has just settled with them. But they refuse and kill him in a battle just before his twentieth birthday. He becomes the famous 'Prince of Martyrs' (*Sultan al-Shuhud*).

His martyrdom is the final act in a long series destined to convert the Bahraich hunting ground into a site dedicated to Islam. Here, hunting represents the taking of possession and martyrdom, the act of accomplishing the conversion which has been gradually elaborated. As soon as he is established in the area, Mas'ūd indulges in hunting expeditions in the jungle and discovers the tank consecrated to the worship of the Sun god. The site is de-sacralised by destroying the tank and turning the area into a garden, which is supposed to be the image of Paradise. The period following Mas'ūd's martyrdom is contradictory. At first, everybody dies, but it seems that later wounded soldiers run away from the battlefield to join Mas'ūd's fencing teacher, Sayyid Ibrāhīm, at the camp of Bahraich and inform him about the death of Mas'ūd. Ibrāhīm then buries the latter under a tree, following the instructions which Mas'ūd passes on to him in a dream. He then kills Suhal Deo and becomes a martyr in turn. Finally, those who are wounded dedicate their lives to the maintenance of the grave.

Ghāzī Miyān under the features of the sovereign Mahmud Ghaznavi

This hagiography should be understood as a text which attaches a lot of importance to the jihad, because it recounts the exploits of a fanatical warrior similar to the pitiless Mahmud Ghaznavi. The hagiography transfers the reputation of his supposed maternal uncle to Mas'ūd. Indeed, he is credited with the feats of arms of the latter, such as the destruction of idols and the murder of infidels. The hagiographer emphasises the capture of the temple of Somnath: its idol is dismembered and reduced to dust, specifically on Mas'ūd's request. It shows him to be determined in his faith. He gives the local populations a single choice: either to convert or to die. By depicting Mas'ūd with the features of a conqueror spreading Islam and bringing down the enemies of the faith, 'Abd al Rahmān creates a heavily Islamised character who fits the Indo-Muslim model of his period, therefore achieving coherence in the eyes of the Muslim elite. The latter had remained uninfluenced by the aspect of the ritual figure of Ghāzī Miyān. He recovers the martyr for orthodox Islam ideology, giving a Muslim legitimacy to his worship. Martyrdom is built on the idea that the premature death of a young, perfectly righteous warrior gives military conquest a religious dimension.

In his introduction, the hagiographer explains what led him to write the text. According to him, there is no complete and coherent historical account of this martyr. His intention is therefore to write a new version of the history of the dynasties of the region where the cult of Ghāzī Miyān had developed, thereby limiting the variety of popular interpretations common at that time. He seeks to put an end to the doubts among the Muslim elite at the beginning of the seventeenth century which surrounded Ghāzī Miyān's authenticity and the merits of his cult.

This hagiography was thus written to meet a precise aim: although members of the elite had written documents proving the existence of a religious organisation attached to the shrine of the martyr, they lacked the possibility to refer to a written narrative of his life that would have strengthened their faith.

The warrior is not the Sufi

'Abd al Rahmān implies in his hagiography that the Muslim conquest was a long process. The sacrifice of one warrior is not enough to ensure the victory of Islam in India. Mas'ūd's martyrdom is thus not followed by irreversible effects to the advantage of the Muslim dominion, such as the conversion of local populations or the attainment of temporal power. The territory between Ajmer – where Mas'ūd was born – and Bahraich – where he died – stayed in the hands of the Hindus for another two centuries. According to 'Abd al Rahmān, only the arrival of the Khwajā Mu'īn-al-Dīn Chishtī's established Islam in India. As a follower of the brotherhood founded by Chishtī, 'Abd al Rahmān can only assign the presence of Islam in India to his master's spiritual authority. For him and his contemporaries, the heroic death of Mas'ūd could not constitute the beginning of the history of Islam in India; this was reserved for the success of the Chishtī Sufi order and the establishment of the Sultanate of Delhi. 'Abd al Rahmān uses the hagiography of Ghāzī Miyān to assert the superiority of the path of the Sufi over that of the martyr particularly in regard to his spiritual master and his order.

Today this hagiography is still prevalent among the upper Muslim and Hindu castes that spread its message. In it, they recognise a character that corresponds more suitably with their idea of a Muslim warrior saint, i.e. clearly indentifying with the warrior fighting against the Hindus and their religion to spread the Islam, than the one of the servants' legend, the ballads and especially the cult. This discourse is the one that most distinguishes, even conflicts with the rituals, as the relation that it maintains with the 'Fair of May-Jun'" and with the marriage of Ghāzī Miyān demonstrates.

Devotional love

On the contrary of the legend which ties the story of Ghāzī Miyān with the "Fair of May-June", the hagiography is mute about it and doesn't evoke his marriage. The upper Muslim castes, generally supported by the upper Hindu castes, spread their own stories of Zohra Bībī, filling the gap which is left by the hagiography. The blind Zohra Bībī, who had heard about him through the narratives of his miracles, visits his grave to find the sight which she had not received at birth sixteen years after the burial of Ghāzī Miyān. She pronounces this wish which he fulfils immediately. She then sees the image of Ghāzī Miyān and decides to settle down near him until the end of her life. According to another version, this marriage was the desire of Zohra Bībī's father, who would not give it up in spite of the fiancé's death. Zohra Bībī spends her life taking care of the grave of the one who should have been her husband.

These two versions depict Zohra Bībī as a devotee. They develop the idea that this young woman can only feel a devotional attachment towards Ghāzī Miyān. Any idea of love or sexual desire is absent. Zohra Bībī's attachment to Ghāzī Miyān is the 'love' (*ishq*) that one feels for God and his saints, of which the different aspects were developed by Sufism. In this sense, these discourses closely fit the hagiographer's thought, whose referent model is the figure of the Sufi. To justify the truth of their interpretation, the higher castes adopt two arguments.

The first one is given by the narrative: Ghāzī Miyān died a virgin. This state is important in the construction of his martyrdom since it makes it more tragic, giving it a higher value. The second argument, based on the ritual, is more interesting because it shows the impregnation of Sufi thought on these upper castes. According to them, the only marriage of Ghāzī Miyān is represented by the festival named *'urs* ('wedding'), commemorating the anniversary of his martyrdom. This festival, which is common to the Indo-Muslim saints, is interpreted by Sufi thought as the union of the feminine soul of the mystic to God's male soul, as we can see in its Arabic name, *'urs*. But, analysis of this festival shows that at Bahraich, it is a question of funerary ritual (Ortis, 2008: 226–296), more than mystic marriage. Participating very actively in this festival, the high Muslim castes attach little importance to the representation of the 'Fair of May-June'. Refuting the evidence of the ritual performances, they do not see the realisation of a marriage but a demonstration of superstition which is, for them, typical of low castes. According to them, it would be enough to educate, i.e. Islamise them by making them give up the celebration of this festival and concentrate on the performance of *'urs*, the only legitimate festival in their eyes. In this double interpretation of the festival in Ghāzī Miyān's honour, we see the perpetuation of the desire to bring him back to a more orthodox Islam, modelled on the cult of the Sufi saints.

The great gap between the Ghāzī Miyān drawn up by the hagiography and the Ghāzī Miyān made by the rituals' cycle shows, more clearly for this discourse than the other two versions, how saints' biographical accounts can deliberately transformed by solicitation and selection. They are like a set of building blocks, each having its specific characteristics, and by placing some to the fore and disregarding others, the adhesion or disavowal of specific parts of the population can be obtained. In the end, it seems that this hagiographical discourse tells us more about the hagiographer, his readers and his epoch than it does about the saint whose life story it conveys.

The ballads of Dafālī: the domestic environment of the Awadhi kingdom

The third discourse is an oral tradition that has taken the form of ballads, sung (*gāna*) in the vernacular languages (Awadhi, Bhojpuri, Hindi and Urdu) and spread by a caste of musicians, the Dafālī. These ballads are not unusual and they are an integral part of Indian oral tradition (cf. Servan-Schreiber, 1999: 7). They are reserved for devotees of Ghāzī Miyān and are performed within the context of the rituals, in particular during festivals ('Fair of May-June' and 'Spring Fifth') where Dafālī have the function of "pilgrim priests" (*pandā*).

In these ballads, Ghāzī Miyān's story does not have quite the same coherence, because unlike the other discourses, they pay little attention to historicity. They describe different episodes of the principal events of his life: his birth, his feats and his miracles. The general thrust is as follows: Ghāzī Miyān is born under the curse of dying as a bachelor; he encounters martyrdom on the very day of his marriage when he tries to save his men and his cattle which are about to be massacred by the king, Suhal Deo.

This discourse takes the domestic background typical of this region of northern India into account, particularly the cattle breeding, the concern for women's fecundity and the marriage of sons. Both latter are important features of the cult of this ritual figure and shape the propitiatory visit as well as the cycle of the festivals. Both the legend and the ballads refer to the local dimension of Ghāzī Miyān, but they vary from one narrative to another and do not evoke the same hero. The legend aims at implanting a foreign warrior, Ghāzī Miyān, in a singular place, Bahraich, conquered by his feats of arms and his martyrdom; however, in the ballads, he is the native child of a larger locality, the Awadhi kingdom (a political unit to which Bahraich belonged), which he already controls as the master of the population of cattlemen (Bhar and Ahir castes).

The ballads underline even more clearly than the legend the influences governing the universe of the Awadhi peasant population, a universe which is culturally irrigated by Islam and Hinduism and which is notable both for its popular and deviant saints and its incarnations of the god Vishnu.

Mu'īn-al-Dīn Chishtī versus *Zinda Shāh Madār*

While the two other discourses link Ghāzī Miyān to the saint Mu'īn-al-Dīn Chishtī and the Pan-Islamic saint Khwāja Khizr,[12] the ballads link him to a major popular Sufi saint of Uttar Pradesh, Zinda Shāh Madār from Mākānpur (a village in Uttar Pradesh). His mother, being sterile, requires the intervention of Shāh Madār in order to give birth to Ghāzī Miyān. By her offerings, she obliges him to fulfil her request favourably, but she makes a mistake which varies in the different versions: either she forgets to thank Zinda Shāh Madār or she acts inappropriately. This infuriates the saint who curses Ghāzī Miyān to die celibate on his very wedding day. There are two lessons to be learned from this essential and formative link.

On the one hand, Zinda Shāh Madār's alleged paternity confirms the disinterest of the oral tradition in historical accuracy. Indeed, the chronology of events is confused since Shāh Madār died (d. 1434) 400 years after Ghāzī Miyān's martyrdom. Nevertheless this timeline is a more accurate historical reflection of the Muslim settlement of North India, which begins at the end of the thirteenth century. On the other hand, the suggested paternity of Zinda Shāh Madār is strikingly different from that of both Khwāja Khizr and Mu'īn-al-Dīn Chishtī. First of all, if two other discourses link the father of the future martyr with Khwāja Khizr, this one links his mother with a popular, specifically Indian saint from Uttar Pradesh. Thus, this oral tradition proposes a local, popular and feminine vision of the procreation of Ghāzī Miyān, which contrasts with the Islamic, erudite and male version of the other two discourses. On this subject, the ballads and the hagiography follow inverse aims. For the latter, the issue is to integrate a local ritual figure into the Muslim universe, through references to Muslim history and its great orthodox saints. It seems to be an attempt by the Muslim high status elite to appropriate a popular form of worship as its own. By contrast, the oral tradition emphasises the multiple relations between the Muslims and Hindu society, accounting for the references to the non-conformist local saint and to the Hindu gods. It is also interesting to note that the Muslim universe is associated with paternal filiation, while the integration into the locality is associated with maternal filiation. Furthermore, the Sufi brotherhood established by Shāh Madār in the fourteenth century, the non-conformist Madariyya, is the antithesis of the Chishtīyya, the brotherhood of Mu'īn-al-Dīn Chishtī.[13]

Ghāzī Miyān under the features of the human incarnations of the Vishnu god

In these ballads, Ghāzī Miyān shares certain characteristics with the human incarnations of the Vishnu god, Rāma and more especially Krishna. To interpret this disconcerting aspect of the personality of Ghāzī Miyān, it is necessary to put it back in their local context. First, the area over which extends the worship of Ghāzī Miyān is also, according to my informants, the region where the events related in the two Hindu epics occurred: Mahabharata and Ramayana. These two epics even are considered by the Muslims as the history of their region. Second, Rāma is the favourite god of Hindu upper castes and Krishna the favourite of Hindu herdsmen and dairymen (the Ahir), these latter dominating the Awadhi region. From my point of view, the shared characteristics is neither a confusion nor an assimilation, but the expression of a category of deities that is shared by Muslims and Hindus, and for which there is still a lack of research.[14]

By his functions, Ghāzī Miyān is close to Krishna. Ghāzī Miyān is presented as having the right to collect the 'gift' (*shagun*) of the milk of 1,600 cowherds (Ahir) and twenty-five thousand cows at the end of every week. The protection of cattle and herdsmen represents the motive of Ghāzī Miyān's sacrifice in war. The broken marriage and the protection of cattle, two major themes of Hindu epics, are indispensable to sublimate into martyrdom the death of the young hero on the battlefield. Both have the same foster parents: Nand and Jashoda. Finally, the servants of Ghāzī Miyān's shrine compare the celebration of his marriage with the celebration of the anniversary of Krishna's birth.

Two poems take up themes from the Ramayana epic, such as the repudiation of women and the struggle against demons. In the first, *The Lay of Saint Amina* (collected and entitled by Greeven, 2010: 24–32), a woman, Amina Sati, is rejected by her husband for having served food to a Muslim, Ghāzī Miyān. The story of this woman is modelled on that of Sītā, the woman of the Rāmāyana's hero, Rāma; she is the example of the virtuous wife, unjustly rejected for having been suspected of infidelity in the absence of her husband. The second poem, *The Demon Palihar* (collected by Greeven, 2010: 8–24) presents the epic demon, Palihar, who fights against Ghāzī Miyān in the final battle of Bahraich.

The ballads show that Ghāzī Miyān is the ritual and thaumaturgical figure of a particular population, defined primarily by their locality and their function and not by their religion. It is not necessary to be Muslim to believe in the miracles of Ghāzī Miyān; his devotees, beyond their religious affiliation, have to share the values which this powerful local figure concentrates in his person. This oral tradition is the vehicle of this sharing of values; it is only sung in the ritual contexts, in particular during the 'Fair of May-June'.

Marriage: axiom of prosperity

In contrast to the hagiographer and like the servants, the Dafālī attach great importance to the marriage celebrated at the 'Fair of May-June', especially because these authors and interpreters are also 'pilgrim priests' (*pandā*) during this festival. Each of the ritual sequences is performed under the Dafālī's supervision, from the pilgrims' point of departure until their return. In particular, Zohra Bībī's 'dowry' (*dahej*), brought in a ceremonial procession called the 'wedding procession' (*barāt*), is given by devotees to servants through their mediation. As we have seen above, their poems affirm that Ghāzī Miyān has been cursed to die on his wedding day. Their participation in the festival and the role which they play thus seems to contradict their discourse. Would this contradiction enlighten the double figure of Ghāzī Miyān, ritual and heroic, emphasising the superiority of the first over the second?

By their performance, the Dafālī materialise the principal attribute of the festival the greatest miracle of Ghāzī Miyān. Every year, thanks to the work of these pilgrimage priests, Zohra Bībī is married to Ghāzī Miyān, with a precise purpose: that everybody benefits from its effects. The effectiveness of this marriage is evident, since it triggers the arrival of the monsoon, thus marking the beginning of a new rice cycle, causes the miraculous cure of lepers and obviously provides income to all those who live from the cult of Ghāzī Miyān, in particular Dafālī and servants. Was not the martyr's greatest miracle to have broken Zinda Shāh Madār's curse by the exemplary nature of his martyrdom, and to have provided exactly what everybody expects of marriage in this society: prosperity? This is what the Dafālī tell us, and also the servants of Ghāzī Miyān who have similar discourses.

This idea, which associates the prosperity of the devotees of Ghāzī Miyān with his marriage to Zohra Bībī, is the logical extension of his royal character. In the king-queen relation, the latter is at the same time wife, kingdom and earth over which the king reigns and to which he provides prosperity thanks to their sexual intercourse. By fertilising the queen, the king makes his kingdom fertile, which becomes apparent by the arrival of timely rain and good harvests, signs of his good governance. Features which are also the ones associated to the marriage of Ghāzī Miyān with Zohra Bībī. This one appears less as a character than as a representation of the soil of every individual village led to Bahraich by the Dafālī, during the 'Fair of May-June'. Each wedding procession represents a village, not a devotees' family. Moreover, the different sequences of this marriage, including the ceremonies of the 'proposal' (*mangnī*) and the 'fixing of wedding's date' (*din tarikh*) performed at the time of and the 'betrothal' during the festival of *Lagan*, are in association with the agricultural cycle and indicate the various stages of its annual fulfilment. Beginning rituals at the time of 'Spring Fifth' and *Lagan* clearly demonstrate that the master of the crop is Ghāzī Miyān.

From the hagiography to the ballads: the origin of the hero

After this hasty and general presentation of the narrative discourses of the life of Ghāzī Miyān and their interpretations of his marriage, I would like to return to discourses presenting the strongest contrasts, the hagiography and the ballads, to reassess the construction of the heroic figure of Ghāzī Miyān through narratives. I think it is necessary to rethink their chronology because the hagiography and the ballads have been inaccurately compared in the scientific literature.

The order of the discourses

As we can read about Ghāzī Miyān in general or particular works about South Indian Islam[15], such as the Islamic Encyclopaedia[16], Districts Gazetteer,[17] or in the reviews of the British ethnographers[18], when these scholars summarise his life, they consider the hagiography to be the original historical text, and they suppose that it reflects the history of North India; on the contrary, they dismiss the ballads as fiction. Nevertheless, considering the introduction the hagiographer gives to his or her work, it is questionable if we should consider him or her a historian (cf. below). It is precisely the Mirror of Mas'ud that renders Ghāzī Miyān so elusive, because its jihadist tone does not match the heroic figures developed in the other two versions (by the oral traditions of the Dafālī and the servants) on the one hand, and it does not mean match with the cult of the local powerful itself, which implies a strict collaboration between Muslim and Hindu followers, on the other.

To understand the way in which the different discourses developed, it would certainly be more judicious to invert the temporal sequence between the hagiography and the oral tradition. Although it is difficult to date the appearance of the first poems, it would seem that they have existed since the fourteenth century at least (see Amin, 2005: 281). They would thus be older than the hagiography from the seventeenth century. Indeed, Ibn Battuta reports in 1341 that numerous wonderful stories circulate about Ghāzī Miyān. Then, from the end of the eighteenth century, it is attested that the Dafālī lead the ceremonial processions of the annual 'Fair of May-June', and that the offerings which they bring to this occasion are accompanied by narrative poems. Finally, the material collected by Amin (Ibid. 283) does not differ from the compilation of the British ethnographer (as Greeven) at the end of the nineteenth century. Thus, the oral tradition would have been established a long time ago. But like the legend, they are based on the cult of Ghāzī Miyān and the traditions of his followers, particularly because they are expressed in the context of worship.

The hagiography could be seen as a modification of the oral traditions in terms of conventional seventeenth-century Islamic thought. To prove the existence of Ghāzī Miyān, in the introduction to his hagiography, 'Abd al Rahmān claims to have established the facts by relying on his Sufi capacity and his ability to communicate with saints from the past, as well as with friends and servants of Ghāzī Miyān. To draft his work, he even settles in the village of Zohra Bībī, at Rudauli (in Bara Banki district, Uttar Pradesh). Through this procedure, relying on the aid of Sufism, he tries to render the martyr more orthodox and his cult more valid.

'Abd al Rahmān claims that his research is based on historic arguments. Furthermore, to prove Ghāzī Miyān's existence and to strengthen his identity, he uses two conflicting sources about the martyr. The first is a book that can no longer be found, which would have been drafted by the servant of Sultan Mahmud Ghaznavi (Ghāzī Miyān's supposed maternal uncle), Mullā Muhammad Ghaznavī. This book is supposed to have essentially dealt with the sultan's wars and to have only mentioned in passing the narrative of the martyrdom of Ghāzī Miyān in its final part. Second, he upholds that the story which he tells is confirmed by a scholar of Bahraich, a Brahmin who had his sources drafted in Sanskrit and preserved in the library of the direct descendants of the murderer of Ghāzī Miyān, Suhal Deo.[19] From our point of view, the hagiographical work of 'Abd al Rahmān does not guarantee the historicity of Ghāzī Miyān; his introduction seems to fall within the sphere of the legend. It seems risky to use this base for reconstructing the history, with the exception of the part concerning the relationship between the Muslim elite and the worship of the Indo-Muslim saints. It seems that essentially Ghāzī Miyān acquires an authenticity that was previously lacking through this written work, which is legitimised by two high-status witnesses: Mullā Muhammad Ghaznavī and a Brahmin scholar.

On this subject, Amin (2005: 279), who tries to reconstruct history through the story of Ghāzī Miyān, recognises that the hagiography does not keep its promises. On the contrary, it contributes to sustain the thesis of the unclassifiable character of Ghāzī Miyān developed by the ethnographers since the nineteenth century, who's a jihadist worshiped by Hindus. Here, the personality of the martyr retains his duality because the hagiography oscillates between three registers: it remains the biography of a historically ambiguous character, it refers to local stories produced by Suhal Deo's followers and finally, it borrows popular Hindu themes. Despite its efforts to revise the heroic figure of Ghāzī Miyān in the mould of conventional Islamic thought, this hagiography has not managed to eliminate all the purely Hindu characteristics. This version belongs to a framework of Hindu connotations, while Ghāzī Miyān is supposed to belong to the Persianate Turkic culture. However, in many circumstances, Ghāzī Miyān behaves like a Hindu. For example he refuses cooked food, complies with food restrictions concerning the consumption of meat and likes chewing areca nut. Concerned about his personal hygiene, he adorns himself with impeccable clothes and perfume so that he is always in a state of great purity. At his father's death, he covers his clothes with ashes, and he protects cattle and herdsmen. These Hindu characteristics are essential to Ghāzī Miyān's personality, seeing as they appear even in this composition as crucial as his relationship to the period of Mahmud Ghaznavi's expeditions.

The ambition of 'Abd al Rahmān underlines, on the one hand, the major role of written evidence for the Muslim elite, and on the other hand, that this elite remained more or less unfamiliar to Ghāzī Miyān's cult, in spite of the visits of its sovereigns. Today, they remain ambivalent towards it and accept all its aspects with difficulty, and even try to render the martyr more orthodox by attempting to modify his cult (introducing a new ritual, like a birthday festival during which a sermon is organized), as 'Abd al Rahmān did in his time while mobilising the reference to Sufism.

A ritual figure

Following the cult, the discourses seem to have been embellished later, with the aim of building a personality through a biographical narrative into what seems to have been principally a local power. In other words, the discourses shaped a model life[20] of a figure of holiness, essentially known as a ritual figure, through the practices of which he is the object. As they were not able to use convincing elements to prove his historicity, they had to justify his affiliation to the Muslim religion as well as the presence of Hindus in his cult. Concerning Zohra Bībī, according to the versions, she is Muslim (for upper castes) or Hindu (for Hindus, servants and Dafālī).

Ghāzī Miyān is certainly not the best saint to guide us through the eventful paths of the history of the encounters of the Muslims and India, in spite of or because of the various heroic figures deployed by his narratives. But the wealth of his cult opens a more interesting way for a synchronic understanding of this encounter, by defining his functions in the society, functions which seem, for me, shared by Muslims and Hindus. Unlike Amin (2005: 279), for example I do not consider the accomplishment of the cults as a form of superstition. This historian relegates them to the category of 'superstitious syncretism' or the 'triumph of thaumaturgy over the historical facts', because for him, the cult tends to obscure the process of the creation of the Indian composite culture. I shall propose the inverse reading. On the contrary, the cult, the rites throw light on, if it is not the process, at least the foundation of this Indian composite culture. Finally, in my view, the annual repetition of this marriage is not proof of the incapacity of the society to accomplish it, as was interpreted by Crooke (1968: 324) and Amin (2005: 283–284). Rather, the hypothesis formulated here is the opposite: the regular repetition of the marriage expresses the hope to profit from the positive effects expected from this uncommon marriage every year. The recycling of the 'Fair of May-June's' offerings shows it. Notably, in the end of the festival, the palanquin of Zohra Bībī is recycled in cradle for the devotees' infants to come.

Conclusion

The construction of this singular figure shows two main ideas: one concerns the discourse, the other refers to the saints. In this article, I tried to show how three discourses build a different personality to the same holiness of a figure that I defined as heroic and ritual. From a general point of view, the discourse is never neutral and it can even show contradictory aims, when it has multiple versions as here. Thus, it should not be understood as a historic source but as a construction of ideological models on the origin of saints. It is also not the only tool of their manufacturing. I also tried to show by reversing the relation between discourse and ritual and by taking support on more stable data that we could otherwise interpret all the facts. The incoherence is always on the side of the researcher not on the side of the society which he or she studies. The ritual participates just as much in this elaboration, particularly because certain elements are sometimes missing to adapt the discourse to the life of its protagonist. The discourse must therefore refer to the ritual to develop itself; it then comes, according to the circumstances, in support of, or in contradiction to the ritual. A saint is not always a great name in history and a witness of his time and society. He can also be an elaboration, the fruit of a society of which the discourse then fabricates a biography. In the case analysed here, the comparison of three types of discourses highlights a society less marked by the opposition between Muslims and Hindus than by the system of castes. Indeed, over time, the different discourses shaped this figure according to the vicissitudes of history, and against the background of different values which varied according to the social status of the narrators and their audience. The protean nature of Ghāzī Miyān's life narratives shows the work of the Awadhi Indian populations to make the life of this Muslim martyr resonate with the values of their society, in which they participate as members of the low castes or members of the upper castes. His narratives give an account of a society with a composite culture and values shared beyond religious divisions, the unity of which is based on the re-composition of the archetype of the warrior-hero, emanating from the theme of the holy war and the Hindu epics. By qualifying Ghāzī Miyān as a specifically Indo-Muslim figure, my aim was not only to be accurate in his geographical localisation but also to emphasise that his creation is as much due to Muslim religion as to Indian civilisation. We deal with a cultural universe where Islam and Hinduism elaborated a holiness figure together.

My analyses follow a precise example, Ghāzī Miyān, whom I defined as a heroic figure. For the moment, he seems atypical in the landscape of Indo-Muslim holiness. This situation is certainly the result of our shortcomings in this domain. Our knowledge on this subject remains incomplete, particularly because the rare studies on the cult of the Indo-Pakistani saints mainly focus on the Sufi brotherhoods. Nevertheless, to grasp Islam in its entirety and its history, it is essential to know how to think about the worship of the saints independent of Sufism. The work of the historian Karamustafa (2006) on the emergence of Sufism shows that it took hold of the worship of saints from the thirteenth century onwards, by beginning to worship its own founders and by appropriating local saints that did not originally have a link to Sufism. Ghāzī Miyān belongs to this category. To accept this, to learn from it and to develop research can open new doors for understanding the modalities of the encounters between the Muslim conquerors and the Hindus.

Historians are in the habit of saying that the mystics followed in the footsteps of the conquerors. If it was absolutely necessary to give Ghāzī Miyān a historic appearance, we would need to connect him to the conquerors and to deduce that the Hindu-Muslim dialogue can't be limited to the one that animated the retreats of the ascetics of both religions.

Notes

1 To report it, I could quote practically all in-depth studies or simple presentations about the Indo-Muslim saints.
2 About this aspect cf. also Dumont (1951: VI) and (1957: 315).
3 My intention is different here from Seale-Chatterjee's article (1990), which studies the inversions, reversions and reversal in a set of Ghāzī Miyān's legends among the population of Benares.
4 In my thesis, I demonstrated that Sufism does not encompass all the expressions of the cult of the saints: there are some places of worship linked with other types of saints, rather than the Pan-Islamic historic or mythological figures and the Sufis as the heroes (Ortis, 2008).
5 The data was collected during three periods of fieldwork between 1996 and 2000 in Bahraich and Uttar Pradesh, funded by the grant 'Fonds Louis Dumont' and the 'Maison des Sciences de l'Homme', Paris.
6 The first Muslim raids crossed the River Ghaghara (a natural boundary in the southwest of the district of Bahraich) after the establishment of the Sultanate of Delhi in the middle of the thirteenth century.
7 Amir Khusrau (1287) is the first writer known to mention the shrine of Ghāzī Miyān.
8 From this period onward, his life is a legend and his grave the sanctuary of a miraculous Bābā, as Zia' uddin Barani explains in his narrative of the visit of Muhammad bin Tughluq (r. 1325–1351) and of the Moroccan traveller Ibn Battuta (1304–1369), or *Sirat-i Firuz Shahi* (of the Sultanate of Bengal, Haji Ilyas, who went to Bahraich to be cured of leprosy).
9 As, for example the historian Siddiqui (1989: 45) who thinks that Ghāzī Miyān must have lived during the first decades of the thirteenth century rather than at the beginning of the fourteenth.
10 The person dearest to Ghāzī Miyān, the Brahman renouncer Sikandar Dīvānā Barahnā, his fencing master, his two servants (ancestors of the current servants), soldiers of his army (assembled in a common grave, the 'Treasury of the Martyrs', *ganj-i-sahīdā*), some relatives (his wife Zohra Bībī and both of her brothers, his nursemaid and his maternal uncle), enemies converted to his cause (The Five Saints and their two bodyguards), and finally, his mare and his bitch.
11 In the year 680, Husain refused to recognise Yazid the first as a legitimate caliph, following a battle at Karbala, where he was tortured and beheaded by the soldiers of the new caliph.
12 A recurrent character of Islamic thought, Khwāja Khizr is conceived of as the double of the Prophet Elie. Having become immortal by drinking from the Source of Life, he has become the greenery covering the driest of lands; initiator of the mystics which have no human master, he is always the sign of a superior initiation. In the legend and in the hagiography, he intervenes in the conception of Ghāzī Miyān. Both narratives explicitly accentuate the causality between Khwaja Khizr's gift of a walnut to Ghāzī Miyān's father and the birth of Ghāzī Miyān. The walnut appears as an agent of fertility here.
13 However, Ghāzī Miyān and Shāh Madār do not share any religious practice. Nevertheless, for the 'Fair of May-June', the servants of Ghāzī Miyān make a black flag for Shāh Madār and prepare a rice and lentil soup called 'mixture' (*kichri*) for 'Spring

Fifth'. In Nepal, the Curaute caste, Ghāzī Miyān's devotees, are also the devotees of this antinomian saint (cf. M. Gaborieau, 1993: 299).

14 Besides, Krishna and Rāma are similarly under a curse, announced by the wise man Nārada, concerning their marriage (cf Chambard, 1991: 3).

15 Cf. Gaborieau (1975 and 1996), Mahmood (1989), Schimmel (1980), Schwerin (1981), Siddiqui (1989), among others.

16 The writer of the article on Ghāzī Miyān is Nizami (1977).

17 The District Gazetteer of Bahraich was written by Nevill, (1903) cf. pages 118–119. For a review of the District Gazetteers of Uttar Pradesh talking about Ghāzī Miyān see Ortis (2008:573–584).

18 I think here of Briggs (1920), Crooke (1968), and Ibbetson (1919).

19 See on these various points, Amin (ibid. 272).

20 On this subject, see the introduction of Centlivres (2001: 7–14).

References

Amin, S. (2005) 'Un saint guerrier. Sur la conquête de l'Inde du Nord par les Turcs au XIème siècle', *Annales* n° 2 (mars-avril): 265–292, Paris: Editions de l'Ecole des Hautes Etudes en Sciences Sociales & Armand Colin.

Briggs, J. (1920) *The Chamars*, London: Oxford University Press.

Cenlivres, P. (ed.) (2001), *Saints, sainteté et martyre. La fabrication de l'exemplarité*, Neuchâtel: Editions de l'Institut d'ethnologie & Paris: Editions de la Maison des Sciences de l'Homme.

Chambard, J-L. (1991) 'La chanson de la terre qui tremble, ou la punition du roi qui avait voulu régner sans sa reine', *Cahiers de littérature orale*, 29, *Rêver le roi* : 125–157.

Crooke W. (1896, 2nd ed 1968) *The Popular Religion and Folklore of Northern India* (2 vol.), Delhi: Munshiram Manoharlal.

——— (1896, 2nd ed 1974) *The Tribes and Castes of the North Western India*, Delhi: Cosmo Publications.

Dermenghen, E. (1981) *Vies des saints musulmans*, Paris: Sindbad.

Dumont, L. (1951, 2nd ed 1987) *La Tarasque*, Paris : Gallimard.

——— (1957, 2nd ed 1992) *Une sous-caste de l'Inde du Sud. Organisation sociale et religion des Pramalai Kallar*, Paris : Edition de l'Ecole des Hautes Etudes en Sciences Sociales.

Gaborieau, M. (1975) 'Légendes et culte du saint musulman Ghâzî Miyân au Népal occidental et en Inde du Nord', Paris: *Objets et Mondes*, XV/3: 289–318.

——— (1993) *Ni brahmanes ni ancêtres. Colporteurs musulmans du Népal*. Nanterre : Société d'Ethnologie.

——— (1996) 'Les saints, les eaux et les récoltes en Inde', *in* Amir-Moezzi M. A. (ed.) *Lieux d'islam. Cultes et cultures de l'Afrique à Java*, Paris: col. Autrement "Monde HS" n° 91/92: 239–254.

Greeven, R. (1898, present ed 2010) *The Heroes Five [Panchon Pir]; An Attempt to Collect Some of the Songs of the Pachpirya Ballad-Mongers in the Benares Division*, Memphis: General Books.

Hocart, A.M. (1950) *The Life-giving Myth and other Essays*, London: Methuen and Co.

Ibbetson, D. (1919) *A Glossary of the Tribes and Castes of the Punjab and the North-West Frontier Provinces*, 2 vols., Lahore: Superintendent Government Printing.

Karamustafa A. T. (2006) *God's Unruly Friends. Dervish Groups in the Islamic Middle Period 1200–1550*, Oxford: Oneworld Book.

——— (2007) *Sufism: the formative period*, Berkeley: University of California Press.

Lingat, R. (1989) *Royautés Bouddhiques. Asoka. La fonction royale à Ceylan*, Paris: Editions de l'Ecole des Hautes Etudes en Sciences Sociale.

Mahmood, T. (1989) "The Dargah of Sayyid Salar Mas'ud in Baraich: Legend, Tradition and Reality", *in* Troll C. (ed.), *Muslim Shrines in India: Their Character, History and Signifiance*, Delhi: Oxford University Press, 24–43.

Merathi, A. (1938) *A'ina-e Mas'udi*, Bahraich: Khalil Book Depot of Bahraich.

Nevill, H. R. (1903) *Bahraich: A Gazetteer, District Gazetteer of Uttar Pradesh* (Vol. XLV), Allahabad: Superintendent Government Printing.

Nizami, K. A. (1977) "Ghâzî Miyân", *Encyclopédie de l'islam*, vol. II, Leiden, London, Luzac and Co: E. J. Brill.

Ortis, D. (2008) *Ethnographie d'un islam indien. Organisation cultuelle et sociale d'une institution musulmane: la* dargāh *du martyr Ghāzī Miyān (Bahraich, Uttar Pradesh, Inde du Nord)*, unpublished thesis, EHESS, Paris.

Schimmel A. (1980) *Islam in the Indian Subcontinent*, Leiden: E. J. Brill.

Schwerin von K. G. (1981) "Saint Worship in Indian Islam: the Legend of the Martyr Salar Masud Ghazi", in Ahmad I. (ed.), *Ritual and Religion among Muslims in India*, Delhi: Manohar, 143–161.

Searle-Chatterjee, M. (1990) 'The Muslim Hero as Defender of Hindus: Mythic [21]Reversals and Ethnicity among Benares Muslims', in Webner P. (ed.), *Person, Myth and Society in South Asian Islam*, Adelaide: Social Analysis 28: 70–82.

Servan-Schreiber, C. (1999) *Chanteurs itinérants en Inde du Nord. La tradition orale bhojpuri*, Paris: L'Harmattan.

Siddiqui, I. H. (1989) 'A note on the Dargah of Salar Mas'ud in Baraich in the Light of the Standard Historical Sources', in Troll, C. (ed.), *Muslim Shrines in India: Their Character, History and Significance*, Delhi: Oxford University Press, 44–47.

Part II

Shrine and circulation

7 Meditative practice, aesthetics and entertainment music in an Indian Sufi shrine

Mikko Viitamäki

Music is incorporated into the rituals of several South Asian Sufi shrines and it contributes to shaping the experiences of those who visit them. This paper analyses two qawwali performance occasions in the *dargāh* of Niẕẕām al-Dīn Auliyā', a major shrine located in New Delhi. I explore how qawwali is used during the death anniversaries of the saints (*'urs*) celebrated in the shrine. A first observation reveals the variety of pilgrims' aspirations and experiences, encompassing spiritual, material and carnivalesque elements.

Discussing pilgrims' aspirations and experiences through analysis of qawwali music is facilitated by certain characteristics of the musical genre. Although it was developed for the Sufi practice of *samā'*('listening as meditation') in the Sufi hospice (*kh*ānqāh) of Niẕẕām al-Dīn Auliyā' (1244–1325) by Amīr *Kh*usrau (1253–1325), qawwali is devoid of the rigidity which is often present in the context of religious performances. In comparison with, for example the *sema* ceremony of the Turkish Mevlevis, qawwali performances are very flexible. In practice, this means that the qawwals adapt their performance according to the needs of different audiences. This is possible because only two items[1] have a fixed place in qawwali assemblies, and they can occasionally be omitted. Otherwise, the qawwals are fairly free to select the items they perform from a vast repository of song texts consisting of poems written in Persian, Urdu and archaic Hindi.[2]

Ever since 'Alī al-Hujvīrī (d. 1073) wrote his treatise *Kashf al-Maḥjūb* ('Revelation of the Veiled') in Lahore, discussions about music in Indian Sufism have revolved around defining the limits of its acceptability as a part of religious practice.[3] Sufi authors have routinely employed legal terminology in an attempt to counteract the stock argument of the critics of *samā'* who have proclaimed it a manifestation of frivolity or useless speech (*laghv*, *lahv*) which is condemned in the Koran.[4] Endless rounds of argumentation have resulted in a portrayal of music in *samā'* as something fundamentally different from other musical performances. In both popular and academic discussions, this has led to qawwali being considered more or less synonymous with the normative practice of *samā'*.[5] This outlook, however, ignores the fact that qawwali is not performed exclusively in *samā'* assemblies, and that as an established art form, it also has aesthetic and entertaining dimensions.

In this paper, I opt for a wider approach to qawwali by explicitly taking into account its aesthetic appeal and the fact that, even in a Sufi shrine, it can first and foremost embody entertainment, albeit religious in character, for some listeners. Yet, I do not side with the critics of *samā'* who contend that qawwali is nothing but merriment in the guise of worship. On the contrary, I acknowledge the significance of aesthetics and entertainment as important elements of the captivating effect of music that is utilized by Sufi masters who speak for *samā'*. Through this approach, I manage to avoid both the normative extremes that either consider aesthetics and entertainment in qawwali superfluous or overlook the religious dimensions of the musical genre.

This paper is based on observations of the *'urs* festivities of Amir *Kh*usrau in November 2006 and Niẕẕām al-Dīn in April 2009 and March 2011. The shrine and its musicians have often featured in works written about qawwali, both scholarly (e.g. Qureshi 2006) and popular (e.g. Devos 1995). Yet, I hope to add a new dimension to the preceding studies. Qureshi conducted her ethnomusicological fieldwork more than three decades ago when Sufism had not yet become a household word for urban seekers of spirituality, and the shrine of Niẕẕām al-Dīn was mainly frequented by Sufi devotees. Since the 1970s, the shrine has become a site of living heritage in Delhi and the attendance has broadened. I will be contrasting the present conditions with Qureshi's findings in the course of this paper whenever it proves significant. Furthermore, instead of approaching the topic from the viewpoint of musicology, I focus on the textual content of qawwali and relate the lyrics to the actual performance occasions, instead of concentrating on their abstracted mystical import as has been done by Claire Devos.

This paper has two distinct parts. I begin by discussing the *dargāh* of Niẕẕām al-Dīn and its role as a centre of Sufi poetry and music. Were the shrine situated in the rural periphery instead of in a capital city, it is unlikely that it would have developed into a major centre of diverse expressions of Sufism. And it would not have acquired the magical aura that in the eyes of qawwali connoisseurs is still largely intact, even though the shrine has long since lost its place at the cutting edge of Sufi music and poetry. In the main part of the paper, I focus on two qawwali performance occasions. First, I discuss a qawwali assembly organized in the meditation cell of Niẕẕām al-Dīn where Sufi disciples gather to practise *samā'* under the guidance of their shaikh. The second assembly, organized at 'Urs Maḥal, differs radically from these intimate settings. There, qawwali is aimed at a non-Sufi audience, and the performers do not concentrate on providing a means for a mystical experience but on giving an enjoyable and polished performance. Although categorizing qawwali performances in this way is, to a certain extent, an academic abstraction and an oversimplification of the multifarious experiences nurtured by individual listeners, I believe it will prove a useful tool for mapping the diversity of aspirations of those who frequent Sufi shrines.

The shrine and its festivities

The *dargāh* of Niẕẕām al-Dīn Auliyā' is a major Sufi shrine, attracting pilgrims[6] from all over South Asia. The shrine is centrally located in a New Delhi neighbourhood named Basti Hazrat Nizamuddin after the saint. In addition to being a residential area, it is a virtual necropolis where Sufis, poets, nobles and royals have been buried over the past seven centuries.[7] However, the devotional activities revolve around two tombs situated on opposite sides of a chequered courtyard in the heart of the basti, namely those of Nizẓām al-Dīn and Amīr *Kh*usrau. Nizẓām al-Dīn, the eponymous founder of the wide-spread Chishti-Nizami order, was a Sufi shaikh whose influence brought about a blooming of the literary culture of the Chishti order. His life and teachings were recorded by literary-minded disciples who thus set a normative example for both Sufi practice and literary genres of subsequent generations. Amīr *Kh*usrau was one of his disciples, and his influence as a poet and musician permeated both the royal court and the Sufi *kh*ānqāh. He has been portrayed as Nizẓām al-Dīn's closest follower since the mid-fourteenth century when the biographical compendium *Siyar al-Auliyā'* ('Deeds of the Saints') was completed by Amīr *Kh*vurd.[8] At the shrine, the significance of Amīr *Kh*usrau is underlined by the pilgrims' practice of presenting themselves by his cenotaph before entering the main mausoleum. The other tombs in the area are generally neglected by pilgrims and *kh*ādims (custodians of the shrine) alike.

Although the reputation of Nizẓām al-Dīn was immortalized in literature, his tomb has significantly helped in diffusing it among people who may have had neither the chance nor the interest in submerging themselves in Sufi writings. Situated in a city that has served as an imperial capital for eight centuries except for minor intervals, the shrine has been frequented by Muslim conquerors and travelers, along with the local elite and common people. At present, a visit to the shrine is included in the official visits of Muslim statesmen. Its *kh*ādims and architectural edifice have enjoyed royal patronage, and the ongoing restoration of the shrine and the surrounding basti, funded by the Aga Khan Trust for Culture, reveals its sustained significance in independent India.

Despite the blows suffered by Muslims and Indo-Islamic culture in Delhi during the brutal suppression of the 1857 uprising and the partition ninety years later, the shrine continues to be an important cultural symbol for the inhabitants of Delhi and Indian Muslims in general. The decade following the commencement of the war on terror has seen the emergence of Sufism, which is portrayed as a form of Islam that is compatible with the secular ideology promulgated by the Indian state authorities. At the same time, a number of people belonging to the urban middle class in Delhi have discovered spirituality that crosses the boundaries of diverse religious traditions and does not involve a political agenda in Sufism.[9] They visit the shrine on Thursday nights in significant numbers in order to experience Sufi spirituality that finds its most accessible manifestation in qawwali music. It is interesting to note that although Thursday-night qawwali is only a faint echo of the music heard in *samā'* assemblies, it appears authentic when compared with recordings that fill the Sufi Music section of upmarket stores like Music World and Planet M. Thursday-night qawwali sessions attract the participation of another visible group of people, namely European and American tourists who are drawn to the shrine by the promise of hearing 'qawwali (Sufi devotional singing)' mentioned in *Lonely Planet: India* (2001: 190). Listening to qawwali and witnessing ecstasy at the *dargāh* of Niẕẕām al-Dīn has also become a recurring feature in present-day Delhi travelogues.[10]

In addition to the religious fervour of Thursday nights, the shrine has its annual cycle of religious festivals which culminates during the *'urs*. *'Urs*, a word referring to marriage festivities, denotes the commemoration of the union of a Sufi saint's spirit with the divine beloved in death. During the *'urs*, the saint is thought to be particularly accessible, and pilgrims engage in spiritual communication with him through prayers and offer him their requests to be mediated to God. In addition to the *'urs* of Niẕẕām al-Dīn on 18 Rabī' al-Sẕānī, the death anniversary of Amīr *Kh*usrau is celebrated on 18 Shavvāl. Despite naming the two occasions as *Baṛe 'Urs* ('The Great *'Urs*') and *Choṭe 'Urs* ('The Small *'Urs*') respectively, they are both large-scale occasions that attract thousands of pilgrims. The festivities begin on the sixteenth day of both lunar months, and draw to a close on the twentieth, although many pilgrims already leave after the main rituals on the eighteenth. The core element of the *'urs* festivities is a ritual called *qul*. *Qul*s are organized in the shrine courtyard, and the attendance, especially during the *'urs* of Niẕẕām al-Dīn, is so high that the *dargāh* compound can barely contain all the devotees. *Qul* begins with a *fātiḥa*.[11] Known by the name of the first *sura* of the Koran, this ritual includes reciting certain Koranic passages and the master-disciple chain (*shajara*) ending with the name of the saint, and conferring the merits of the recitation to his spirit. This is followed by a supplication (*du'ā*) for the general well-being of humankind. Afterwards, the sweets and other items that had been placed in front of the Sufi dignitaries conducting the ritual are distributed as blessed items (*tabarruk*).

The ritual is, however, incomplete without music and the hereditary qawwals attached to the shrine perform items called *Qaul* and *Rang* after the *fātiḥa*.[12] In addition to the ritual context, qawwals perform virtually around the clock during the five days of *'urs*. The sheer abundance of qawwali performances renders music the major attraction of the celebrations – alongside the saint, of course. At the shrine, there are relatively few other attractions to compete with qawwali.[13] There is no full-fledged fair (*melā*) with stalls and merry-go-rounds organized in the neighbourhood, or non-religious events such as the All India Industrial Exhibition that takes place during the *'urs* of *Kh*vāja Bandanavāz Gesudarāz in Gulbarga.

Qawwali in the shrine of Niẕẕām al-Dīn is particularly interesting, because it is performed in highly heterogeneous contexts for diverse audiences. In contradistinction with the practice in smaller shrines where the participants of the *'urs* attend all the programmes as a single group, in Niẕẕām al-Dīn the celebrations spread to various locations. Some pilgrims practically spend the entire *'urs* in the courtyard of the shrine and take part in whatever programmes take place there, while others stay with their specific Sufi order. Yet others follow a particular qawwali group from one function to another.

For qawwals, *'urs* is a lucrative period. They have a possibility to practise their profession on multiple occasions over a short period of time. Even if they do not act as religious functionaries[14] like Sufi shaikhs and *kh*ādims, they are crucial to the proper execution of *'urs*. Their services are in high demand, and since Delhi is home to a relatively small number of qawwali groups, the shrine has to rely on qawwals arriving from outside the city in order to meet the demand for performers. The need for qawwals is all the more pronounced at present as it seems that the Sufis who lay claim to qawwali connoisseurship are reluctant to listen to the hereditary qawwals of the shrine.[15] The senior qawwal of the shrine, Mi'rāj Aḥmad, who during Qureshi's fieldwork in the 1970s was at the height of his career and the chief performer in any *maḥfil*, has not been able to transmit his musical and poetic skills to his sons, and thus lacks well-trained accompanists. Other hereditary qawwals have drifted away from the musical and poetic standards expected by the Sufi elite in their quest for new audiences, and they rarely appear in the *maḥfil*s arranged outside the shrine courtyard.

On the other hand, qawwals like Muḥammad Aḥmad Vāris̤ī and Mājid Vāris̤ī, both from Rampur, have endeared themselves to the discerning audiences with their trained voices, musical idiom conforming to the conventions of Hindustani art music and their poetic repertoire consisting of Sufi classics and contemporary poems. In addition, Iftikhār Aḥmad Amrohavī has achieved prominence in Delhi. Qureshi (2006: 38, 102) characterized him as a young amateur performer with limited musical abilities. However, over the past three decades, his continued training and mastery in setting poetry to music have made him one of the most sought after performers. These qawwals are able to enthrall elite Sufi audiences who value Old Persian poetry and qawwali performances that adhere to the conventions of art music, as well as listeners whose notion of qawwali has been formed by popular commercial recordings. This versatility becomes evident in the following chapters.

A *Samā'* assembly at Cilla Sharīf

The first qawwali performance occasion closely follows the norms delineated for the practice of *samā'* in literary sources.[16] These norms relate to both the outward comportment of participants and their inner orientation. The art of qawwals is indispensable to this assembly, but simultaneously it has an essentially instrumental value as an aid for the listeners' spiritual practice. The assembly in question is organized at Cilla Sharīf in the late morning of the seventeenth day of both *'urs* festivities. Cilla, the meditation cell used by Niz̤z̤ām al-Dīn, is situated about one kilometre east from the *dargāh*, adjacent to the north wall of the Mughal emperor Humāyūn's tomb. The rediscovery of the place has been claimed by a prominent Sufi shaikh, author and hereditary custodian of the Niz̤z̤ām al-Dīn *dargāh*, *Kh*vāja Ḥasan Niz̤z̤āmī (1878–1955), and he initiated the practice of holding *samā'* assemblies there. The Cilla is located away from the thoroughfares of the neighbourhood, and casual passersby rarely stray in. Most listeners are disciples (*murīd*) in the Sufi order headed by *Kh*vāja Ḥasan S̤s̤ānī Niz̤z̤āmī, the son and deputy of *Kh*vāja Ḥasan Niz̤z̤āmī, and the atmosphere is very intimate. The *'urs* is a rare opportunity for *murīd*s to enjoy the company of their shaikh as *Kh*vāja Ḥasan S̤s̤ānī is not very active during the rest of the year due to his considerable age.[17] As a result, the five days spent with the shaikh during the *'urs* become an intensive period of Sufi training. The assembly organized at the Cilla represents an important aspect of pilgrimage to Sufi shrines that is sometimes overlooked: the focus of the pilgrims is not exclusively on the dead saint, but also on being in the company of a living shaikh.

On regular days, the people visiting the Cilla engage in their devotions in the gallery facing the meditation cell that also functions as a mosque. During the *samāʻ* assemblies, the cell is opened and *Kh*vāja Ḥasan Ṣ̤ānī takes his place inside, thus explicitly assuming the role of Niẕẕām al-Dīn's present-day representative. His relatives, closest *murīd*s and visiting Sufi dignitaries gather around him, while the rest of the listeners and qawwals take their seats in the gallery.

The assembly opens with a *fātiḥa* that is followed by the qawwals' performance. In April 2009, three qawwali groups attended the assembly at the Cilla.[18] First to perform is Miʻrāj Aḥmad with the hereditary qawwals attached to the *dargāh*. As their head, he is entitled to perform the ritual songs, *Qaul* and *Rang*. The text of the *Qaul* is very short, and it consists of the Arabic hadith, *Man kuntu maulāhu fa-ʻaliyyun maulāh* ('Whose master I am, his master is Ali') set to music by Amīr *Kh*usrau. For the Shia, the hadith proves Ali's inheritance of both the spiritual and worldly authority of the Prophet Muhammad. For the Sufis, the significance of the hadith rises from Ali's role as the heir of the Prophet's esoteric knowledge, as well as from his being the first link in the master-disciple chain of most orders. While performing the *Qaul*, Miʻrāj Aḥmad sang inserted verses (*girah*) in order to augment the otherwise brief text and open new vistas into the import of the hadith for the listeners to explore. Many of these verses were stock items which were sung during most performances. However, he sang something rare for the discerning audience, namely a seldom-heard Persian verse attributed to Maulānā Rūmī:

Whose master I am, his master is Ali
As long as the picture of earth remains and time remains, will Ali remain
As long as the form of the world keeps together, will Ali remain
Whose master I am . . .

*Kh*vāja Ḥasan Ṣ̤ānī and his main guest, Vāriṣ̤ Ḥusain Cishtī, a *kh*ādim from the shrine of Muʻīn al-Dīn in Ajmer, are stirred by the verse and it becomes the culminating point of the performance. *Kh*vāja Ḥasan Ṣānī instructs the qawwals to sing the phrase *'alī hast 'alī būd*[19] ('Ali is, Ali will remain') in different variations. A successful performance of the verse that appeals to the mystical and aesthetic sensitivities of the audience leads to the offering of notes to the head of the assembly. The money constitutes the reward of the qawwals, but it is given to the head of the assembly instead of the performers. This emphasizes the listeners' focus on the Sufi master, and offers them a chance to establish physical contact with him by kissing his hand or bowing their heads to his knee when presenting the offering.

In Delhi, *Qaul* is always followed by *Rang*, a Hindi poem that is also attributed to Amīr *Kh*usrau. This poem describes the meeting of a young lady with her beloved during the Holi festival when the revelers throw coloured powders and water on each other, and the social norms regulating the dealings between the sexes are relaxed. Through this imagery, the poem evokes the meeting of a *murīd* and his Sufi master. Thus, *Qaul* and *Rang* express in poetry and music the concept of the master-disciple relationship that was evoked during the *fātiḥa* by the recitation of the entire lineage from the Prophet to *Kh*vāja Ḥasan Nizẓāmī. These items acquire pronounced significance when the audience consists of listeners who share the experience of being a *murīd*.

After the obligatory items, *Kh*vāja Ḥasan Ṣānī indicated that Mi'rāj Aḥmad's group should give way to other, more accomplished performers. Mi'rāj Aḥmad's son, however, inquired in a hurt voice if that was all the time given to the Delhi qawwals. In the end, they were allowed to sing one more item. The choice was a poem often sung on festive occasions, Amīr *Kh*usrau's ghazal *'Īd-gāh-i mā gharībān kū-yi to* (*'Id-ground for us poor is your lane'*). The first two verses describe the lover at the lane of the beloved, where he has arrived to receive alms of love and beauty:

Id-ground for us poor is your lane
Seeing the joyous day of Id, your face.

I offer you a hundred crescent moons of Id
Crescent of ours, the arch of your eyebrows.

The following verse turns the focus of the poem onto Nizẓām al-Dīn:

Nizẓām al-Dīn, the Divine Beloved
All lovers sacrifice themselves for the sake of your face.

The audience was thrilled. This verse turns the poem into a depiction of the relationship between a *murīd* and his master that in the collective imagination of the Chishti-Nizami order is epitomized by the bond between Amīr *Kh*usrau and Nizẓām al-Dīn. This relationship is an ideal of present-day *murīd*s, and the performance provoked them to approach *Kh*vāja Ḥasan Ṣānī with an offering.

Although the ghazal is a stock item in the repertoires of all qawwals, Mi'rāj Aḥmad's version is highly original as it contains several verses which are not found elsewhere.[20] The following verses employ images of passionate love:

We destitute have arrived to your lane
[To perceive] the affairs of God from the beauty of your face

Extend your hand towards our [begging] basket
Praise to your hand and to your arm!

What do I know about the Kaba and the temple?
I keep prostrating in front of your face.

How long will you be asking what killed Khusrau?
It was your coquettish glance, your eyes, your eyebrows.

Once he had finished, Mi'rāj Aḥmad had to give way to Muḥammad Aḥmad Vāriṣ̤ī. The latter had previously been given a privileged place in the assemblies of *Kh*vāja Ḥasan Ṣ̤ānī. However, assuming the role of a representative of authentic qawwali outside the Sufi context, and even prioritizing a concert over *'urs* festivities on one occasion impaired his status. In 2006 and 2009, *Kh*vāja Ḥasan Ṣ̤ānī frequently made critical remarks about Muḥammad Aḥmad's singing and his understanding of poetry. For a well-trained and self-assertive qawwal hailing from a family of musicians formerly attached to the Rampur court, this verged on public humiliation. Even so, Muḥammad Aḥmad kept attending his assemblies. In 2011, when the public attention around him had somewhat abated, the relationship between the Sufi master and the qawwal markedly improved.[21] Whenever he is performing for *Kh*vāja Ḥasan Ṣ̤ānī and his disciples, Muḥammad Aḥmad seeks to demonstrate his musical skills and command over a wide array of poetry. In the assembly organized in 2009, he begun with the concluding verse (*maqṭ̤a'*) of a ghazal by Amīr *Kh*usrau:

Cry out in front of his door, Khusrau, because that king
Knows that it is his servant calling.

It is the normal practice among qawwals to perform select verses of a ghazal instead of singing the entire poem. However, only singing the concluding verse is highly unusual. Muḥammad Aḥmad builds the entire performance on musical variations of this single verse. The emphasis he places on purely musical considerations is somewhat uncharacteristic of qawwali. The verse describes Amīr *Kh*usrau at the door of a king announcing his presence with a cry. The verse plays with the meaning of the poet's pen name, *Kh*usrau ('emperor'). He is only a supplicant at the door of 'that king' (*ān sulṭ̤ān*) – a phrase that indicates Niẓ̤ām al-Dīn, the King of Shaikhs (*Sulṭ̤ān al-Mashā'ikh*). The verse manages to take into account the actual performance context as well: the participants sit in front of the door to the meditation cell of the King of Shaikhs.

After completing *Kh*usrau's poem, Muḥammad Aḥmad continued with a Persian ghazal written by Shāh Niyāz Aḥmad Barelvī (1742–1832). A positive response to poems by this eminent Sufi is guaranteed anywhere in South Asia. This time the qawwals concentrated on delivering the textual message, rather than engaging in vocal artistry. In the poem, Niyāz utilizes conventional hyperbolic idiom in praising Niẓ̤ām al-Dīn:

You are an ocean of blessing and guidance, a teacher of the knowledge of poverty
From head to toe you are a life-bestowing charm of all the beauties the heart longs for.

You are a pearl in the ocean of seclusion, a rose in the garden of solitary ascetic practices
In the appearance and form of a human being, you manifest the essence of God.

Some verses, on the other hand, rely on erotic themes to praise the saint. The following verse describes the emaciation of the lover:

> *The passion for the divine beloved has made me like this*
> *Were an artist to paint my picture, he would make it into the form of a sigh.*

Conceptualizing the relationship between a disciple and his master or between a human being and God in the framework of passionate love features prominently in Sufi poetry written in India prior to the mid-nineteenth century. Notwithstanding that this poetic convention has become increasingly rare in modern Sufi poetry and public qawwali performances, such poetry is still an essential component of intimate *samā'* assemblies like those organized at the Cilla.

The last group to perform also hailed from Rampur. Mājid VāriṢī continued with the theme of passionate love by performing a ghazal by *Kh*usrau:

> *You robbed the spirit from the body and yet are within the spirit*
> *You gave me pain but are the medicine as well.*
>
> *With the sword of coquetry you ruined the kingdom of heart*
> *And yet, you are the ruler of this wasteland.*
>
> *'Both worlds!' you told the price of yourself*
> *Raise the bid, as it still sells cheap.*
>
> *Old age and worship of beauties don't go well together*
> *Kh*usrau, how long will you remain agitated?

The qawwals began with an extended vocal introduction (*alāp*) that is reminiscent of the *kh*ayāl style of singing and inserted lengthy improvisatory passages between the verses as well. Their musical skills were lauded by *Kh*vāja Ḥasan Ṣānī. The group concluded with a more energetic number, a ghazal by Niyāz in praise of Mu'īn al-Dīn, the fountainhead of the Chishti order in India. After a succinct performance, *Kh*vāja Ḥasan Ṣānī concluded the assembly with a *du'ā*. The sugar candies blessed during the *fātiḥa* were distributed as *tabarruk*, and the crowd dispersed.

A qawwali concert at 'Urs Maḥal

In the twentieth century, qawwali has found its way to concert stages both in South Asia and abroad.[22] Perhaps surprisingly, qawwali is also performed in concert-like circumstances during the *'urs* festivities at the venue called 'Urs Maḥal. The main programme at 'Urs Maḥal differs fundamentally from the intimate settings of the Cilla. Rather than a component of spiritual practice, qawwali is performed as an expression of Sufi culture to a largely non-Sufi audience.

'Urs Maḥal is a pillared hall, open from one side, situated on the eastern side of the *dargāh* next to the sixteenth-century tomb of a Mughal noble, Mirzā 'Azīz

Kokaltāsh. The edifice was inaugurated in 1962 under the auspices of the president at that time, S. Radhakrishnan. Since then, its express function has been to offer a stage for a programme that state dignitaries requiring strict security measures can attend, and so either the president or the prime minister has regularly been present as a guest of honour. The functions at 'Urs Maḥal are presided over by Pīr Aḥmad Nizẕāmī, son and deputy of the late Pīr Ẕāmin Nizẕāmī (d. 1993). Pīr Ẕāmin was a *kh*ādim who campaigned actively for the portrayal of Sufism as an integral part of the shared cultural heritage of independent India.

'Urs Maḥal is cleaned, whitewashed and decorated prior to both *'urs* festivities. The performers sit on a stage that is situated in the middle of the back wall. Rows of chairs reserved for the general public fill the space on its right side, while a dais for the guests of honour is on the left. The main programme takes place in the evening on the nineteenth and it consists of a poets' gathering (*mushā'ira*), Pīr Aḥmad Nizẕāmī's speech that portrays Sufis as emissaries of peace and universal humanism, *fātiḥa* and a qawwali performance. The distinctive feature of the event is that it is broadcast live by All India Radio. All the qawwals are introduced by an announcer and the time allotted for each group is, in principle, limited to five minutes. This effectively rules out the prospect of lengthening the performance by repetition of poetic phrases which are required in the case of a listener experiencing a mystical state. Besides, the layout of the venue is such that the performers and listeners sit quite far away from each other, and keeping an eye on the reactions of an audience numbering several hundred at best is practically impossible. The listeners sit relatively far from the performers and the head of the assembly. Only guests of honour sitting nearby engage in the conventional offering of notes, and the qawwals receive little money. Notwithstanding the lack of interaction with the audience and modest prospects of income, a chance to be broadcast live is enough to attract more qawwals to 'Urs Maḥal than to any other programme organized during the *'urs*.

The programme of the nineteenth showcases Sufism for an audience which is not necessarily acquainted with even its basic tenets. This attempt to reach beyond traditional Sufi circles affects the qawwali performances as well. The preferred languages are Urdu and Hindi, both commonly understood by the live audience and the listeners in front of their radios. The majority of the lyrics performed at 'Urs Maḥal fall into one of two categories: the texts in the first category have relevance outside the immediate Sufi context, and thus manage to represent Sufism as a part of the common cultural heritage. The Hindi poems ascribed to Amīr *Kh*usrau, who in modern India has become a champion of Indo-Islamic composite culture, are a case in point. During the programme organized on the occasion of the *'urs* of Amīr *Kh*usrau in November 2006, *Gh*ulām Ḥusain Niyāzī performed *Torī ṣūrat ke balhārī* ('A sacrifice for the sake of your face'), a poem that was made famous by several recording artists. Muḥammad Aḥmad opted for *Kāhe ko byāhī bides* ('Why do I have to marry outside my village?'), a poem sung in wedding celebrations and films as well as in *samā'* assemblies.

The second category of lyrics comprises texts that connect Sufism with the reformist rhetoric concerning orthodox Islam.[23] If Hindavi poems target non-Muslims, these lyrics are aimed at non-Sufi Muslims. In an attempt to prove orthodox credentials of Sufism, such lyrics engage in the debate raging around the correct practice of Islam instigated by reformist movements in the nineteenth century. In November 2006, Ifti*kh*ār Aḥmad sung in celebration of visualization (*taṣavvur*) and acts of worship (*'ibādat*) in a ghazal that ends in the rhyme 'and I am' (*aur maiṅ hūṅ*). The rhyme trivializes the state of annihilation (*fanā'*) during which the self of the perceiving subject is effaced and only the object remains. The person undergoing the experience may act in ways that are considered improper from the point of view of the orthodox establishment. Upturning the conventional poetic imagery is particularly evident in the third verse which adds 'I' where traditionally there has only been the beloved and the mystic turned into a mirror:[24]

> *I visualize you and I am*
> *I experience the joy of worship and I am.*
>
> *I am afraid that your hand might seek for me*
> *There is the sanctuary, there is the place of retreat and there am I.*
>
> *I sacrifice myself for the face of the beloved*
> *There is the glance, there is the mirror and there am I.*

Adhering to the unambiguously religious frame of reference does not thwart the qawwals' ability to entertain. In spite of the fact that the lyrics sung at 'Urs Maḥal are fairly sober, the performances can be surprisingly showy, even frivolous. The best example in November 2006 was the last qawwal to perform, Yūsuf Malik Qavvāl. Already his appearance was in stark contrast to the conservative dress code followed by qawwals: he donned formal trousers, a short jacket with glitzy embroidery and a blue fur hat. His accessories included a pendulum worn prominently around the neck and a gold watch that flashed whenever he raised his hand. He gesticulated vehemently while singing and engaged the audience's attention by inserting small questions into the song. In the manner of popular qawwali idiom, the main bulk of the lyrics consisted of *girah* verses joined together by a single-line refrain. The profuse use of *girah* verses stems from the fact that their often surprising interaction with the main text adds a dimension of enjoyable verbal entertainment to the performance. In the following, every *girah* finds its full meaning in the refrain:

> *This is the mercy of the one wearing a blanket* [i.e. Muhammad].
>
> > *Upon taking your name, I obtained honour*
> > *Lord, continue to bestow your mercy upon the slave like this!*
> > *Because my head does not bow down on anyone else's threshold*
> > *I find success on every stage.*
>
> *This is the mercy of the one wearing a blanket.*
>
> > *The one has seen the end result of love*
> > *Who has given his life for Muhammad like the men at the battle of Uḥud.*

And in the Prophet's Mosque it seems
As if Bilāl was still calling people to prayer.

This is the mercy of the one wearing a blanket.

Going to Medina, I press a kiss on the earth
If my life is required, I shall relinquish it.
[Recording unclear] *I would give to your lips*
Even then Bilāl would say, 'I'll give the call for prayer anyway'

This is the mercy of the one wearing a blanket . . .

The engagement with the Muslim cause emerges in the mention of Bilāl, the first *mu'azzin* known for his beautiful voice. As the prohibition of broadcasting the call for prayer is perceived as a definite sign of repression by non-Muslims, Bilāl has come to represent the protection of the rights of Muslims.

More than any other qawwal, Yūsuf Malik was able to enthrall the audience. Some young men left their seats in the audience and flocked in front of the stage. Leaning forward, they expressed their admiration for the performers whenever they reached the refrain. After each number Yūsuf Malik asked the audience, 'More?', and since he was not interrupted by the head of the assembly, he continued for almost half an hour with the encouragement of the rowdy youngsters. In contrast, the enthusiasm among the guests of honour was somewhat mild, and Pīr Aḥmad Nizẓāmī actually dozed off during the raucous performance before finally closing the assembly with a *du'ā*.

Conclusion

Material collected at the *dargāh* of Nizẓām al-Dīn during the *'urs* festivities offer useful insights for the discussion pertaining to the pilgrimage to Sufi shrines in South Asia. As a major shrine, it attracts pilgrims from various backgrounds, ranging from Sufi adepts to middle-class seekers of spirituality. They all bring their individual aspirations to the shrine and this guides their participation in various programmes organized at the shrine and in its vicinity. Qawwali music plays an integral role in these programmes, and it acquires multiple meanings in addition to merely being a genre of music used in meditative practice.

The structure of a qawwali performance is open to myriad variations. These variations reveal more about the fabric of the audience and the qawwals' notion of what it wants to hear than about the performers' predilection. The qawwals are also adept in utilizing other features such as the venue of the assembly and the *murīd*s' affection to their master in the process of maximizing the effect of their performances. In practice, this leads to both a deeper experience for the listeners, and an increase in the performers' remuneration.

At the Cilla, the qawwali performances are set in the context of normative practice of *samā'*. While performing, the qawwals highlight the significance of the Cilla by repeatedly evoking the presence of Nizẓām al-Dīn. Along with Amīr

*Kh*usrau, he epitomizes the master-disciple relationship in the memory of the Chishti-Nizami order, while most listeners hold it as an ideal of their own experience of being a *murīd*. At the Cilla, the audience is largely acquainted with the deeper tenets of Sufism, and the head of the assembly, *Kh*vāja Ḥasan Ṣānī, has the reputation of being an eminent Sufi shaikh and a scholar and connoisseur of music and poetry. Hence, it is not surprising that the qawwals adhere to the conventions of Hindustani art music and usually sing classic items written in Persian and Hindi. Poetic imagery in these languages is often ambiguous in the sense that it evokes the relationship between a disciple and his master, or human and divine in the terms of passionate love – something shunned in more public contexts, like 'Urs Maḥal. Outside the more formal context, entertainment can also emerge as the prominent concern of the qawwals. This is discernible in the programme organized at 'Urs Maḥal. The site has little connection with Niẕẕām al-Dīn and the audience does not share parallel religious orientation. The qawwali performances reflect a more general desire to introduce Sufism to an audience that is not necessarily familiar with it. The qawwals sing poems that are either relevant outside the immediate Sufi context or lend Sufism an aura of what is currently thought to constitute Islamic orthodoxy. The former are aimed at non-Muslim listeners, while the latter are intended to appeal to non-Sufi Muslims. The performances are usually more entertaining and open to popular influences than on other occasions. This is evident, for example in the profuse use of witty *girah* verses. It is interesting to note that although the performances at 'Urs Maḥal may be more playful than at the Cilla, the lyrics are more sober and leave no doubt as to their intended interpretation in an expressly religious framework.

These two performance occasions reflect the different dimensions of Sufism centred on shrines. At the Cilla, music becomes an aid to meditative practice and the entire context reinforces the bonding between a living Sufi master and disciples committed to following him. At the 'Urs Maḥal, the scope of the programmes extends beyond the committed Sufi disciples and the performances are targeted toward the pilgrims who wish to benefit from the saintly intercession without necessarily adopting a regime of Sufi practices. The programme is much like any concert and the music acquires a role as a central attraction of the festivities. The qawwali performances at the 'Urs Maḥal are also tied to discussions on Sufism in broader cultural and religious contexts. The 'Urs Maḥal is open and easy to approach, whereas the assembly at the Cilla is attended by the inner circle of Sufi disciples.

In spite of the differences, the two performance occasions have much in common. In both cases, aesthetic enjoyment and entertainment are crucial to shaping the experience of the listeners. Even if the possibilities for interaction between the audience and the performers are limited at the 'Urs Maḥal, even there the qawwals make an effort to tailor their performances so as to ensure a favourable reception. Unrestricted by predefined conventions dictated by ritual requirements, the qawwals capitalize on the liberty to choose the items they sing, and freshness and surprise are important elements of both assemblies.

In the broader context of the fabric of Islam in South Asia, the employment of music and sung poetry as vehicles for conveying religious views and shaping religious experiences seem to give shrine-centred Sufism a certain advantage over its reformist critics. Both Sufis and reformists take recourse to books, pamphlets and sermons in disseminating their views, but only the former include music in their practice of Islam. In Basti Hazrat Nizamuddin, the members of Tablighi Jamaat have to content themselves with printed materials and preaching in their attempts to reform those who attend the shrine. However, it is hard to make scriptural argumentation, however eloquent, as appealing and as entertaining as sung poetry. This hopefully stimulates discussions on the significance of aestheticization of religion, entertainment and fun for the sustained popularity of Sufi shrines in South Asia.

Notes

1 The word 'item' (*cīz* in Urdu) refers to a unit of performance that consists of a text and the music it is set to. The performance items are commonly referred to by the first words or the opening line of the poetic text.

2 In addition to these languages, poems in Siraiki and Punjabi are performed in Pakistani Punjab. However, the significance of these languages is localized and they are never utilized, for example in the Deccan. Other areas, like Sindh and Bengal, have their respective traditions of Sufi poetry and music. For a discussion on general features of qawwali repertoires, see Viitamäki 2009: 315–23.

3 For the views of al-Hujvīrī on *samā'*, see al-Hujvīrī 1967: 508–46. For an English translation, see al-Hujvīrī 1999: 393–420.

4 See, e.g. Quran 23:1, 25:72 and 31:5. See Lawrence 1983 (also Ernst & Lawrence 2002: 34–45) on the early Chishti approach to *samā'*. For Indian Sufi texts employing legal terminology in discussing *samā'*, see, e.g. *Risāla Uṣūl al-Samā'* (Zarrādī 1889) by Niẕẕām al-Dīn's deputy Fa*kh*r al-Dīn Zarrādī (d. 1347) and *Samā'* (Ṣiddīqī n.d.) by 'Abd al-Qadīr Ḥasrat Ṣiddīqī (d. 1962). For a critical view on *samā'*, see e.g. Thānavī 1904.

5 See, e.g. Huda 2007 and Latif 2007.

6 The word pilgrim, *zā'ir* (lit. 'visitor'), is seldom used in Urdu parlance, whereas the words 'pilgrimage' (*ziyārat*) and 'place of pilgrimage' (*mazār*, i.e. a saint's tomb), derived from the same Arabic root, are in common use. The word *ziyārat* denotes the visit to the shrine and the rituals performed there, not the act of peregrination. Thus, both those who arrive at the shrine from a longer distance and those who live in its vicinity and may attend the shrine on a daily basis perform *ziyārat*.

7 Detailed information on various tombs and their locations in and around the shrine can be gleaned from the margin notes of *Niẕẕāmī Bansurī* by *Kh*vāja Ḥasan Niẕẕāmī (Niẕẕāmī 1990). On the architectural development of the mausoleum of Niẕẕām al-Dīn and its adjacent mosque, see *Khān 2003*: 291–4. [Please include the full reference in the reference list]

8 See al-Kirmānī 1885: 301–5.

9 Several coffee table books on South Asian Sufi shrines – affordable only to the higher income classes – have appeared in recent years. On Niẕẕām al-Dīn and his shrine, see Currim and Michell 2004: 24–39; Dhaul 2006 and Quraeshi 2009: 166–85.

10 See, e.g. Dalrymple 2003: 279–81 and Mackintosh-Smith 2005: 93–6.

11 For a detailed discussion on *fātiḥa*, see the paper of Mauro Valdinoci in this volume.

12 For more information on *Qaul* and *Rang*, see the following chapter.

13 Besides qawwali, food is the other important attraction. *Kh*ādims urge their guests to sponsor lavish *langar*s that include the ever-present dishes of rice cooked with meat (*biriyānī*) and meat stew (*qorma*) served with rich bread (*shīrmāl*) or oven baked

flatbread (*tandūrī roṭī*). Needless to say, such dishes are beyond the means of most pilgrims.

14 Qureshi (2006: 97–8) has likened the qawwals to service professionals in the hierarchy of the shrine.

15 See Qureshi (2006: 96–102) on the hereditary qawwals in the shrine.

16 See, e.g. the lengthy chapter on *samā'* in *Siyar al-Auliyā'* (al-Kirmānī 1885: 491–534) and the remarks on *samā'* made by Nizẕām al-Dīn in *Favā'id al-Fu'ād* (Sijzī 2007: 248–50, 254–6, 464–70, 904–8, 972–4).

17 This applies to many other Sufi orders based in Delhi as well. The relative inactivity manifests in the absence of weekly congregational zikr gatherings and monthly *samā'* assemblies which are core activities of the Sufi scene in, for instance, Hyderabad.

18 Although the examples are taken from a single assembly for the sake of coherence, the selection of items by the qawwals, as well as the audience's reactions to them have been strikingly uniform during all the assemblies organized in this location during the fieldwork.

19 Consolidating poetic and musical metres lies behind the pronunciation of 'is, will remain' *būd* instead of *buvad*. The Perso-Arabic script facilitates both readings, although the latter is grammatically correct.

20 Interestingly, the compilation of qawwali poetry collected by Mi'rāj Aḥmad, *Surūd-i Rūḥānī*, only contains the standard four-verse version (Qavvāl 1998: 70).

21 A similar case of conflict between stardom and Sufi practice that aims at obliterating the ego has been discussed by Robert Rozehnal (2007: 222–4). He notes that a deputy of the Chishti-Sabiri shaikh, Zauqī Shāh, Shahīd Allāh Farīdī refused to allow either the Sabri Brothers or Nusrat Fateh Ali Khan to perform in his assemblies because he deemed their celebrity incommensurate with the practice of *samā'*.

22 For a discussion on popular qawwali, see Qureshi 1992, 1995 and 1999.

23 The contest over defining the correct Islam is a salient element of the religious scene in the basti. After the *dargāh*, the most important religious institution in the neighbourhood is the Delhi Centre of Tablighi Jamaat. Members of this movement are notorious for their aggressive preaching and zeal to reform Muslims who do not share their religious views.

24 It is worth noting that in other contexts, Ifti*kh*ār Aḥmad performs poems which extol *fanā'* and discuss the metaphysics of the singleness of existence (*vaḥdat al-vujūd*).

References

Currim, M. and Michell, G. (photographs by K. Lewis 2004) *Dargahs. Abodes of the Saints*, Marg, Special issue 56 (1), Mumbai: Marg Foundation.

Dalrymple, W. (1993; 2nd ed 2003) *City of Djinns*, New York: Penguin Books.

Devos, C. (1995) *Qawwali. La musique des maîtres du soufisme*, Paris: Éditions du Makar.

Dhaul, L. (2006) *The Dargah of Nizamuddin Auliya*, New Delhi: Rupa & Co.

Ernst, C.W. and Lawrence, B.B. (2002) *Sufi Martyrs of Love. The Chishti Order in South Asia and Beyond*, New York: Palgrave Macmillan.

Huda, Q. (2007) 'Memory, Performance, and Poetic Peacemaking in Qawwali', *The Muslim World*, 97 (4): 678–700.

al-Hujvīrī, 'A. (1967) *Kashf al-Maḥjūb*, ed. V. Zhoukovskii, Teheran: Cāp Gulshan.

——— (1999) *Revelation of the Mystery*, trans. R.A. Nicholson, Accord: Pir Press.

al-Kirmānī, A.K. (1885) *Siyar al-Auliyā'*, Delhi: Matṣba'-i Muḥibb. *Kh*ān, S.A. (2003) *Āṣār al-Ṣanādīd Vol. I*, ed. K. Anjum, New Delhi: National Council for Promotion of Urdu Language.

Latif, A, (2007) 'The Performance of Perplexity: A Sufi Approach to the Paradoxes of Monotheism', *The Muslim World*, 97 (4): 611–635.

Lawrence, B.B. (1983) 'The early Chishtī approach to *samā'*', in M. Israel and N.K. Wagle (eds) *Islamic Society and Culture. Essays in Honour of Professor Aziz Ahmad*, pp. 69–93, New Delhi: Manohar. *Lonely Planet: India* (2001) London: Lonely Planet Publications.

Mackintosh-Smith, T. (2005) *The Hall of a Thousand Columns. Hindustan to Malabar with Ibn Battutah*, London: John Murray.

Qavvāl, M.A. (1998) *Surūd-i Rūḥānī. Qavvālī ke rang*, New Delhi: n.p.

Quraeshi, S. (2009) *Sacred Spaces. A Journey with the Sufis of the Indus*, Ahmedabad and Delhi: Mapin and Timeless Books.

Qureshi, R.B. (1986; 2nd ed 2006) *Sufi Music of India and Pakistan. Sound, Context and Meaning in Qawwali*, Karachi: Oxford University Press.

——— (1992) 'Muslim devotional: Popular religious music and Muslim identity under British, Indian and Pakistani hegemony', *Asian Music* 24 (1): 111–121.

——— (1995) 'Recorded Sound and Religious Music: The Case of *Qawwālī*', in L.A. Babb & S.S. Wadley (eds) *Media and the Transformation of Religion in South Asia*, pp. 139–166, Philadelphia: University of Pennsylvania Press.

——— (1999) 'His Master's Voice? Exploring Qawwali and "Gramophone Culture" in South Asia', *Popular Music*, 18 (1): 63–98..

Rozehnal, R. (2007) *Islamic Sufism Unbound. Politics and Piety in Twenty-First Century Pakistan*, New York: Palgrave Macmillan.

Sijzī, A.Ḥ.'A (2007) *Favā'id al-Fu'ād*, ed. and trans. *Kh.*Ḥ.Ṣ. Nizẕāmī, New Delhi: n.p.

Thānavī, A.'A. (1904) *Ḥaqq al-Samā'*, Delhi: Matṣba'-i Mujtabā.

Viitamäki, M. (2009) 'Where Lovers Prostrate: Poetry in the Musical Assemblies of Chishti Sufis', *Studia Orientalia*, 107: 311–343.

Zarrādī, F. (1889) *Risāla 'Uṣūl al-Samā'*, Delhi: Matṣba'-i Muḥibb.

8 Evolution of the Chishtī shrine and the Chishtīs in Pakpattan (Pakistan)

Muhammad Mubeen

Pakistan and Sufism are so interconnected that one cannot separate them from each other. Although the Sufis' message of peace reached almost every corner of the Indian Subcontinent, it particularly struck a chord with the common folk in the areas that comprised Pakistan after the Partition of 1947. The majority of Muslims in Pakistan follow the popular Barelvī Sunni School, which favours the propagation of popular Sufism that developed in the region as a result of the acculturation of Central Asian Sufism to the local, predominantly Hindu reality.[1] This popular Sufism became the form Islam took locally in the countryside and among the urban common folk.

Since the thirteenth century, the Chishtiyya (Chishtī Sufi order) has remained the most prominent and dominant Sufi brotherhood throughout the Subcontinent. Originating in Afghanistan, the order spread rapidly in India, where the highly revered Muʿīn al-Dīn Ḥassan Sijzī (d. 1236) introduced it (Ernst and Lawrence 2002). Three important attributes of Chishtī Shaikhs helped them to become established in this region: their personal piety, a system of offering food and shelter to the poor and travellers, and their introduction of Islamic beliefs and Sufi tradition in vernacular languages, thus making alien ideas familiar within the local cultures. Moreover, their convents (*jamāʿat-khānas*) were open to non-Muslims; they consoled the pilgrims through their spiritual blessings (*baraka*) and introduced a comprehensive system of spiritual guidance for their chosen disciples. Each master in the order would send deputies (khalīfas) to propagate his teachings in his spiritual jurisdiction *(vilāya)* and appoint a spiritual successor at the head of his lodge (khānqāh) (Digby 1986: 55–77). With the passage of time, succession became hereditary, and the shrines (*dargāhs*) of past luminaries became centres of devotional veneration. Thus, from the beginning of the fourteenth century, the major Sufi shrines became popular religious places, even for non-Muslims, and a permanent and respected symbol of local Muslim culture in the Subcontinent (Feener 2004: 118, Rozehnal 2006: 29–47).

The crystallization of the culture of the Punjab also began with the advent of Sufism. Gradually, the Sufis' message became part of the people's lives and consciousness. Rich tributes are paid to the former masters on their death anniversaries in the form of jubilant celebrations or fairs known as *ʿurs* (final mystical 'marriage' to God) or *melā*, the latter emphasizing the festive aspect of the celebrations. Every year these festivals are celebrated in many shrines across the entire province.

The same is true in the case of the shrine of a renowned thirteenth century Chishtī Sufi saint, Shaikh Farīd al-Dīn Mas'i ūd Ganj-i Shakar (d. 1265), popularly known as Bābā Farīd, Bābā Ṣāḥib or Bābā Jī in the area of the shrine and in Sufi spheres.[2] It is situated in Pakpattan, a small town in what is now Pakistani Punjab. For more than 700 years, this institution has developed to a considerable extent in both its structural and influential spheres. From a single tomb attracting an insignificant number of visitors, it has transformed into a big shrine complex (known as Bābā Ṣāḥib), receiving millions of visitors per annum. For centuries, this shrine has played a very important socio-economic role in the lives of the people around it. In recent times, the Indo-Pak Partition (1947) has also elevated the shrine's position due to the immigration of a large number of devotees, as well as descendants of Bābā Jī from eastern Punjab and Rajasthan. The creation of the 1947 boundaries has completely changed the sphere of influence of Chishtī Sufi because it has made it difficult for the pilgrims of Pakistan to visit major Chishtī shrines in India. As a result, Pakpattan now stands as the unrivalled centre of Chishtī Sufism in Pakistani Punjab.

A large number of hagiographical volumes have been produced about the saint, but very little effort has been expended to explain the nature of his heritage in the form of his shrine and his lineal descendants in Pakpattan. Some researchers like Khaliq Ahmad Nizami (*The Life and Times of Shaikh Farid-ud-Din Ganj-i-Shakar* 1998), Richard Maxwell Eaton ('Court of Man, Court of God: Local Perceptions of the Shrine of Baba Farid, Pakpattan, Punjab' 1982 and 'The Political and Religious Authority of the Shrine of Bābā Farīd' 1984), and David Gilmartin (*Empire and Islam: Punjab and the Making of Pakistan* 1988) have tried to touch some aspects, related to certain episodes of this institution. However, a thorough study is still required in order to understand its history, the evolution of its management and the level of its social penetration (the level of intimacy and interaction between people and the institution) in public spheres concerned directly or indirectly to it.

The legacy of Bābā Farīd can be described from different angles, i.e. his Sufi teachings, his poetry,[3] his spiritual and lineal descendants, and his shrine comprising his tomb and some other relevant buildings. A large number of hagiographical books on the saint's Sufi teachings, his poetry and his spiritual successors (*kh*alīfas)[4] are available. However, very little literature is found on his lineal descendants and his shrine.[5]

The shrine of Bābā Farīd and his lineal descendants are key factors in the political, economic and socio-religious evolution of the city of Pakpattan. It is evident from the change in the name of the town from Ajūdhan (the name of the town in the medieval period) to Pakpattan (meaning 'the holy ferry'), due to the sanctity of the place in relation to the saint. Today the city is generally called Pakpattan Sharīf (the noble Pakpattan). The purpose of the present study is to briefly introduce different important episodes and aspects of the history of this institution. Therefore, this study deals with the evolution of two aspects of the town of Pakpattan related to the legacy of Bābā Farīd: his shrine and his following headed by his lineal descendants in Pakpattan. Accordingly, the paper is divided into two main parts. The first part deals with the beginning of the shrine, its gradual development, changes in its management and its historical importance for the people, its locality, the state and the Chishtiyya itself. The second part deals with the hereditary custodians of the shrine of Bābā Farīd who are the focal point of the local authority of the shrine in the region.

The shrine of Bābā Farīd: its beginning, development, management and importance

Structural development of the shrine complex

The shrine of Bābā Farīd started after an interesting episode concerning the saint's burial on the eve of his demise. At the time, the question was to decide on his burial place, and different opinions were being put forth. The prevailing Sufi tradition was to bury the saint at the place of his worship and meditation, which was outside the city wall. However, that would have certainly minimized the respect and reputation of his family members. The view of Khʷāja Niẕām al-Dīn, a son of the deceased Shaikh, was that it would be more appropriate to bury him inside the walled town for two reasons. First, visitors would come to the family while visiting the shrine and they would gain the same respect; second, the charity for the *jamāʿat-khāna* would be enough to meet all the requirements which, it was feared, would decrease otherwise.[6] Similarly, burying the saint inside the town meant that the unsolicited offerings (*futūḥ*) would continue to pour in, along with fame and respect (Anjum 2009: 72).

Therefore, after Bābā Farīd's death in 1265, he was buried in his living chamber. His simple tomb was built by his chief spiritual successor, Niẕām al-Dīn Auliyā (d. 1325) (Khan 2003: 72) which was, later on, reconstructed by Sultan Muḥammad Tughlaq (r. 1320–1325) (Khan 1990: 63). After Bābā Farīd's burial at the site inside the town, the long career of his shrine began, and it has been running for the last seven and a half centuries.

Research of Ahmad Nabi Khan states that there are different phases of the expansion of Bābā Farīd's shrine complex (Khan 1990; Khan 1997; Khan 2003). At first, it was a single tomb in a big courtyard, but later many other graves of family members of the saint were placed around it, and a mosque and many *ḥujra*s (separate chambers for prayer and receiving guests) were constructed.

During the custodianship (*sajjāda-nishīnī*) of Shaikh i'Alā al-Dīn Mauj Daryā (1281–1334), the second *sajjāda-nishīn*[7] of the shrine of Bābā Farīd, a number of structures became part of the shrine complex. In fact, Shaikh iAlā al-Dīn, unlike his father and grandfather, welcomed the patronage of the Delhi Court, which led to the tremendous increase in physical development at the Bābā Ṣāḥib during the contemporary Tughlaq dynasty (1320–1398). The new structures, which were constructed by the Tughlaqs in the early decades of the fourteenth century, included the Jāmī/*jāmeʿ* mosque,[8] the Muṣalla-i Niẕāmīyya (the prayer mat of Niẕām),[9] a *bārah-darī*[10] and three *ḥujra*s known as *burj* for different disciples of Bābā Farīd.[11] A massive community kitchen (*langar-khāna*) was also established in the southwestern part of the courtyard. After the death of Shaikh iAlā' al-Dīn Mauj Daryā in 1334, his big tomb was also constructed by Muḥammad bin Tughlaq (1325–51) in the mid-1330s (Khan 1990: 63; Khan 1997: 82). This was the last major construction carried out in the early centuries.

Two major sources indicate that there were only three main structures inside the shrine courtyard – the tomb of Bābā Farīd, the big tomb of his grandson and an old mosque – until the early decades of the British colonial era. The first source is a description of the shrine given by a British officer in 1837 (Mackeson 1837: 192). The second source is a sketch drawn in 1871, in an official correspondence regarding an incident that occurred during the annual *'urs* of March 1871 (*Proceedings*, April 1872). This sketch was only meant to describe the nature of the incident, and many structures were ignored because they had no relevance in the official correspondence. However, it can be ascertained from the above-mentioned descriptions that no major development had taken place in the Bābā Ṣāḥib's structure until the early decades of the colonial era, since the main constructions of the early fourteenth century described above.

The next major wave of structural developments came in the second half of the colonial era (1849–1947). Until the second decade of the twentieth century, the shrine edifice did not receive much serious attention from the custodians. A picture taken in 1911 reveals the crumbling condition of the mausoleum in which the *bārah-darī*, a passage leading to the tomb from the southern side, was roofless, while the whole structure was deteriorating as is shown in Figure 2. The small structure of Muṣalla-i Niẕāmīyya was also roofless. Dīvān Said Muḥammad (d. 1934), the twenty-fifth *sajjāda-nishīn* of the shrine, carried out a number of developments at the shrine during the last decade of his custodianship. He renovated the structure of the tomb and the attached veranda. A number of small *ḥujra*s were also constructed along the southern boundary of the courtyard, in between the existing *burj*s of Bābā Farīd's disciples, to assist visitors staying near the tomb.[12]

In 1960, the shrine of Bābā Farīd was taken over by the West Pakistan Auqāf Department. Until the late 1980s, the shrine looked quite derelict. The Auqāf Department started its developmental projects when the high government authorities took an interest in the matter, realizing the importance of this institution. Therefore, over the last few decades, a great deal of renovation and building of extensions has taken place. In the 1990s, different democratic governments (including federal and provincial) announced a number of projects (for expansion and renovation), but due to regular changes of political regimes, these projects were constantly interrupted. Renovations were carried out and new structures were built, including a mosque, a library, a VIP complex, an underground car park, a dispensary, toilets, bathrooms, a *waṣū-khāna*[13] and three multi-purpose halls attached to the mosque.

The shrine and its main rituals

The tomb itself is made of white marble. Inside the tomb, besides the grave of the saint, there is another grave where his son, Shaikh Muhammad Badr al-Dīn Sulaimān (d. 1281), the first *sajjāda-nishīn*, is buried. These graves are always covered with flowers and ornate sheets of cloth brought by the pilgrims. The tomb has two doors: the one on the eastern side is called Nūrī Darvāza,[14] and the one on the southern side is the famous Bahishtī Darvāza.[15] The *mazār* (the shrine complex) is vast and spacious. The saint's tomb stands next to the big mausoleum of his grandson, Shaikh iAlā al-Dīn Mauj Daryā (d. 1334). The area in front of the eastern door is called Sama' Khāna. Here, the *sajjāda-nishīn* of the shrine conducts the ceremonies of the annual *'urs*. A small prayer area is situated between the saint's tomb and his grandson's tomb, known as Muṣalla-i Nizāmiya (the prayer mat of Nizām). There is another important chamber on the western side of Bābā Farīd's tomb, which contains the grave of Shahāb al-Dīn Ganj-i 'Ilm, one of the sons of the saint. There was an old mosque in the complex, but when the new expansion took place in the late 1990s, it was demolished to make space for the construction of the new one.

In addition to the saint's resting place, which is the central site of his *baraka*, and the lineal descendant *(sajjāda-nishīn)* of the shrine who are the living representatives of the saint, there are certain 'tools of attraction' at the shrine complex which bring a large number of devotees throughout the year, especially during the annual *'urs* (i.e. the Bahishtī Darvāza). These attractions include the daily routine (including many rituals like the running of *langar-khāna*), daily singing of Sufi poetry (*qavvālī*),[16] the preservation and distribution of different relics (*tabarrukāt*)[17] and the mosque where devotees pray five times a day.

The *Javāhir Farīdī* records how the major rituals had been instituted in the early days of the shrine's career. They include the tying of the turban (*dastār-bandī*),[18] regular singing of *qavvālī* at the shrine, the functioning of *langar-khāna*, and the tradition of the *sajjāda-nishīn* opening the Bahishtī Darvāza of Bābā Farīd's tomb on the occasion of the shrine's annual *'urs*.

The *'urs* of Bābā Farīd, his death anniversary, is celebrated every year from the twenty-fifth of Dhū al-Ḥaja to the tenth of Muharram. Primary hagiographical sources like *Rāḥt al-Muḥibbīn* of Amir Khusrau (d. 1325) suggest that the commemoration of Bābā Farīd by way of celebrating his death anniversary in the shape of annual *'urs* began just after his death (Chaghatāi 1968). During *'urs*, devotees assemble in large numbers and pay homage to the memory of the saint. Multitudes from all walks of life throng the shrine distributing offerings. The key event of the annual *'urs* is the opening and crossing of the Bahishtī Darvāza. The Bahishtī Darvāza is opened once a year, for five nights, from sunset to sunrise, from the sixth to the tenth of Muharram, and hundreds of thousands of people pass through it. Eaton opines, 'In the Bihishti *melā* the theme of salvation through loving devotion was made far more explicit than in most other Indo-Muslim shrines, since it was literally acted out by all participants', and '. . . the Bihishti ceremony served ritually to act out and confirm the sense of spiritual hierarchy that pervades the whole ethos of the shrine' (Eaton 1982: 56). Before Partition, this fair was called Bahishtī Melā (Sahar 1983: 43).

Evolution in the shrine management

Traditionally, the Sufi shrines in the history of the Indian Subcontinent remained in the managerial control of the lineal descendants (*sajjāda-nishīn*s and *pīr*s) of the buried saints inside them. During the medieval period, different monarchs as well as the nobles (*'umrā'*) used to extend their generous patronage, through grants of lands (*jāgīr*s) to their custodians cum managers for the better running of these socially and religiously acclaimed sacred sanctuaries. However, they never ventured to interfere directly in the administrative affairs of such institutions unless they became a local or national threat. The management of the shrine of Bābā Farīd remained with its traditional custodians, the *sajjāda-nishīn*s, of the shrine in the pre-colonial scenario. Even during the early colonial period, after the annexation, there was no direct concern or interference from the Colonial Government regarding managerial matters of the shrine. The only event that attracts any attention is the management of the shrine's annual fair security by the district police, whereas in the past, it was overseen by the *sajjāda-nishīn*'s own managerial team.

In the mid-1930s, following the succession of a minor *sajjāda-nishīn* and a heated family dispute over succession, the British decided, in the case of Pakpattan, to include the management of the shrine in the management of the estate. This was realized through the 'Court of Wards'[19], an institution that was established to give economic stability to the local intermediaries by preserving the estates of families facing crises as a result of debt or succession (Kirpalani, Bombay: 1993). This, no doubt, simplified the overall administration of the shrine and minimized internal conflict. Nevertheless, it also put the government in the difficult position of supervising the shrine's *'urs*. One annual Court of Wards administration report for the estate declared, 'The management of this estate presents peculiar difficulties, and great tact is needed on the part of the manager, as the elder ward, Dīvān *Gh*ulām Qu*t*b al-Dīn is the Gaddi Nashin of an important shrine at Pakpattan. The Court of Wards has to see that those religious ceremonies which the *sajjāda-nishīn* has to perform are properly done' (File 601/10/24/88, Board of Revenue Punjab, Review of the Administration of the Pakpattan Estate, September 1938). Another very interesting issue was the education of the minor *sajjāda-nishīn*. The authorities sent him to Chief's College in Lahore which was an institution offering a Western type of education. At the time, many Chishtī elders objected to this move by the government, explaining the requirement for being a Chishtī head or *faqīr* or *darvesh* (Ernst and Lawrence 2002: 103).

After Partition, in January 1961, the West Pakistan Auqāf Department took over the management of the Bābā Ṣāḥib from Dīvān *Gh*ulām Qu*t*b al-Dīn (d. 1986), the twenthy-sixth *sajjāda-nishīn* of the shrine (Notification No. 3(4)-Auqaf/60 dated 17/01/1961, Take-over File).[20] With the takeover by the Department of Auqāf, the Government took control of all the shrine's affairs, including management, property and daily cash income. Pakpattan was made part of the Multan Zone of the Auqāf Department of the West Pakistan Government. Later on, in the mid-1990s, Pakpattan was declared an independent new Zone of the Punjab Auqāf Department.

The importance of the shrine of Bābā Farīd

Ajūdhan (present Pakpattan) was not well known when Bābā Farīd (d. 1265) arrived and settled in the city. At the time, the walled town was surrounded by shrub forest, which was inhabited by wild animals (Nizami 1955: 36; Khan 2003: 72). It is important to note that many medieval Sufi saints chose totally uninhabited and tough locations as their seats of residence. Hence, one finds Pakpattan, which is now a bustling Sufi town in the Punjab, chosen by Bābā Farīd, has evolved from a barren site to a densely populated centre. The famous mid-eighteenth-century classical Punjabi Sufi poet, Vāriṡ Shāh, has acknowledged this idea in his well-known poem *Hīr*.[21]

After Bābā Farīd's arrival, Ajūdhan became a site of attraction due to his large following. Bābā Jī established his *jamā't- khāna* (Sufi lodge), which hosted a large number of his disciples. Nizami describes the lifestyle of Bābā Farīd and his *kh*ānqāh as follows, 'teeming crowds flocked to it and found spiritual solace in his [Bābā Farīd's] company. A calm spiritual atmosphere pervaded his dwelling, and men who were secretly tormented by flames of mundane ambitions, found in his *kh*ānqāh "the refreshing breeze of a different world" ' (Nizami 1955: 1). His *kh*ānqāh remained a popular place in his lifetime and became a meeting place for people from different origins and backgrounds. After Bābā Farīd, many of his disciples successfully built a network of shrines, which owe their renown to their association with Bābā Farīd's shrine, and render reverence to this central place of pilgrimage.

It is believed by a huge following, and depicted in the different hagiographical sources, that since its existence the shrine has always protected the inhabitants of the city from invaders. One can observe this phenomenon as early as the fourteenth century, when Tamerlane, the Mongol invader, spared the majority of the inhabitants who had not left the city out of respect for the saint whose shrine ensured the safety of the town (Irving 1911. 71). About a century later, Babur (r. 1483–1530), the first Mughal emperor in India and a descendant of Tamerlane, again invaded the area but the town remained safe, and Babur returned from Dīpālpur, the adjoining town (Roe and Purser 1878: 29–30).

Different local rulers as well as famous personalities of the pre-colonial period had great respect for the saint. Many of them visited the shrine, and gave charity and lands to it. Among the famous people who have visited the city due to this shrine over the centuries are the famous explorer, scholar and traveller Ibn Baṯṯūṯa in 1334, Tamerlane in 1398, and latterly, according to the *Janam-sākhī*s (birth stories), Guru Nanak, the Founder of Sikhism in the 1520s, and Jalāl al-Dīn Akbar (r. 1556–1605), the Mughal Emperor, who visited the city twice. The Sikh ruler, Mahārājā Raṇjīt Singh (r. 1799–1839), had a great deal of respect for Bābā Farīd and used to send money and gifts for the shrine and its caretakers. In the last few decades, almost every ruler of Pakistan has visited the shrine during her or his tenure.

As the shrine's wealth increased, it became a major economic power in the locality. In fact, the shrine had its own political economy where public donations were used for public needs. Philanthropic activities were encouraged and a type of circulation of money developed on its premises. The *melā*, held around this shrine for centuries, became the main source of economic activity in the town, as it not only attracted a large number of pilgrims, but also those in business circles who came to generate their annual earnings. It is said that people used to earn their income for the whole year ahead from this *melā*.[22] Now the markets, which have developed around the shrine, and are also generally referred to as 'Bābā Ṣāḥib', are the representatives of its economic importance.

When the Auqāf Department started its operations, the department was organized in a number of 'Auqāf Administrative Zones' in different Divisional Headquarters. Pakpattan was included in the Multan Zone of the Auqāf Department of the West Pakistan Government. Bābā Farīd's shrine was the highest income point from cash boxes in that zone (Jamal Malik 1990: 93). Later, in the mid-1990s, realizing the importance of the presence of a large shrine, Pakpattan was declared an independent new Zone of the Punjab Auqāf Department. The importance of this shrine for the Auqāf Department can also be determined by the fact that its *sajjāda-nishīn* is the only custodian in the Punjab province who is paid a heavy stipend per annum by the Auqāf Department.

The Chishtīs of Pakpattan: lineal descendants of Bābā Farīd

For centuries, Pakpattan remained strongly under the influence of the *sajjāda-nishīn*s of the shrine of Bābā Farīd. These custodians acted as intermediaries between the local populations and the rulers, from the Sultans to the Mughals and the British. The lineal descendants of the saint are represented at the shrine, of which they remained the managers and the guardians until the Auqāf Department gained control of the shrine in the early 1960s, under Ayyūb Khān (r. 1959–1969). They enjoy a sanctified reputation and receive the honorific appellation of Dīvān (financial manager or chief officer).[23]

Unlike the worldly kings, it is not necessary that the successor of a Shaikh or Sufi is one of his offspring. The spiritual succession is often nominated by the Shaikh during his lifetime and it might be anyone, either his son or any disciple. The chief spiritual successor of Bābā Farīd was Shaikh Niẕām al-Dīn Auliyā who was nominated by Bābā Jī himself, but the caretaker, custodian and the beneficiary of the earnings of the saint's shrine was one of his lineal descendants. Thus, the *sajjāda-nishīnī*, the institution of the hereditary custodianship of a Sufi shrine that grew in the thirteenth century, went to the hereditary heirs of Bābā Farīd, and the spiritual successor went to Delhi to avoid any confrontation. In the words of Tanvir Anjum, '(. . .) in actual practice, the descendants failed to inherit the spiritual domain (*wilayat*) for themselves, while the disciples failed to gain the control of the shrine . . . ' (Anjum 2009: 64).

As the custodianship of the shrine was held by one family, the shrine and its endowments and gifts from local leaders and the central authorities helped to entrench the power of Bābā Farīd in the shrine itself (Bigelow 2010: 381). With the passage of time, the role of the *sajjāda-nishīn*, as the centre of that power has taken many shapes. The *sajjāda-nishīn* was initially a patron saint, and on certain occasions, a government official, at times a ruler, a feudal lord, an influential elder of the area, an intermediary between the government and the local masses, a dependent, a king maker, a politician and a ceremonial but prestigious figure. Eaton's study of Bābā Farīd's shrine in Pakpattan gives a clear idea of this evolution in the pre-colonial period (Eaton 1984: 333–356).

After the demise of the saint, his son Shaikh Muḥammad Badr al-Dīn Sulaimān (d. 1281) acquired the seat (*sajjāda*) of his father with the consent of both the lineal and spiritual heirs of Bābā Farīd. He was the disciple of two Chishtī Shaikhs, Khʷāja Zovār and Khʷāja *Gh*aur, from Chisht. Although he was not the disciple of Bābā Jī, his style of living followed that of the saints of Chisht (Nizami 1998: 61). After the death of Shaikh Badr al-Dīn Sulaimān, his son, Shaikh iAlā al-Dīn Mauj Daryā (d. 1334), succeeded him as the second *sajjāda-nishīn* in office. He was known for his piety, godliness and austerity as indicated by the contemporary hagiographical and historical works (Nizami 1998: 61–62).[24]

Bābā Farīd, being a firm follower of the Chishtī doctrine, remained distant from the political spheres of his time. He avoided kings, government officials and the rich. He also advised his spiritual khalīfas and disciples (*murīd*s) to avoid their company. Ernst and Lawrence write, 'Perhaps no Chishtī master was as renowned for his withdrawal from society at large and the company of kings in particular as Shaikh Farīd al-Dīn of Pakpattan' (2002: 5). However, less than a century after his death, the descendants and managers of his shrine accepted land grants and cash stipends from the Delhi Sultans. During Mauj Daryā's tenure of custodianship (1281–1334), the family was approached by the Sultans of Delhi and we note in the accounts of Ibn-i Baṭṭūṭa (1304–1377) for the year 1334 that at that time the town of Ajūdhan was granted to him as a fief by the ruling Sultan (Ibn-i Baṭṭūṭa 1973: 396–97). The need of additional financial resources for the necessary running of the *jamāʿat-khāna* and the *langar-khāna* might have been one of the reasons for this decision, as they needed a sustainable source of income to continue the legacy of Bābā Farīd. After the Delhi Sultans, the Mughal Emperors also offered land grants to *sajjāda-nishīn*s, and this process continued with the British government who donated large amounts of land to the shrine in order to secure its *sajjāda-nishīn*'s loyalty.

'Over centuries, the shrine of Bābā Farīd got precedence over *jamāʿat khāna*, which became less significant as an institution' (Anjum 2009: 73), and 'the prestige and authority of a *sajjāda-nishīn* came to depend on the extent of *langar* and the splendor of the *ʿurs* festival' (Gilmartin 1988: 43, 45). During the medieval period (Sultanate and Mughal periods fourteenth – eighteenth century), even the requirements for becoming a *sajjāda-nishīn* gradually shifted from spiritual merit to political loyalty to the central government. Thus, the descendants of Bābā Farīd started to deviate from their ancestors' teachings and the norms of the Chishtī order by initiating the acceptance of endowments from the Sultans, Rajas and Navābs as well as high-ranking officials. They also received the government share of all crops on which revenue was levied in kind (Eaton 1984: 348). This was in addition to the revenue of the shrine, which in itself was considerable. Consequently, these descendants enjoyed social prestige and economic prosperity, along with religious, spiritual and political authority in the ensuing centuries. It can therefore be assumed that the custodian of the shrine was no longer a saint of Bābā Farīd's type but a feudal elder with worldly desires for land and power.

Property attached to the shrine in 1894 was worth one and a half lakh rupees, which was a large amount at that time. 'The descendants of Bābā Farīd possessed, by the twentieth century, a tenth of all the land in the Pakpattan Tehsil in which the shrine was situated, some 43,000 acres in all' (Talbot 1988: 24). Part of this land had come to them as state gifts during Sikh rule (Talib 1974: 43–44). The British Colonial Government rewarded Dīvān Said Muḥammad, the twenty-fifth *sajjāda-nishīn*, for war services after World War I. He received seven squares of land. Similarly, the custodians of the shrine of Bābā Farīd are included in the list of those who were rewarded for their loyal services and awarded 125 acres of land (Ali 1989: 105–06). Many villages were granted to the *sajjāda-nishīn* around the town of Pakpattan. Over the years, the shrine custodians acquired large amounts of land, as grants from the State, in addition to the considerable *Waqf* endowments, which they received from individuals. Hence, they became landed magnates. Such large landholdings became instruments not only of economic viability but also of political authority for the *sajjāda-nishīn*s who remained, in the colonial period, as British collaborators.

In a few decades, after the demise of Bābā Farīd, his lineal descendants also gradually stepped into the local political arena of the region, and the town of Pakpattan eventually came under the political control of the *sajjāda-nishīn* of the shrine of Bābā Farīd. Therefore, these 'Sons of Bread'[25] in Ajūdhan (modern Pakpattan) could not keep themselves away for long from the political spheres and the patronage of the Delhi Court. The local political authority of the custodians of the shrine of Bābā Farīd, in addition to their socio-religious authority in the region, was materialized half a century after the demise of the founding saint. The Khiljī Sultāns (1290–1320) were not interested in the affairs of the shrine, but the situation changed with the ascendancy of Tughlaqs (1321–1414). Shaikh iAlā al-Dīn Mauj Daryā, the second *sajjāda-nishīn*, had two sons, Shaikh Mu i'iz al-Dīn (d. 1348) and Shaikh ʿAlm al-Dīn. The inclination of political involvement was further enhanced when both of his sons were dragged, by Sultan Muḥammad bin Tughlaq (r. 1325–1351), into the active political arena of the Delhi Court. Shaikh Mu i'iz al-Dīn (d. 1348), the elder son of Shaikh i'Alā al-Dīn and the third *sajjāda-nishīn* at Pakpattan, was called to Delhi by the Sultan, and then sent to the Gujarat Province as Deputy Governor (Eaton 1984: 339). His brother ʿAlm al-Din was also appointed as the Shaikh al-Islām of Hindustan in the Delhi Court.[26] Even in the next generation, Shaikh ʿAlm al-Dīn's son was also appointed as Shaikh al-Islām (Nizami 1998: 63). Therefore, they both became government officials as well as playing a part in the political spheres of the time.

During these centuries (fourteenth–eighteenth), the lineal descendants of Bābā Farīd enhanced the political prestige of the office of the *sajjāda-nishīn* by adopting a number of measures, which ultimately led to a substantial evolution of the local shrine culture in Pakpattan. These included the socio-religious patronage of, and the political attachment to, different Jāt and Rājpūt clans who gradually established themselves in and around Pakpattan (Eaton 1984: 333–356). This was materialized through the kinship ties of inter-marriages between the family of the *sajjāda-nishīn* of the shrine of Bābā Farīd and the the families of different heads of these neighbouring clans, where the family of the *sajjāda-nishīn* was only the recipient of brides from others.[27] This phenomenon enhanced the socio-political prestige of the family of the *sajjāda-nishīn*s, and tied other clans to the shrine even more powerfully than economic or political connections.

David Gilmartin is of the opinion that the declining authority of the Mughals in Delhi heavily shook the scenario of traditional Muslim leadership in the Punjab because of a breach in the centuries-old arrangement of political patronage from the central political authority. This state of affairs led to the rise of many powerful figures who established their local chieftainship (Gilmartin 1988: 489). As it might be supposed, the Dīvān, being an influential person, a powerful elder and owning a brick fort at Pakpattan[28] as well as a substantial strength of armed personnel, held ambitions to be independent if possible. After the gradual decline of the Mughals, the mid-eighteenth century *sajjāda-nishīn*, Dīvān ʿAbd al-Subḥān (d. 1766) had asserted his autonomy from the Mughals and had fought against other local tribal and Sikh chieftains, gaining political control of a substantial area in the north, the west and southwest of the present Pakpattan, estimated to yield a revenue of 30,000 rupees. He is thought to have become independent in 1757 (Roe and Purser 1878: 35).

The Dīvān organized his Jāt *murīd*s and entered into an alliance with Mubārik Khān of Bahawalpur (a princely state in southwestern united Punjab), and joined an attack on the Bikaner (a princely state of pre-partition Rajasthan) Raja. The outcome of this was that he acquired some land on the southern side of the Sutlej River. He then fought the Nakkai Sikhs (a Sikh confederacy) and defeated them. The Bhangīs (another Sikh confederacy) then occupied his territory. After the expulsion of the Bhangīs, the succeeding Dīvān recovered the territory until Mahārājā Raṇjīt Singh (d. 1839) appropriated it in 1809. Therefore, from 1767 to 1809, the region around the town remained under the full political authority of the *sajjāda-nishīn.*

Mahārājā Raṇjīt Singh (r. 1799–1839) took control of the Punjab and created his kingdom, which lasted up to the annexation of the Punjab by the British East India Company in 1849. The Mahārāja gave a semi-independent feudatory status to the *sajjāda-nishīn* of the shrine of Pakpattan regarding the town's political control and, to some extent, for its economic affairs. The *sajjāda-nishīn* was allowed to have a revenue of 1,000 rupees derived from the town duties of Pakpattan, as well as a quarter share in four small villages in the neighbourhood of the town (Mackeson 1837: 192–3). After the death of the Mahārāja in 1839, the *sajjāda-nishīn* of the shrine of Bābā Farīd retained the same status under Dīvān Sāvan Mal (d. 1844) and his son Dīvān Mul Rāj (d. 1850), the successive Governors of Multan. This was the state of affairs until the arrival of the British in the region in 1849 (Roe and Purser 1878: 35–36).

After the annexation, British relations with many shrines grew from the local political pressures they faced in establishing their rural administration. Recognizing the importance of Sufi shrines as a major focus of regional identity and the power of hereditary Sufi leaders as moral exemplars and mediators, the British colonial administration actively incorporated Sufism into its system of local politics and patronage (Rozehnal 2006: 34). Many *sajjāda-nishīn* were honoured with prestigious posts like that of divisional, provincial and even vice-regal *darbārī* (courtiers).[29] Sometimes they were also given positions in the local administration, especially in the southwestern Punjab where they were among the most influential personages in social and landholding contexts (Hassan 1987: 559).

David Gilmartin observes that under colonial rule, the Sufi shrines' traditional position as a hinge between the culture of the locality and the larger Muslim community remained intact, while the role of the saint's living heirs was increasingly politicized (Gilmartin 1988: 39–52). In fact, the political role of the *gaddī*,[30] in the colonial period, started with the introduction of the electoral process in the Subcontinent. Their role in Punjab politics during this period must be seen in relation to the Unionist Party, representing the interests of Hindu, Sikh and Muslim landowners, and to the British administrative policies which had helped to produce it. Many of the *sajjāda-nishīn*s, particularly those associated with the older pre-Mughal shrines, were very strongly tied to these same rural administrative structures, which lay behind the development of the Unionists. The role of the Court of Wards in the case of the Pakpattan *sajjāda-nishīn*, at the time of the release of his controlled lands, can be viewed in this reference.[31]

The Partition of 1947 was a major turning point in the history of the town of Pakpattan as it resulted in a number of phenomenal changes. On one hand, the Partition changed its religious demography, on the other hand, the shrine attracted a large number of Chishtī elders (having Chishtī *gaddī*s) and families from eastern Punjab and Rajasthan to Pakpattan. This phenomenon resulted in the development of *pīrī-murīdī* culture in the city.[32] Nowadays, one can see a number of small Chishtī shrines in and around the city that are devoted to the descendants of Bābā Farīd.

In the colonial period, although the *sajjāda-nishīn* was very influential in all the affairs of the town, there was no direct participation in the politics of the area. During the first decade after Partition, his stature in town was further boosted by the changing demographics of Pakpattan. The departure of Hindu and Sikh landlords left him the only influential landlord in town, while his social and religious standing was improved by the arrival of a large number of Chishtī families from the eastern districts, who had reverence for the saint as well as for the *sajjāda-nishīn*. In this context, the *sajjāda-nishīn* favoured one political group or the other at different times, assuming the role of king maker. Later, the fledgling Pakistani state, in its effort to embed Islamic symbols in its political ideology, continued the British policy of direct control over Sufi shrines and Sufi leaders. The state's hegemony over religious spaces and local religious leaders was formally institutionalized with the passage of the West Pakistan *Waqf* Properties Ordinance of 1959.

With the takeover by the Department of Auqāf in the early 1960s, the Government took control of all the shrine's affairs, including management, property and daily cash income. Only some rituals were left with the Dīvān of the shrine. To overcome his loss of power,[33] the Dīvān started to participate directly in the political affairs of the area, and for the first time, Dīvān Ghulām Qu*t*b al-Dīn (d. 1986), the twenty-sixth *sajjāda-nishīn*, became a Member of the National Assembly

(MNA) in the 1965 General Elections. The *sajjāda-nishīn* became an elected politician and was declared winner without any contest. He participated again in the National Assembly Elections of 1970, but was defeated. From then onward, the Dīvān decided to oversee shrine and family matters, leaving political affairs to his family members, especially to his brother-in-law and his cousins.[34] However, he continued to influence later elections according to his capacity. In a couple of cases, the *sajjāda-nishīn* of the shrine of Bābā Farīd even played the role of king maker due to his socio-economic and religious influence.[35]

'Initially, at least, two conditions were considered prerequisite to qualify the *sajjāda-nishīnī* in Ajūdhan: first, the *sajjāda-nishīn* must possess some degree of godliness and piety; and second, he must be a direct descendant of the deceased Shaikh. With the passage of time, the second precondition emphasizing the lineage of a *sajjāda-nishīn* seems to have taken precedence over the first one' (Anjum 2009: 74). As a result, the issue of *sajjāda-nishīnī* became a bone of contention among the different members of the custodian family of the shrine of Bābā Farīd at Pakpattan. Earlier, in the pre-colonial period, the Chishtī elders solved these issues, but in the colonial period, the British interfered directly in the administration of local shrines like Pakpattan, going as far as to mediate succession disputes in official courts established after the annexation. The Colonial Government even took control of the shrine and the attached properties, thus making the *sajjāda-nishīn* a dependant of the state in all its affairs.

The tussle for the possession of *gaddī* remained a very important factor in the history of the shrine especially in the colonial and post-colonial period. This tussle itself is the depiction of its importance for the custodians. The main attraction of this post comes from the fact that it is one of the most prestigious *gaddī*s in the Subcontinent with a heavy influence over a wide Chishtī shrine circle in and around the region. Another determining factor is the social, political and economic prestige of the *gaddī* in the minds of the followers of the saint.

The course of litigation began after the death of Dīvān Allāh Javāya, the twenty-fourth *sajjāda-nishīn* of the shrine of Bābā Farīd, in December 1884. Pīr ʿAbd al-Raḥmān, the uncle of the deceased, succeeded to the *gaddī* as the nearest agnate to the deceased. However, Saʿīd Muḥammad (d. 1934), the deceased's daughter's son, sued for its possession in the District Court. It was decided, four years later, in 1888, that the late *sajjāda-nishīn* had the power under the custom of the shrine to appoint a successor to the *gaddī*, and accordingly, Dīvān Saʿīd Muḥammad was installed as the twenty-fifth *sajjāda-nishīn*. Pīr ʿAbd al-Reḥmān appealed against this decision in the Chief Court of the Punjab, in which he succeeded and was consequently reinstalled in April 1890. Dīvān Saʿīd Muḥammad made a further appeal to the Privy Council, but before any decision was made, Pīr ʿAbd al-Raḥmān died and was succeeded by his son Fateḥ Muḥammad. Saʿīd Muhammad's appeal to the Privy Council was accepted, and Fateḥ Muḥammad had to vacate the *gaddī*, which was retaken by Dīvān Saʿīd Muhammad in November 1894. Then, after the death of Dīvān Saʿīd Muḥammad in December 1934, another dispute started between the son of the deceased *dīvān* and the descendants of Pīr Fateḥ Muḥammad. This case also remained in court for almost a decade and was, at last, decided in favour of the preceding *dīvān*'s son, Dīvān Ghulām Quṯb al-Dīn (d. 1986), from the Lahore Chief Court. After Dīvān Ghulām Quṯb al-Dīn's death in 1986, the dispute started again between his brother Bakhtiyār Sa'īd Muḥammad and the son of the deceased Dīvān, Maudūd Mas'ūd. This is still in the process of litigation although Maudūd Mas'ūd is the declared *sajjāda-nishīn* at the moment.

Eaton is of the opinion that these succession cases had nothing to do with the following of Bābā Farīd in Pakpattan as he quotes one of the witnesses from the proceedings of the 1935–42 succession case, 'I am a follower of the Gaddi Nashin whosoever may be occupying it' (Eaton 1982: 59).

Holding a high socio-economic position, as well as being the venerated elder of the town, the *sajjāda-nishīn* assumed another socially prestigious role in the pre-colonial and colonial periods when a 'Kachehrī of Dīvān Ṣāḥib'[36], which is a courtyard of Divian Shaeb developed which was intended as a place to resolve the local disputes of the people of the area.[37] This was a key institution that depicted the shrine custodian's good reputation and influential position in the region. 'It was the center of socio-political activity of the area'.[38] This *kachehrī* gradually lost its worth with the introduction of a legal court system in the Subcontinent by the British administration[39] and came to an end when the Government of Pakistan took over the management of the shrine and its properties in the early 1960s. In recent years, the *kachehrī* is regaining its worth under the headship of Dīvān 'Azmat Sa'īd Muḥammad Chishtī, the younger half-brother of the current *sajjāda-nishīn*.

Explaining the worthy religious status of the *sajjāda-nishīn* of the shrine of Bābā Farīd, Eaton remarks, 'It is worth noting that because only the Dīvān opened the gate [the Bahishtī Darvāza], it was only through his agency that devotees gained access to Bābā Farīd, and only through the saint's agency that they gained access to Heaven' (Eaton 1982: 56).

Conclusion

To conclude, it can be said that the study shows the gradual expansion, changes in organization and historical prominence of Bābā Farīd's tomb in the context of locality and state, while on the other hand it throws light on the ever-changing role and stature of the hereditary custodians of the shrine through the colonial and post-colonial eras.

The shrine of Bābā Farīd al-Dīn Mas i' ūd Ganj-i Shakar has known tremendous development in different areas, i.e. its structure, its influence, its prestige and its political as well as economic importance. It has transformed the old town of Ajūdhan into the strong Chishtī Sufi centre of Pakpattan Sharīf, a spiritual symbol of the Chishtiyya in the Pakistani Punjab. Over centuries, the city has been distinguished as the home and last resting place of Bābā Farīd and the seat of his shrine, with its Bahishtī Darvāza and its famous *'urs* or *melā*. In a broader context, in the pre-colonial and colonial periods, the shrine of Bābā Farīd with all its 'daughter shrines' played a major role in the Chishtī landscape of India. After Partition, it emerged as the sole significant Chishtī centre in Pakistan, playing a considerable role in enhancing the religious, social and political importance of the Chishtī elite in the whole country.

The study also discusses the gradual nonconformity of Bābā Farīd's descendants to his teachings in the form of receiving benefactions and gifts from the contemporary elite and entering into the political arena. The most important aspect of this evolution is the shift of spiritual values of the office of *sajjāda-nishīn* to political loyalties and its economic empowerment along the passage of time. This gradual shift transformed Bābā Jī's descendants into socially esteemed and economically affluent figures who occupied positions of religious, political and spiritual authority. The local political authority of the shrine and its *sajjāda-nishīn* has decreased greatly in the colonial and post-colonial eras. Nonetheless, certain changes of historical importance, as well as the prestigious position of the custodians of this shrine in the last few centuries, have been a catalyst to make it an essential site for local rulers as well as for the Chishtī devotees in Pakistan and in South Asia at large.

Notes

1 The Barelvīs are members of a movement that arose in late nineteenth century northern India under the leadership of Maulānā Aḥmad Raẓā *Kh*ān Barelvī (1856–1921). On the Barelvīs, see Sanyal, Delhi: 1996.

2 Sufi sphere here means the group of people who are known for their active following of Sufi doctrines.

3 For being recognized as the first poet of the Punjabi language.

4 Mainly *Shaikh* Niẕām al-Dīn Auliyā (d. 1325) and Alā al-Dīn Sābir Kalyār (d. 1291), whose followers are termed as 'Chishtī Niẕāmī' and 'Chishtī Sābrī' respectively.

5 Two hagiographical sources are important in this reference, i.e. *Sayyar al-Auliyā* (lives of saints) of Amir Khurd, which was written half a century after the demise of Bābā Farīd, and *Javāhir Farīdī* (gems of Farīd) (1623) of Ali Asghar Chishti, which was written in Emperor Jahangir's time (1605–27). Later researchers have mainly depended on these sources with the help of certain other contemporary historical works produced in royal courts.

6 *Jamāʿat-Khāna* is a space for the spiritual disciples of a saint where they are provided with spiritual, religious and moral education. For them, it is also a place of worship.

7 '(. . .) literally, the Persian and Urdu word *sajjāda* is used to refer to a prayer mat, throne or seat; the Arabic word *sujjāda* has a similar meaning, although it is pronounced differently. The term *sajjāda* has often been used in a symbolic sense to denote authority as well. Thus, the term is used both in its literal sense as well as its symbolic connotation. Nonetheless, the translation of the term *sajjāda* into English as 'the spiritual seat' is far more satisfactory. This translation confuses the concept of *sajjāda-nishīnī* with the *kh*ilāfat or spiritual succession. While using the semantic construct of 'spiritual seat', one is likely to assume that all the *sajjāda-nishīn* were necessarily the spiritual successors of the Sufi *Shaikh*, whereas, as a matter of fact, it was not a prerequisite for *sajjāda-nishīn*' (Anjum 2009: 67).

8 Ahmad Nabi Khan names the old mosque as Jāmī Mosque. However, in some sources its name is given as *jāmeʿ* mosque (a mosque worthy of conducting Friday prayer called *jumʿa*). The mosque was constructed in the northwestern part of the courtyard by Sul*t*ān Muḥammad bin Tughlaq (1325–1351) in the early years of his reign; (Khan 1997: 82; Khan 1990: 116).

9 Beside the northeastern corner of Bābā Farīd's tomb.

10 Bārah-darī is a veranda with twelve doors or columns. It was constructed on the southern side of the tomb of Bābā Farīd, leading towards the Bahi*sh*tī Darvāza.

11 These *ḥujra*s were constructed on the southern periphery of the shrine courtyard. The *burj*s were named after their occupants. First was the Jamālī Burj, named because of the occupancy of *Shaikh* Jamāl al- Dīn Hānsvī (d. 1260), one of the main disciples of Bābā Farīd. Second was the Niẕāmī Burj, named because of the inhabitation of *Shaikh* Niẕām al- Dīn Auliyā (d. 1325), who was elevated as *kh*alīfa-i-ā*ʿzam* (chief spiritual successor) of Bābā Farīd and was the founder of the Niẕāmīyya branch of the Chishtīyya. Third was the Ṣābirī Burj, which was named after *Shaikh* ʿAlāʿ al-Dīn ʿAlī Aḥmad Ṣābir (d. 1291), who was a disciple of Bābā Farīd as well as the son of his sister and was the founder of the Ṣābirīyya branch of the Chishtīyya.

12 According to the Auqāf Records, there were thirty-nine *ḥujra*s, which were demolished during the extension of the shrine complex in the late 1990s.

13 A proper place for making ablution.

14 'Gate of Light', the eastern door, commonly used for access to the graves inside the tomb.

15 'Gate of Paradise', the southern entry to the tomb, only opened during the annual fair. It is made of silver, and floral designs are inlaid with gold sheet. The first mention of the Bahishtī Darvāza appears in the *Javāhir Farīdī*. It is mentioned that at the time of the burial of Bābā Farīd, *Shaikh* Niẓām al- Dīn Auliyā had a vision of the Prophet Muḥammad with his principal companions saying that whosoever passed through the door would be sanctified.

16 Qavvālī is a genre of Sufi devotional music, which plays an important role in the Chishtī rituals and is very popular in South Asian Sufi spheres. A regular feature of the daily life of the *mazār* is the continuous singing of *qavvalī*. In the evening and at night, a large number of devotees gather around the group of singing *qavvāl*. On *qavvālī*, see Regula 1986, Cambridge.

17 These are of two types: one, the eatables distributed at the shrine; two, the articles for the personal use of the saint that were preserved. The preserved *taburrakāt* include *naʿlain* (shoes of the saint), wooden bread, fruits that have been turned to stones, a stone which used to hang around the neck of the saint, *kh*irqa/*jubba* (a woollen cloak) and a *ʿAlm* (banner).

18 The ritual of the tying of the turban (*dastār-bandī*) was established in the earliest days during the lifetime of Bābā Farīd when some prominent saints of Chishtiyya from Chisht visited Ajūdhan. Bābā Farīd asked them to tie the turban on the head of his descendants. The turban used at the shrine for the purpose of *dastār-bandī* is a symbol indicating the formal inheritance of Bābā Farīd's spiritual authority. A special saffron-coloured turban is reserved only for the *sajjāda-nishīn*, which is physically touched with the Bābā Farīd's grave before being placed on the candidate's head.

19 The British Government introduced the Court of Wards in the Punjab under The Punjab Court of Wards Act 1903. In the case of the shrine of Bābā Farīd, see Report, Lahore: 1936–46.

20 'The nationalization had three aims: firstly, the administration wanted to extend and protect its interest, since these endowments are often in the form of religious schools, estates and shrines. . . Secondly, the State was interested in the financial resources accruing from shrines and schools . . . Thirdly, nationalization meant the bureaucratization of shrine-culture and of endowments which, in association with Folk-Islam, was striving for autonomy' (Malik 1990: 64).

21 The fifth quatrain or stanza of the poem *Hīr* by Vāris̤ *Sh*āh describes how the fate of the Punjab changed or blossomed due to Bābā Farīd's arrival in Pakpattan and how his *baraka* has made it peaceful.

22 Interview, Syed Afṣal Ḥaider, December 10 2009.

23 Dīvān, literally meaning financial manager, is the title adopted by the *sajjāda-nishīns* at some later stage, because there is no evidence available in the earliest records related to the shrine in hagiographical and contemporary historical sources.

24 Nizami quotes works of Amīr *Kh*usrau, Amīr *Kh*urd and Ṣiī al-Dīn Baranī. Baranī calls him 'an embodiment of virtue and devotion'. (Not sure why the names are in inverted commas.)

25 *Farzand-i nānī* or 'Sons of Bread' is the term used by Bābā Farīd himself for his successors by lineage, narrated by *Shaikh* Niẕām al-Dīn Auliyā (Anjum 2009: 63).

26 The '*Shaikh* al-Islām' was the representative of the *ʿulamāʿ* and it was his duty to bring to the notice of the king anything he thought detrimental or prejudicial to the interest of his religion, and the king had little option in acting upon his advice.

27 Writer of *Javāhir Farīdī* (1623), ʿAlī Aṣ*gh*ar Chishtī had given detailed descriptions of different *sajjāda-nishīns* of the shrine of Bābā Farīd who married themselves as well as other male members of their families to the females of different clans living around Pakpattan (Chishtī 1623: 101–110). The significant aspect of this association was that the shrine custodians only accepted daughters, for themselves as well as males in their immediate family, from other clans and never gave their daughters to them, thereby affirming the religious and social superiority of their status (Eaton 1984: 350).

28 Pakpattan is a walled city. In the Sultanate period, some Sultans used it as a frontier post.

29 Dīvān Allāh Javāya (d. 1884), the twenty-fourth *sajjāda-nishīn* was given a seat in the Viceroy Darbār (The Court of the Viceroy). Later, his successor remained a member of the Divisional as well as Provincial Courts (*List of Divisional Darbārīs* and *List of Provincial Darbārīs*, 1873, 1912, 1919–33).

30 '*Sajjāda* is also referred to as *gaddī* (literally meaning a throne or a seat of authority), and thus, *sajjāda-nishīn* is also referred to as *gaddī-nishīn*. However, the term *gaddī* and *gaddī-nishīn* seemed to have been coined at a later stage' (Anjum 2009: 76).

31 The minor Dīvān was obliged to support the Unionist Party in order to obtain the release of the *Waqf* lands attached to the shrine from the possession of the Court of Wards in the early 1940s (Interview, Syed Afṣal Ḥaider, December 10 2009).

32 Pīrī-Murīdī is a master-disciple relationship of a spiritual nature.

33 Another trend that developed in this period was that the legislators of the assemblies gradually became the executive and economic powers of their constituencies.

34 His brother-in-law Mīyān *Gh*ulām Muḥammad Mānekā (d. 2011) was twice elected as MNA, and thrice as Member of the Provincial Assembly (MPA). His nephew, Mīyān *Gh*ulām Farīd Chishtī (d. 2006), constantly participated in the General Elections for the Provincial Assembly of the Punjab from the constituency of Pakpattan and was elected four times as MPA. Dīvān ʿAẕmat Saʿīd Muḥammad Chishtī, younger son of Dīvān *Gh*ulām Qu*t*b al-Dīn, contested a number of Provincial Assembly elections and was elected as MPA in 1997. He was also elected as Tehsil Nāẕim (elected administrator-mayor) of the city in the 2005 Local Government elections.

35 Mīyān *Gh*ulām Farīd Chishtī only succeeded in the 1985 elections for provincial assembly due to the favour of his maternal uncle, Dīvān *Gh*ulām Qu*t*b al-Dīn (Saghar 1986: 261).

36 Traditional local court of justice in a courtyard in front of the Dīvān's residence where he resolved local disputes.

37 Interview with Sayyid Afẕal Ḥaidar, December 10 2009 (79 years old).

38 Idem.

39 After the annexation of the Punjab by the British East India Company in 1849, the Company introduced legal courts that applied principles of justice, equity and good conscience. After 1857, the Government was transferred from the Company to the British Crown, which paved the way for the gradual process of codification of laws (Menon and Banerjea 2003: 232–33).

References

Primary sources

List of Divisional Darbaris of the Punjab and List of Provincial Darbaris of the Punjab (1873, 1912, 1919–33), Lahore: Punjab Government Press.

Secondary sources

Ali, I. (1989) *The Punjab under Imperialism*, 1885–1947, Delhi: Oxford University Press.

Anjum, T. (2009) 'Sons of Bread and Sons of Soul: Lineal and Spiritual Descendants of Bābā Farīd and the Issue of Succession', in S. Singh and I. Dayal Gaur (eds) *Sufism in Punjab: Mystics, Literature and Shrines*, pp. 63–79, Delhi: Aakar Books.

Bigelow, A.B. (2010) *Sharing Saints, Shrines, and Stories: Practicing Pluralism in North India*, New York: Oxford University Press.

Chaghatai, M.A. (1968) *Pakpattan and Baba Farid Ganj-I-Shakar*, Lahore: Kitab Khana Nauras.

Chishti, A.A. (1883–84) *Javāhir Farīdī*, Lahore.

Cunningham, A. (1871) *The Ancient Geography of India*, London: Trübner and Company.

Eaton, R.M. (1984) 'The Political and Religious Authority of the Shrine of Bābā Farīd', in B. Metcalf (ed.) *Moral Conduct and Authority: The Place of Adab in South Asian Islam*, pp. 333–356, Berkeley: University of California Press.

——— (1982) 'Court of Man, Court of God: Local Perceptions of the Shrine of Baba Farid, Pakpattan, Punjab', in R.C. Martin (ed.) *Islam in Local Contexts*, Contributions to Asian Studies 17, pp. 44–61, Leiden: Brill.

Ernst, C.W. and Lawrence, B.B. (2002) *Sufi Martyrs of Love: The Chishtī Order in South Asia and Beyond*, New York: Palgrave Macmillan.

Ewing, K.P. (1997) *Arguing Sainthood: Modernity, Psychoanalysis, and Islam*, Durham, N.C.: Duke University Press.

Feener, R.M. (2004) *Islam in World Cultures: Comparative Perspectives*, Santa Barbara, California: ABC-CLIO Publishers.

Gilmartin, D. (1988) *Empire and Islam: Punjab and the Making of Pakistan*, Berkeley: University of California Press.

Hassan, R. (1987) 'Religion, Society, and the State in Pakistan: Pirs and Politics', *Asian Survey*, 27 (5): 552–565.

'Ibn Batuta at Ajodhan in 1334', *The Punjab Past and Present* Vol. VII, Part II, no. 14 (October 1973), pp. 396–97.

Irving, M. (1911) 'The Shrine of Baba Farid Shakarganj at Pakpattan', *Journal of the Punjab Historical Society*, 1: 70–76.

Kirpalani, S.K. (1993) *Fifty years with the British*, Bombay: Oriental Longman.

Sahar, Kanwar Mohinder Singh Bedi (1983) *Yadon Ka Jashn*, Delhi: Summer Printers.

Khan, A.N. (1990) *Islamic Architecture of Pakistan: An Analytical Exposition*, vol. 1, Arab and Central Asian Contribution, Islamabad: National Hijra Council.

——— (2003) *Islamic Architecture in South Asia: Pakistan, India, Bangladesh*, Karachi: Oxford University Press.

Mackeson, F. (1837) 'Journal of Captain C.M. Wade's Voyage from Lodiana to Mithankot by the River Satlaj, on His Mission to Lahore and Bahawalpur in 1832–33', *The Journal of the Asiatic Society of Bengal*, 6: 169–217.

Menon, N.R. Madhava and Banerjea, D. (eds) (2003) *Criminal Justice India Series: Punjab, 2002*, New Delhi: Allied Publishers.

Nizami, Khaliq Ahmad (1998) *The Life and Times of Shaikh Farid-U'd-Din Ganj-I-Shakar*, Dehli: Idārah-i Adabiyāt-i Dillī.

Qureshi, R.B. (1986) *Sufi Music of India and Pakistan: Sound, Context and Meaning in Qawwali*, Cambridge: Cambridge University Press.

Roe, C.A. and Purser, W.E. (1878) *Report on the Revised Land Revenue Settlement of the Montgomery District in the Mooltan Division of the Punjab 1878*, Lahore: Central Jail Press.

Rozehnal, R. (2006) 'Faqir or Faker? The Pakpattan Tragedy and the Politics of Sufism in Pakistan', *Religion*, 36 (1): 29–47.

Saghar, Tariq Ismail (1986) *Election 1985: Fervrī 1985 key Intkhābāt per Tafṣīlī Report*, Lahore: Maktaba Int*kh*āb wa Jamhūr.

Sanyal, U. (1996) *Devotional Islam and Politics in British India, Ahmad Riza Khan Barelwi and His Movement, 1870–1920*, Delhi: Oxford University Press.

Shahzad, G. (2009) *Taʿmīr-O Tausīʿ Khānqāh Bābā Farīd Ganj-i Shakar*, Lahore: Sang-i Mīl Publications.

Singh, C. (1991) *Region and Empire: Panjab in the Seventeenth Century*, Delhi: Oxford University Press.

Talbot, I. (1998) *Punjab and the Raj 1849–1947*, Delhi: Manohar Publications.

Talib, Gurbachan Singh (1974) *Bābā Shaykh* Farīd *Shakar Ganj*, Delhi: National Book Trust.

9 The mother and the other

Tourism and pilgrimage at the shrine of Hiṅglāj Devī/Bībī Nānī in Baluchistan[1]

Jürgen Schaflechner

The Hiṅglāj/Nānī shrine is located in a cave in the Hingol National Park on the western side of the Hingol River in the district of Baluchistan, Pakistan. The cave is about 250 kilometres west of Karachi and 20 kilometres inland from the Arabian Sea. I will argue in this paper that the remote location of the cave plays a crucial role in the historical depiction of the goddess Hiṅglāj Devī/Bībī in literature and related ritual events. In earlier times, the extreme hardship of the journey was a significant characteristic of the pilgrimage, contributing to its spiritual value. Today the shrine's significance is measured in different terms, taking into consideration its increased accessibility and the presence of the modern 'tourist' there. Located along ancient trading routes between the Middle East and South Asia (Kamphorst 2008: 253), the cave and the goddess residing in it have a historical relationship with merchant castes, nomadic pastoral groups and the local aristocracy.[2] The goddess Hiṅglāj/Nānī has frequently been associated with other goddesses in Asia, a relationship that is often emphasized in the literature to legitimize her importance. The pilgrimage to the goddess's abode, mainly done on foot until the beginning of the 1980s, was seen as a purifying process for devotees before entering her sacred valley. This sacrificial journey inspired many stories about the shrine and led authors and poets to praise the *yātrā* (pilgrimage) for its religious benefits.[3] Today, especially after the construction of the Makran Coastal Highway in 2003, the shrine's importance among Hindu communities in Pakistan has increased, and this has various implications for the rituals performed at the shrine.[4]

In part one of this article, I will give an outline of the history of this ancient site, followed by a summary of its most important receptions in vernacular and colonial sources. In part two, I will further argue that these sources and their repeated mention of hardship, kinetic experience and immense spiritual benefits lead to a distinction among visitors at the shrine between the label of the 'pilgrim' and the 'tourist'. But aside from current discussions about details of such differentiations (Coles 2004, Olsen and Timothy 2006, Swatos 2006 *et al.*), I will state that this divide is mainly drawn by the visitors at Hiṅglāj themselves and serves as an important marker for their identity. But such differentiation is not due to certain intrinsic characteristics of any of these terms, but rather due to a lost ideal, a fantasy structure (Zizek 1989) built and perpetuated within the literature, which collides with the experienced reality at Hiṅglāj. The result is the construction of the 'tourist', a label with no ontic content, rather used as a canvas for the projection of an alleged lost spiritual unity between the goddess and her devotees somewhere in the shrine's history. In this way the tourist functions as an *Other*, a designation of a lack that attempts to close the gap between fantasy and experienced reality at the shrine.

Part I

The cāraṇī sagatī *and the* ādiśakti *Hiṅglāj*

In his book, *The Alchemical Body* (1996), David Gordon White mentions a passage from Ctesias' fifth-century B.C. Greek work, *Indika*, which can be read as the earliest reference to the Hiṅglāj/Nānī shrine in Baluchistan (205). In this text, Ctesias mentions a place in the desert and some kind of ritualistic behaviour related to the sun and the moon. He also describes the location and says that one could reach this area within fifteen days from 'Mont Sardo', probably a mountain where the Sardo gem was found.[5] King describes these mountains as being fifteen days' walking distance from the desert between Cutch and Multan (1865: 297). This could certainly be a reference to the valley of Hiṅglāj/Nānī. The symbols for the sun and the moon are found there, carved into the stone opposite the shrine. Today it is said that these symbols were made by Lord Rāma himself when he visited Hiṅglāj. So far, this quote is the oldest reference to the site that I have found.

Aside from these historical references, there are many *mytho-historical*[6] narratives of pastoral groups from the western Indian Subcontinent, namely the Bharvāṛ, the Rabārī and the Cāraṇ, that imply the great age and influence of the cult of the goddess, Hiṅglāj, in the area. The Cāraṇ[7] in particular have a special bond with Hiṅglāj in Baluchistan, and their pilgrimage to her shrine is mandatory for many of them at some point in their lifetime (Westphal and Westphal-Hellbusch 1974: 311). This requirement obviously became problematic after the creation of the Indo-Pakistan border in 1947, and resulted in an entirely new set of dynamics within the Cāraṇ communities' ritual expression.[8]

At this point, it will be useful to devote a few words to the historical relationship between the Cāraṇ communities and the local rulers, since it was the particular combination of political and religious power between the two groups that helped give rise to the *cāraṇī sagatī* (Kamphorst 2008), the tradition of apotheosis amongst Cāraṇ women. This practice led, according to Tambs-Lyche, to a widespread goddess cult starting from the seventh to the ninth century in the west of the Subcontinent, unique in its structure and thus distinct from other *devī* traditions in the area (1999).

From mythological times, many Cāraṇ were employed as bards and poets, serving kings and aristocrats as genealogists, and even more significantly, assembling and composing the histories of their masters' dynasties. In this way, the Cāraṇ played an important role in stabilizing the monarchs' reign. Their poetry connected the rulers of their day to those of mythological times, thereby placing current administrations inside a timeless *dharma* and legitimizing the rulers' claims to power. Cāraṇ were also warrantors for contracts, and guaranteed the adherence to certain agreements between two parties with their lives. They did this by threatening to commit *traga* (self-immolation)[9] in which Cāraṇ wounded or even killed themselves or members of their community to show that injustice had been done, and the evil-doer was directly responsible for the death of a Cāraṇ. The ghosts of the deceased were feared, especially those of females, because they embodied the horrific aspect of the goddess. The threat of *traga* served as a guarantee for everyday agreements like loans or the settlement of disputes, but also for politically sensitive topics such as contracts between two kings (Tambs-Lyche 2004). As an embodiment of *dharma*, the Cāraṇ community retained a powerful position that helped them develop a strong bond with local rulers, a connection that lasts to this day. This relationship between the Rājpūt clans and the Cāraṇ community was symbiotic in many ways. While the Cāraṇ legitimized Rājpūt authority by facilitating a connection to an eternal order, the Rājpūt were instrumental in the Cāraṇs' upward social mobility.

Many Cāraṇ communities consider the *devī* to be their creator who formed their *jāti* (caste) out of her own body (Basu 2004: 182). In conversations with Cāraṇ in India, I was told that when a boy is born into the community, a bell rings at the Hiṅglāj shrine in Baluchistan. They also said that it is the responsibility of every male Cāraṇ to visit the goddess at Hiṅglāj before his sixtieth birthday, otherwise a rock will tumble down into the sacred valley. The goddess also grants Cāraṇ men the ability to write and compose stories and poems. She is their muse, and they imagine her sitting on a poet's tongue and quickening his creativity. The women's relation to the goddess goes even further: the *devī* herself promised to incarnate as a Cāraṇ woman periodically to bring change and prosperity to the community. Such deified Cāraṇī are considered full or partial incarnations of *śakti* (the divine female energy) and according to caste narratives, Hiṅglāj herself was once a Cāraṇī (Samaur 1999: 503). In fact, she was the first of countless incarnations of the goddess in this world. Janet Kamphorst writes:

> I think it is best to keep in mind that the attribution of the same heroic deeds and/or names to different Charani goddesses can be understood as a part of a narrative tradition that casts all Sagatis as forms of Hinglaj and/or major or minor incarnations of each other, and this means that, in the end, it is the Mahashakti Hinglaj herself who is credited with the heroic deeds of all her *avatārī*s.
>
> (Kamphorst 2008: 244)

This circle of incarnations, the *cāraṇī-sagatī*, has a long tradition in the west of the Subcontinent, and it is from these communities that the 'more important Goddesses' of the area emerge (Tambs-Lyche 2004: 124). The practice still exists today; the most recent famous incarnation was Cāraṇī Āī Śrī Sonal Mātājī, a social reformer, who died in 1975. She supported the education of young women in her community, preached against alcohol abuse and spread ideas that were inspired by the politics of Gandhi (Basu 2004).

There are not many stories about the alleged Cāraṇ woman whose life is associated with the goddess Hiṅglāj. Samaur believes the goddess's origins lie in the 'Gaur'viyā Cāraṇ' branch from Thatta, a city in the south of Sindh (1999). Kamphorst mentions the name 'Charani Deval' (2008: 236) and dates her appearance and the beginning of the *devī* tradition to the eighth century. These narratives describe her as a knowledgeable woman, initiated by Kanphaṭa Yogis, who gave her the name Hiṅglāj (Westphal and Westphal-Hellbusch 1974: 31). The narratives of one branch of the Cāraṇ, the Tūṃbel of Gujarat and Sindh, also describe Hiṅglāj as a deified Cāraṇī who lived in the Hala mountain range, not far from the present location of the shrine. The Tūṃbel spread the goddess's fame in Las Bela, and so Hiṅglāj decided to settle in a cave close to the Hingol River, where she has been worshipped since as early as the ninth century by the Cāraṇ and other communities (Kamphorst: 236).

Many other incarnations exist in the west of the Indian Subcontinent that are associated with the *ādiśakti* (Sanskrit, 'primeval power') of Hiṅglāj, and one of the most important of these is the goddess Karṇī. After the separation of Pakistan and Hindustan and the restriction of movement that followed, her shrine in Deshnok, Rajasthan, became the most important place of pilgrimage for Cāraṇ and other worshippers of the *cāraṇī-sagatī* in India (*ibid.* 245). Karṇī is seen as a partial incarnation of the *ādiśakti*. While Karṇī's father was undertaking the pilgrimage to Hiṅglāj, the goddess appeared to her mother and foretold the coming of the *devī*. Karṇī was born in the year 1388 and soon revealed her divine nature through her miracles and influential charisma (Westphal and Westphal-Hellbusch 1976: 174). In those days, Rao Shekha was the ruler of the area, and it is said that with the blessing of the goddess Karṇī, he was able to defeat his enemies and establish stable rule (Tambs-Lyche 1999: 66). Karṇī also supported Ridmal, whose son Jodha later conquered Jodhpur. But Bika Rathore, Jodha's younger son, received special patronage from Karṇī Mātā. She provided him with 500 oxen for his conquest, and at a later date miraculously drew the bows of the army of Bikaner, allowing them to defeat their enemies from a safe distance (Kamphorst 2008: 248). In exchange for her beneficence, the heirs to Bikaner's throne remained loyal to the goddess, and in time, her temple in Deshnok became elaborately adorned. Related myths speak of the strong connection between the goddess and the ruling elite of the area, a relationship that is reiterated in the songs and poetry of the Cāraṇ and the Rājpūts.

Following the cited works of Tambs-Lyche (1999; 2004) and Kamphorst (2008), one can therefore assume that the goddess cult of the western Indian Subcontinent started between the seventh and the ninth centuries, and incorporated ritualistic behaviour that might have already existed at the shrine of Hiṅglāj/Nānī in Baluchistan. Further, the goddess Hiṅglāj is understood by some as being the first incarnation, the *ādiśakti*, and thus the centre for many variations of goddess worship in western India (Tambs-Lyche 1999: 64). The *mytho-historical* narratives of the bards and the Rājpūt communities reveal a strong connection between the establishment of ruling dynasties of the area and the apotheosis of Cāraṇ women. Such cultural memories may bear witness to a consistent theme of religiously intertwined governance in western India, in opposition to a modern typological separation of religion and politics; an assumption that, notwithstanding its intriguing character, can't be discussed at this point. The deification of the Cāraṇī was often related to their social and material status and went hand in hand with the connection they had to local rulers. Over time, these various local incarnations became anchored to the shrine of Hiṅglāj and were further interpreted in its light. With the establishment of these links to the place in Baluchistan, a continuous history was created that is reiterated and perpetuated to this day by the stories and poetry of the bards, the Rājpūts and devotees in meetings, festivals and even in monthly magazines.

The śākta pīṭha *and Hiṅglāj*

In contemporary Pakistan, various stories circulate concerning the origin of the shrine in Baluchistan, most of which build upon the famous myth of Satī and her father Dakṣa Prajāpati. Due to the importance of this story to the present study, I will provide a short account here.

In mythological times, the great goddess incarnated into the body of Satī, the daughter of King Dakṣa. Satī had married the god Śiva against her father's will, so when Dakṣa performed a sacrificial ceremony, he invited every god in the pantheon except Śiva. Satī was deeply upset by her husband's humiliation, and to express her anger, leaped into the sacrificial fire, thus taking her own life. When Śiva heard of this, he was furious and called upon his armies to interrupt the ritual and kill Dakṣa. He then took the burnt body of his beloved Satī in his arms, and wild with grief, began to dance the *tāṇḍava*, the cosmic dance performed by Siva, that threatened to destroy the whole world. To save the universe and to relieve Śiva from his pain, Viṣṇu and the other gods cut the body of Satī into many parts that fell out of Śiva's arms and were scattered all over the Subcontinent. Wherever these parts of the body of Satī fell, the soil became holy and soon the places became known as *śākta pīṭha* (Sanskrit, 'seats of power').

This version forms the core of a story I heard frequently from people at the shrine, although Viṣṇu's intervention is sometimes omitted. One of the first versions of this narrative is found in the Mahābhārata (XII chapters 282–83) with variations evolving in the Kumārasaṃbhava of Kālidāsa in the fourth or fifth century C.E., and later in the Bhāgavata (IV, 5, 20–21) and the Kālikā Purāṇa (XVII 42–49) (Sircar 2004: 5). In the earlier version, we only find the characters Satī and Dakṣa, and it is not until the later Purāṇas that the humiliation of Satī by her father and the eventual murder of Dakṣa by her husband Śiva become crucial parts of the story. The association of the goddess's limbs with certain places of worship is the latest development and originated no earlier than the fourteenth or fifteenth century (*ibid.* 6 fn. 3). Over time, different texts gave different figures for the number of associated holy places, and eventually fifty-one *śākta pīṭha* were enumerated in the Mahāpīṭhanirūpaṇa. The text itself claims to be a part of the Tantracūḍāmaṇī, but was, according to Sircar, composed in the seventeenth or eighteenth century (*ibid.* 3).

As for the question of which part of the goddess's body came down to earth at the shrine, different people give different answers. Some state that the upper part of Satī's head fell onto Baluchistan, while others claim that it is the goddess's navel or womb that fell there. Support for the first interpretation is often given in the etymology of the name Hiṅglāj, which relates to the Sanskrit word '*hiṅgula*', meaning 'vermilion' or 'cinnabar'.[10] As a pious, married Hindu woman, Satī wore vermilion ('*sindūr*') in her hair, and so after the upper part of her head fell in Baluchistan, the place became known by the name Hiṅgula, from which the name Hiṅglāj eventually developed (Billimoria 1944: 93). Narratives claiming that it was the womb that came down to earth in Baluchistan may be connected with one of the central rituals of the shrine where pilgrims crawl through a small tunnel signifying the womb of the goddess from which they are born again. Before a pilgrim is permitted to enter this tunnel, he/she has to follow a rigid pattern of purification and worship (see e.g. Rathi 2008).

Besides a broader corpus of Sanskrit literature and the sources of *cāraṇī sagatī* worship in the western Subcontinent, colonial texts also play a significant role in the discourse surrounding the shrine. In the following section, I will provide some samples of these sources and the way they describe the site.

Colonial perspectives on Hiṅglāj

There are several colonial sources dealing with Baluchistan that mention the shrine and the pilgrimage associated with it. The first remark about Hiṅglāj by a British officer is probably the one found in the 1816 travelogue of Sir Henry Pottinger. Disguised as a Hindu merchant and ostensibly on a mission to buy horses for the market in Bombay, he travelled to Baluchistan to collect strategic information about the area for the East India Company. In Pottinger's account, we learn that the whole region was virtually unknown to the British until the expedition of Captain Grant of the Bengal Native Infantry, who travelled through the Southwest in 1809 (300 f.). Pottinger's book gives an insight into the means of travel in those days, the mutual misunderstandings between him and the people of Baluchistan and their respective perceptions of one another.[11] He briefly mentions the shrine, and from his description of the environment, one can guess that he did not actually go there.[12] But Pottinger's remark that the place was visited by 'many thousand pilgrims yearly' (297) is crucial for this study, for one can conclude that some kind of structured pilgrimage route was already active and conspicuous at the beginning of the nineteenth century, and probably for decades before that.[13] Pottinger also mentions the strong influence of local Hindu communities on the trade in Sonmiani, the main port in Las Bela. He estimated that Hindus comprised about 12–15% of the overall population of 2,000 houses in this town. They 'enjoy[ed] great security and protection in their mercantile speculations, under the mild and equitable government of the Jam' (19 folio).

Another very detailed account of the shrine and its connected pilgrimage from the middle of the nineteenth century is given by Captain Hart in his two articles, 'A pilgrimage to Hinglaj' (1839) and 'Some account of a journey from Kurrachee to

Hinglaj, in the Lus territory' (1840). While the first narrative focuses explicitly on the journey, its stopovers and mythological significance, the second article reflects more on the strategic and geographical interests of the East India Company at the time. Hart went on the pilgrimage accompanied by Thaomul, a merchant from Hyderabad, who years before had prayed for the blessing of male offspring at the shrine of the goddess Āśāpūrī.[14] After his wish had been granted, he revisited the valley of Hiṅglāj to offer the boy's hair in return. The party consisted of around forty individuals, and they set out from Karachi under the guidance of the 'Agwa',[15] the spiritual leader of the group orchestrating all the necessary rituals. Hart says that the Agwa had to be obeyed by the Brahmins regardless of his caste. Interestingly, when the party arrived in the valley of Hiṅglāj, the ritual shaving of Thaomal's son's hair was not performed by the Agwa, but by a local 'Mahomedan' instead (95). It was also a Muslim who cut the throat of a sacrificial goat that was offered to the goddess Kālī. Overall, due to his participation in the pilgrimage, Hart is able to provide a very detailed and useful account of its structure, making his report a valuable document for the purposes of this study.

Charles Masson wrote about the shrine some years later in 1842. Masson, whose actual name was James Lewis, had worked for the East India Company as a soldier, and he tells us that:

> The sacred locality is called Hinglátz. It is understood to be consecrated to Parbatí, the goddess of nature, the universal mother, & c., or Diana, the moon, & c. By the Máhommedans, by whom it is alike revered, the shrine is considered as one of Bíbí Nánī, the lady Nání, or the motherly lady. It is possible they have preserved the ancient name NANAIA, that of the goddess of the old Persians, and the Bactrians, and now so well known to us by coins. There is a small mat or temple at Hinglátz, but the chief attractions appear to be natural objects, as a kand, or reservoir of water; a well, of unfathomable depth, above the mat; and the semblance the mural disposition of the rock presents, in a certain spot, to that of a fortress. There are also said to be figures of the sun and the moon hewn on the rock, in an accessible site.
>
> (1972: 390 f)

Here we find some crucial points: the appearance of the name Bībī Nānī, and again, a reference to a certain Muslim influence at the shrine. Masson also assumes that the name Nānī is linked to other goddesses to the west of the Makran. These conceptions remain connected to the shrine and are a recurring theme in later publications about Hiṅglāj.[16]

A final writer whose work is relevant to this overview is Thomas Holdich, an English geographer who worked for the Survey of India and travelled widely in the border areas of the Empire. His books, *India* (1904) and *The Gates of India* (1910), are a compilation of notes from his extensive journeys during these years (1910 vi). In the introduction to *The Gates of India*, Holdich praises the bravery of earlier explorers like Pottinger, Masson and Cunningham, whose work he wished to revive in his writing (*ibid.* vii folio). He reiterates the possible association of

Hiṅglāj/Nānī with other goddess traditions in Asia, and describes her influence as extending 'from the Euphrates to the Ganges' (1904: 45). He also mentions the shrine's importance for both Muslims and Hindus, but according to him, neither are: '[. . .] recognizing that the object of their veneration is probably the same goddess who was known to the Chaldeans under the same old world name (Nana) a thousand years before the time of Abraham' (*ibid.*). With this statement, Holdich asserts the antiquity of the shrine, surpassing both Islam and Hinduism, thus putting the goddess in an independent position, untouched by any present religious. These books have had a significant influence on today's literature on the shrine in Baluchistan, and by their constant reiteration, they have formed an enduring narrative of Hiṅglāj/Nānī.

The association with other goddesses

This short survey of the shrine's appearances in nineteenth-century colonial literature can, of course, only illustrate certain highlights in the discourse. I have provided a very selective picture here, as important writers and adventurers like Alexander Burns or George Briggs have not been mentioned. But I think that the snippets of information introduced here are paradigmatic for a colonial 'style' of writing that described, but somehow also prescribed, an image of the location and the history of the residing deity.

Because of the shrine's remote position in the desert of Baluchistan, firsthand accounts of journeys to it were rare, so the travelogues of British officers were among the few sources available for devotees and researchers. Thus, it is not surprising that to this day it is often through the eyes of colonial authors that the place and its history are described. In particular, the association of the shrine with the worship of goddesses of Persian, Bactrian or Chaldean origin is an aspect of the site for which colonial sources are preferentially mentioned. Apparently, Charles Masson was one of the first who hypothesized a connection to an ancient Near Eastern goddess, an idea that from then onwards became integral to the description of her. In 1913, William Crooke quoted Masson's idea in his article 'Hinglāj', written for the *Encyclopedia of Religion and Ethics* (ERE), a piece that was frequently quoted in later literature. Besides Masson's allusion, Crooke also describes the circumambulation at the shrine and compares it to other rituals in Europe and Egypt (715). I certainly lack the expertise to adequately evaluate the relation of the shrine to other traditions of goddess worship in the West, but I find it intriguing that this concept reappears and is integrated into contemporary writings by Sindhi authors. Some examples follow.

Ishtiaq Ansari's 2001 book *Dhartī Mātā* (in Sindhi) is based on extensive research on Hiṅglāj, and more generally, on goddess veneration in South Asia. Concerning indications of Hiṅglāj/Nānī's incorporation into Chaldean, Persian and even Egyptian contexts, Ansari quotes, among others, the work of Ali Ahmad Brohi, a Sindhi scholar, and Thomas Holdich, mentioned above (Ansari 2001: 19). For further emphasis, Ansari cites from the *Las Bela Gazetteer* (1907) which also mentions this relationship. The *Gazetteer* gives a description of the goddess's importance for Hindus and Muslims alike, and also introduces the possibility that the deity might be related to a Chaldean tradition, thus dating the deity to a thousand years before Abraham (36). Scrutinizing the quote within Ansari's argument, one finds that the *Gazetteer* account does not build upon new, independent research, but is in fact also derived from Thomas Holdich's book *India* (1904).

Badar Abro's argument has a similar structure to Ansari's in his 1991 book *Hinglaj & Lahoot*. Aside from the work of Ahmad Brohi, mentioned above, and that of James Frazer, Abro makes special reference to an article by M.N. Billimoria from 1944. Although Billimoria's contribution seems, at first, to build on new research, he again quotes Holdich (1910) when it comes to the illustration of the goddess's history and her connection to older traditions (Billimoria 1944: 94 f.). Billimoria also refers extensively (often without citation of direct quotations) to Crooke's 1913 article in the ERE (Billimoria 1944: 93).[17] As stated earlier, Crooke quotes Masson's argument to provide support for his own thesis, thus creating a direct connection between Badro's synopsis and Masson's writing from 1842. Billimoria also cites more than five pages directly from Captain Hart's travelogue from 1839. His contribution to the study of the goddess Hiṅglāj is therefore an accumulation of older sources, rather than a new approach to the question of her origin. On the basis of these arguments, mostly taken from the work of Billimoria, Abro places the goddess in a distant sphere where she is 'related to the human past'[18] – that is, detached from a specific creed – and hence removed from any kind of communal conflict (42). He also connects Hiṅglāj to the mother goddess from Mohenjo-Daro, and adds that she is not different from 'Nānyā,Anāhītā, Kālī, Durgā [or] Pārbatī' (51). By viewing all of Hiṅglāj's attributes collectively (as the goddess of victory, the mountain dweller, etc.), he finds hints and references to all female divinities in Asia and incorporates them into a timeline centred on the shrine of Hiṅglāj. Since Hiṅglāj is now every goddess, beyond any communal dispute – according to his argument – she is all-embracing, transcending and surpassing all the other goddesses. In addition, her existence is scientifically evident to the author from the archaeological discoveries in Mohenjo-Daro (Abro 1991: 50 f.). Abro uses these arguments, based broadly on the texts of colonial writers, to include the shrine in an ancient tradition of goddess veneration, exceeding the borders of present religion, and thus integrating Hiṅglāj/Nānī into a broader Sindhi-national discourse.[19]

But it is not only Sindhi authors who link the goddess to more ancient worship. In a recent Hindi publication about Hiṅglāj, Omkar Lakhavat (2011) also mentions the possible connections to other Asian goddesses. Supporting his argument, he mainly quotes from the work of Holdich, Masson, Billimoria and Ansari (115), thus relating to the same corpus of scriptures, and eventually drawing the same conclusions as the authors before him.[20]

Similar to the history of the Cāraṇ, we find a broader field of narratives (in this case, 'scientific' narratives) organized around one central theme, the shrine of Hiṅglāj/Bībī Nānī. Here, the goddess serves as the reference point, structuring, but also creating the field of articulation and group identity. With the equation of Hiṅglāj to Nānī to Nanea to Anahita and so forth, the shrine is incorporated into a wider nexus of goddess cults, lending it more legitimacy and disconnecting the goddess from any form of communal friction. In this discourse, the colonial sources are cited as the main testaments to the shrine's antiquity. However, these sources of verification can ultimately be traced back to the mere assumptions of a few authors. This does not mean that I challenge the shrine's ancient origins in any way, but I assert that only a handful of descriptions and limited data were repeatedly quoted over time with the same purpose: to prove the influence and significance of the desert shrine to a broader audience.

Part II

Walking through history: an overview of the pilgrimage

I shall provide a short introduction to the pilgrimage as found in three types of sources: mythological narratives, historical records and travelogues in poetry and prose. In most of these references, we find a strong focus on the *kinetic* (Coleman and Eade 2004) aspect of the shrine's ritual *network*,[21] demonstrating the importance of the walking tradition. The story of Rāma's journey to Hiṅglāj/Nānī is one example of this type of kinesthetic emphasis. This story appears in the 'Hingool Pooran' (Hart 1839: 79), but I mainly learned of it through conversations I had at the shrine and at other temples in Sindh.

In mythological times, King Rāma was advised to make the pilgrimage to Hiṅglāj to purify himself of the sin of killing the demon Rāvaṇa, who was a Brahmin. Rāma set out towards Hiṅglāj with his army and *vāhans* (vehicles), but they were intercepted in the desert by the goddess, who challenged them. When Rāma asked why, she told him that he should go back to the area which is now called Karachi and return as a humble pilgrim. So Rāma left his entourage and vehicles behind, peregrinating like a simple man to the shrine, accompanied by his closest friends. Only then did the goddess permit him to enter her abode. Following this sacrificial and physically challenging journey, Rāma was finally granted the purification he sought from the *devī*.

Unfortunately, there is sparse information in the pre-colonial literature about the actual orthopraxy of walking to the Hiṅglāj/Nānī shrine. There are a few records from the *akhāṛās* (the pilgrim shelters) in the city of Thatta, which shed some light on the pilgrimage in mediaeval times. Various Sindhi authors quote these annals as historical evidence of royal visits to the shrine (Chhabria 2007, Jethmalani 1994, Ansari 2001). According to these records, before the Mughal Period, the kings of Rajasthan would stay in the city of Thatta on their way to receive the *darśana* (Sanskrit, 'divine gaze') of the goddess. The journeys of Raja Todarmal (1508), Raja Madhu Singh (1792) and Raja Jagat Singh (1801) receive particular mention in these documents.[22]

Shah Abdul Latif (1689–1752), the famous Sindhi poet, provides another description of the pilgrimage. Latif accompanied a group of Yogis on their way to the goddess's shrine in 1710 (Ansari 2001: 22). His experience is captured in the verses of his *magnum opus* 'Risālo', giving another indication of a long and enduring tradition of walking to the shrine.[23] Unfortunately, from these limited sources, it is difficult to estimate the extent and influence of the pilgrimage in pre-colonial times beyond the experiences of kings and certain religious groups, but it is likely that the practice of walking to the shrine was already common among many people of the western Subcontinent at that time.

Devadatta Shastri's 1978 travelogue 'Āgney Tīrth Hiṅglāj' provides a more recent and prosaic representation of the pilgrimage. Here, the journey is described from the perspective of a *yātrī* (a pilgrim) who gives a detailed account of his struggles along the way and the difficulties his fellow pilgrims faced. The experience of the walk itself forms the core of Shastri's narrative, and the book is important for today's literature because of its detailed depiction of the pilgrimage.

The current pilgrimage network

As discussed above, the pilgrimage to Hiṅglāj/Nānī has been performed for centuries by certain sects, the regional aristocracy and local persons. Rājpūts in particular claim a continuous relationship to the shrine as they often link the establishment of their dynasty to the goddess's spiritual intervention. But despite its ancient history, the rise of the shrine's influence among Hindu communities, including an institutionalized annual pilgrimage, is a fairly recent phenomenon, which can be attributed to several notable changes in Sindh and Baluchistan. Although the increased utilization of the valley by Hindu communities as a stage for religious and ritual performance is a complex topic that must be dealt with in detail elsewhere, I will give a brief overview of the factors contributing to it.

One of the components leading to the shrine's increased importance for Hindu communities was the establishment of the annual pilgrimage. In colonial times many Hindu communities performed initiation rituals such as the *upanayana* ceremony at the temple (Hart 1839). However, Ashok Jethmalani's 1994 book *Hinglājtīrth* describes how, after the colonial period and the eventual hardening of the border between India and Pakistan – especially in the aftermath of the 1965 war – the number of pilgrims from Baluchistan, (Pakistani) Punjab and Sindh visiting the shrine each year declined dramatically. In 1982 Seth Tarvamal, a resident from the town of Lyari approximately 90 kilometres east of the shrine, began guiding pilgrims there again on a somewhat regular basis. But the idea of establishing an annual *melā* (festival) there was, according to Jethmalani, conceived in 1985[24] by one individual, Vasrup Chand Tulsi.[25]

This decision had numerous implications for Hindu devotees. In the following year, Tulsi helped to establish the 'Hinglaj Sewa Mandli' (HSM), an organization that facilitated transportation and distributed information to pilgrims. The HSM also fixed the date of the yearly pilgrimage, usually a weekend in the beginning of April. In 1988, the building of a link road between Aghor village and the Āśapūrī temple at the entrance to the Hiṅglāj/Nānī valley made transportation to the shrine easier, but already from 1986 onwards the HSM assumed responsibility for bringing pilgrims there on an annual basis. Since then the HSM has organized the pilgrimage for thousands of national and international clients, a development that has gradually led to the solidification[26] of Hindu traditions at the shrine.

Another major development leading to the shrine's increased importance to Hindu communities was the completion of the Makran Coastal Highway (MCH) in 2003. Built with aid from the Chinese government (The Telegraph: 12.02.2011), it links Pakistan's commercial metropolis, Karachi, with the port of Gwadar in the far West of the country. Running along the Coast of Makran, the MCH also had a tremendous impact on life in the shrine's valley by linking it to the rest of the country and making it reachable in just three and a half hours by bus from Karachi.

While prior to the 1980s, the place was surrounded by a dangerous, exclusive and sacred ambiance created by the arduous pilgrimage and perpetuated in literature and oral traditions, in recent years the shrine has become increasingly accessible to everyone, particularly through the work of the HSM. Combined with certain infrastructural developments and ultimately the completion of the MCH, the pilgrimage has changed from a rare, kinetic and even potentially life-threatening spiritual endeavour to the biggest annual social gathering of Hindu communities in Pakistan today.[27]

The 'tourist' and the 'devotee'

During my research at the shrine in the spring and autumn of 2010, I encountered a broad array of motivations for people's visits to the valley. These reasons varied from mere curiosity or a leisure activity to the fulfillment of an ancient family tradition. The embassy of one European country even took their employees to the shrine to show them the culture and history of Pakistan.[28] This type of visit often aroused comments from devotees like, '*bas, picnic manāne āte haiṃ*' (Urd/Hin. 'They just come for a picnic'). My informants thereby created a hierarchical structure of motivations, drawing a line between themselves and the 'picnicking' others. But in doing so, they not only referred to the '*baṛe log*' (Urdu/Hindi, 'important/rich people') in their chauffeur-driven Toyotas and sunglasses; they also dismissed fellow pilgrims and members of other (Hindu) communities as lacking serious devotion. This divide between the '*picnic manānevāle*' – equal to the modern 'tourists' – and the 'devotees' was a prominent feature in my conversations with people in the valley and at other temples in Sindh. Interestingly, no one ever perceived himself[29] or his group as 'tourists', but many people would lament the increasing shallowness of the journey and the simplistic motivations of others. The following is a part of a conversation I had with a Sindhi visitor who started to come to Hiṅglāj already from the end of the eighties:[30]

Q. You came here for the first time in 1989, so tell me what has changed?

A. Everything, how the people come and go, how they dress, their attitude . . . everything changed! The worst thing is that they forgot the name of the mother!

Q. And such people keep coming to the shrine?

A. Yes! They constantly come. They turned it into a picnic, a sight (*ghūm 'daede a rsation partnerin 2012. e end of the eighties*: ne kī jagah) where people just come and go as they please. It didn't use to be a picnic, it was just you and the goddess. Now they even take baths in the ponds! They do not come for the darśan.

Here, one of the main reasons for the 'spiritual' decline at the shrine is connected to the swelling crowd and the people's attitude of forgetting the goddess. For this man the place changed from a spiritual place where one only meditated on the name of the goddess to a site where people come for their enjoyment.

Similarly, on another occasion a different visitor told me that the goddess no longer resides at the shrine because she has become annoyed with the crowd. He added that if I wanted to meet her, I ought to climb up to Caurāsī, a two and a half hour ascent into the mountains, to a pond where she had taken refuge.[31] This explanation attempts to connect the kinetic part of the journey to the present time, where one again has to make a physical effort to be able to receive the goddess's blessing.

Through these conversations, I have the impression that the label of the 'tourist' merely serves as the projection of a deficiency or lack, an *Other* at the shrine, a quality that is only found in the fellow visitors not in oneself, and thus filled with a variety of vague complaints used to express a general resentment about recent developments at the shrine. The term serves as a canvas, on which projections of an alleged past and, indeed, a lost unity are combined and personified. In this way, the 'tourist' stands for the connection of the shrine to an urban Pakistan and the accompanying changes at the site.

Michael Stausberg argues in his latest book about religion and tourism that there is a fairly blurry distinction between pilgrimages and tourist activities. For example visits to churches are often embedded in cultural and city tours, while pilgrimages are sometimes embroidered with shopping stops and museum visits (2010). Although the church visit might only be a part of the visitor's interest in the culture and history of a place, they may also take the opportunity to light a candle and say a little prayer for loved ones. Individual motivation will be difficult to grasp in qualitative or quantitative research, and as Humphrey and Laidlaw argue, people impose various meaningful narratives onto ritualistic behaviour by themselves (1994). Interesting in the Hiṅglāj case is the obvious divide, the line that is drawn by *pūjārīs* (Sanskrit, 'priest'), organizers and the pilgrims themselves to distinguish the serious from the non-serious, the pilgrims from the tourists. In this way the pilgrimage site at Hiṅglāj thwarts current discussions of what separates the activity of the 'tourist' from that of the 'pilgrim'.

Such distinction is not drawn along lines of orthopraxy. The performance of rituals is not sufficient to serve as a marker of 'seriousness', a quality that people deny the tourist. Devoted pilgrims might follow all the necessary rituals and *bhajans* (religious songs) in praise of the goddess and still be seen by others as '*picnic manānevāle*'. Younger visitors in particular, mostly teenagers from Hindu settlements in Karachi, have a bad reputation for having 'fun' at the shrine. However, this group provides a huge stock of volunteers ('*sevā kar 'nevālā*') in Hiṅglāj/Nānī to cook and clean for others. I even met a clique of young men riding the 260 kilometres from Ranchor Line, a part of Karachi, to the Hiṅglāj/Nānī shrine on their 125 CC motorbikes. This is an almost epic journey with great risks, where the earlier dangers of being robbed on the way are substituted by the daring driving style of the truckers frequenting the MCH.

The MCH plays an important and rather ambiguous role within the pilgrimage *network*. Over the past few years, the MCH has been responsible for giving many people the chance to experience the shrine. The increasing number of visitors draws, on the one side, more attention to the goddess and the various narratives at the shrine, which in itself emphasizes the importance of the tradition. But on the other side, such an accumulation of individuals, together with the smooth access to the shrine, contradicts the danger and exclusiveness of the pilgrimage experience as it is perpetuated in many stories and travelogues.

In the light of these developments and the widely varying assortment of visitors to the shrine, it seems clear that there are no hard and fast guidelines for distinguishing 'authentic' pilgrims from 'picnic tourists'. Thus, the 'tourist' is merely a figure of general resentment among certain visitors at the shrine. The rapid changes in recent years and the consequent diminishing of the kinetic experience, characterized by reiteration of the grueling journey in oral traditions and literature, leads to a gap between the 'ideal' picture and the reality of the pilgrimage. This gap has to be filled with shape and meaning, a fantasy structure that has led to the construction of the 'tourist', who embodies the lack of the arduous and purifying journey known from various sources.

This phenomenon suggests another split within the already fairly heterogeneous group of pilgrims at the shrine. However, as can be seen by the annual number of visitors, some aspects of this place and the residing goddess also have the potential to harmonize widely varying sets of ideas and characteristics, making it possible to attract large numbers of visitors. The question remains as to where this wide appeal originates and how Hiṅglāj/Nānī is able to unify so many different concepts and demands.

Conclusion

The shrine of the goddess Hiṅglāj/Nānī is probably already mentioned in the work of Ctesias more than 2,000 years ago. Over time, the place in Baluchistan became associated with many different goddesses and religious currents in the region and established a stable pilgrimage system. Religious groups and several *jātis* in India, but also all over the world, have until today a strong bond with the shrine and the residing goddess.

In the last thirty years, the pilgrimage of Hiṅglāj/Nānī has undergone significant changes and shifted from being a singular kinetic experience, a once in a lifetime event, to a social gathering for many different Hindu communities in Pakistan. This reached a point where the April festival is currently said to be the biggest Hindu *melā* in the country. This development was induced by intentional (e.g. HSM) as well as non-intentional actors (e.g. MCH) that influenced the socio-religious life at the shrine on different levels. With the shrine's increased accessibility and growing presence in literature, public interest in the place grew, and in turn, led more authors to attempt an exploration of its history. These publications with their repeated mentioning of the pilgrims' physical effort had an enormous influence on the solidification of the rituals, narratives and traditions of the shrine, and retold the stories of the hardship and deprivation of those who had set out to walk there. Through the reiteration of these narratives, the gap between the ideal and the present becomes apparent, and it has to be filled with a certain *Other* of the kinetic experience: the 'tourist'. But this label has no particular ontic content, rather it encompasses all kinds of attitudes and rituals. The image of the 'tourist' has therefore come to represent certain participants' resentment towards particular aspects of the shrine today that are not in balance with the picture given in the widespread oral traditions and publications.

Notes

1 I am very grateful to Prof. Hans Harder and Prof. William Sax for their valuable criticism. I also want to thank Lillian Langford for her useful comments and Zaki Hussain, who helped me with the translations from the Sindhi originals. All vernacular words in the text are of Hindi/Urdu origin, if not mentioned otherwise.
2 See Tod (1920) & Westphal and Westphal-Hellbusch (1974 and 1976).
3 See Devadatta Shastri (1978), Sircar (2004), Rathi *et al.* (2008).
4 In this article, the terms 'Hindu' and 'Muslim' are used to speak of broader identity conceptions. The question of the legitimate use of these terms is contentious, but it can't be discussed here.
5 'Les Indiens, dit-il, sont les plus justes des hommes; il parle de leurs us et coutumes et de ce territoire consacré en plein désert qu'ils honorent sous le nom du Soleil et de la Lune; on y parvient en quinze journées à partir du mont Sardo' (Ctesias 1959: 136).
6 The term *mytho-historic* is inspired by the work of Babb (2004) and Jan Assmann (1997), who both use mythological traditions to gain insight into the past, as well as the present situation of a certain community. In this way, *mytho-historic* narratives discuss an alleged past and its impact on the present.
7 The strong heterogeneity of the Cāraṇ *jāti* led to the assumption that the only link between the pastoral communities, merchants and bards of the caste is the shared name (Westphal and Westphal-Hellbusch 1976: 93).
8 Notwithstanding the difficult relationship between the two countries, each year several groups from India manage to obtain visas and travel to Pakistan to visit the shrine. This is a unique situation with interesting political and religious implications that must be dealt with separately.
9 The transcription of this term is taken from Tambs-Lyche 2004.
10 For a different interpretation, see Billimoria 1944: 104.
11 ' [. . .] by recalling two questions that were put to us, by the very person who had spoken of his intimacy with the Resident in Sinde, and who might, from that circumstance alone, have been supposed to know little better: he very gravely inquired if I knew whether the Firingee, *i.e.* European governor of Bombay, was a Hindoo or a Moosulman? and [sic] a few minutes after he made use of the word "Company", and wished to be informed how old she was. At first I could not conceive his aim; but he soon explained it, by saying he had always understood that the "Company" was an old woman, with an immense deal of money' (45 f.).
12 '[. . .] close to the temple, in the bed of the Nudee, is a famous well, which is called from its depth the "Uneel ka Koond", or the unfathomable abyss; a man who had been there, assured me he had seen some hundred fathom of rope let down without coming at the water, and the natives believe it to have been dug by the tutelary goddess of the temple. The water of the pagoda is very fine and esteemed good for many disease' (302).
13 In a later section, I will show that Chhabria *et al.* (2007) give some information about the earlier pilgrimage, and further, state that it could be traced back to the fifteenth century.

14 Āśapūrā Dharamśālā is the place of the goddess Āśāpūrī, who is said to fulfil wishes. It is at this place, at the beginning of the valley of Hiṅglāj, that the pilgrims used to stay one night to rest before they proceeded to the cave of Hiṅglāj, just a few hundred metres further into the valley.
15 From Hindi, *aguvā*, a guide, a leader.
16 Interestingly I have not found any publications with narratives about the life story of Bībī Nānī yet. Nowadays, the worship of the goddess, Nānī, is mostly associated with the Ẓikrī community from Makran, and rarely finds extensive mention in broader Hindu publications.
17 The paragraph, 'The title of Bibi Nani may be identified with Nanea, the mother-goddess worshipped in Syria, Persia and Armenia, and other parts of Asia under the names Anaiti, Anaea, Aneitis or Tanais, the primeval Babylonian goddess Nana, the lady of the temple E-anna of her city Uruk', corresponds almost exactly with the wording of Crooke's article, as does the following paragraph. Consequently, I think it is highly likely that this part was taken directly from the ERE (see ERE 1913: 715 f.; see also Billimoria: 99 f. and ERE: 716).
18 Sindhi. '*insān jo māẕi*'.
19 For more information on Sindhi nationalism and its various facets, see Verkaaik 2010.
20 In his book 'Gorakhnāth and the Kānphaṭa Yogis', Briggs quotes the same two authors, Holdich and Masson, when he speaks of the history of Hiṅglāj and her association with other goddesses (1998: 106).
21 The term *network* is inspired by the work of Bruno Latour, who understands it as a metaphor for human 'collectives'. A *network* is an assembly of traces left behind by the agency of both human and non-human actors and thus can portray a wider scope of cause and effect not merely limited to human intentionality (2005). The Makran Coastal Highway is one of these important non-intentional actors within the broader Hiṅglāj *network*.
22 Chhabria, Jethmalani and Ansari all agree on the years of Madhu Singh and Jagat Singh's visits. For the journeys of other kings, the exact dates vary. See Jethmalani 1994: 21 and Ansari 2001: 22.
23 Apparently, an ancient tradition exists among the Jogis of Sindh to walk to Hiṅglāj. Unfortunately, I have not been able to gather any precise data on this yet (see Newsline, August 1992: 83).
24 In contrast to Jethmalani's account, Chhabria (2007) cites the year 1982.
25 Here we already find some varying myths entwined with the establishment of the pilgrimage (see: Musakhel 2006). But since I heard this version of the story from contemporaries of Vasrup Chand Tulsi as well, Jethmalani's account is presumably fairly accurate.
26 By 'solidification' I refer to a complex process in which certain actors with access to public articulations, intentionally or unintentionally, stiffen the borders of a particular tradition by their research, community work or media presence. 'Solidification' is the reiteration of a particular body of narratives and practices that describes, but also captures and hardens the borders of a phenomenon in this process.
27 To understand this development, one must look at earlier statistics: in 1992, the festival had 300 visitors, the biggest gathering at the place since the creation of Pakistan (Jethmalani 1992: 31). While in 2000, the festival attracted 15,000 people (Musakhel: 2006). According to the HSM, it reached its climax to date in 2010 with 45,000 visitors.
28 The impending arrival of this group became evident as a huge number of police and military personnel spread out over the valley hours before the convoy appeared.
29 All of my respondents were men, an imbalance I have so far been unable to avoid in my fieldwork in Pakistan. I am sure one could write an alternative story of the events at the shrine from female perspectives.
30 The interview took place during the April *melā* in Hiṅglāj in 2012.
31 *Caurāsī kuṇḍ*, a pond of fresh water in the mountains around the valley, has its own significance within the narrative surrounding the pilgrimage, to be discussed at length in a future publication.

References

Abro, B. (1991) *Hinglaj & Lahoot*, Karachi: Sangam Publications.

Ansari, I. (2001) *Dhartī Mātā*, Karachi: Sindhica Academy.

Assmann, J. (1997) *Das kulturelle Gedächtnis*, München: C.H. Beck.

Babb Lawrence, A. (2004) *Alchemies of Violence*, New Delhi: Sage Publications.

Basu, H. (2004) *Von Barden und Königen*, Frankfurt am Main u.a.: Peter Lang GmbH Europäischer Verlag der Wissenschaften.

Billimoria, N.M. (1944) 'Hinglaj, an ancient site of pilgramage [sic] in the Las Bela state', *Journal of the Sind Historical Society*, Karachi: Daily Gazette Press. Pp. 29–37.

Briggs, G.W. (1998) [1938] *Gorakhnāth and the Kānphaṭa Yogīs*, Delhi: Motilal Banarsidass.

Chhabria, T.L. (2007) *Hinglaj Mata*, Raipur (Chhattisgarh): Shadani Publications.

Coleman, S. and Eade, J. (2004) 'Introduction Reframing pilgrimage', in S. Coleman and J. Eade (eds) *Reframing Pilgrimages. Cultures in Motion*, New York: Routledge.

Coles, T. and Timothy, D.J. (2004) 'My field is the world' conceptualizing diasporas, travel and tourism', in T. Coles and D.J. Timothy (eds) *Tourism, Diasporas and Space*, London: Routledge.

Crooke, W. (1913) 'Hinglāj', in *Encyclopedia of Religion and Ethics*, vol. 6, New York: Scribner's. Pp. 715–716.

Ctesias (1959) *Indika*, in Photos, Bibliotheca, 6 vols, translated by Rene Henry, Paris: Les Belles Lettres.

Dilgir, Hari and Anju Makhija (2005) *Shah Abdul Latif. Seeking the Beloved*, New Delhi: Katha.

Gold, A.G. (1988) *Fruitful Journeys: The ways of Rajasthani pilgrims*, Berkeley-Los Angeles: University of California Press.

Hart, S.V.W. (1839) 'A pilgrimage to Hinglaj', in *Proceedings of the Bombay Geographical Society*, E.A. Webster, vol. 3, Bombay: American Mission Press. Pp. 77–105.

——— (1840) 'Some accounts of a journey from Kurrachee to Hinglaj in the Lus territory, descriptive of the intermediate country and of the port of Soumeanee', *Journal of the Asiatic Society of Bengal*, Calcutta: Bishop's Colleges Press. Pp. 134–154.

Holdich, T. (1904) *India*, London: Oxford University Press.

——— (1910) *The Gates of India*, London: Macmillian.

Hughes, A.W. (1877) *The country of Baluchistan, its Geography, Topography, Ethnology and History*, London: George Bell & Sons.

Humphrey, C. and Laidlaw, J. (1994) *The Archetypal Actions of Ritual*, New York: Oxford University Press.

Jethmalani, A. (1994) *Hinglāj Tīrtha*, Karachi: Āl Hindu Śiva Dhārmi Esosīaytśan.

Kamphorst, J. (2008) *In Praise of Death*, Leiden: University Press.

Khan, D.S. (2004) *Crossing the Threshold*, London: I.B. Publishers.

King, C.W. (1865) *The Natural History of Precious Stones and Gems*, London: Bell and Daldy.

Lakhavat, O. (2011) *Hiṃglāj Śaktipīṭh*, Pushkar: Tīrth Pailes Prakāśan.

Latour, B. (2005) *Reassembling the Social*, New York: Oxford University Press.

Masson, C. (1972) [1842] *Narrative of Various Journeys in Baluchistan, Afghanistan, and the Punjab; Including a Residence in those Countries from 1826 to 1838*, Karachi: Oxford University Press.

Musakhel, M.Y. (2006) 'Socio-ecological and economic impacts of Hinglaj Mata festival on Hingol National Park and its resources', Protected Areas Management

Project, Hingol National Park, Uthal (Source: http://www.scribd.com/doc/33863665/Hinglaj-Mata-Festival-Hingol-National-Park-report).
Olsen, D.H. and Timothy, D.J. (2006) 'Toursim and religious journeys', in D.H. Olsen and D.J. Timothy (eds) *Tourism, Religion and Spiritual Journeys*, New York: Routledge.
Pottinger, H. (1816) *Travels in Beloochistan and Sinde*, London: Longman, Hurts, Rees, Orme and Brown.
Rathi, J. (2008) *Hinglāj Devī Mātā*, Karachi: Lānghanī Brādaras.
Samaur, B.S. (2005) [1999] *Rājasthānī Śakti Kāvya*, Delhi: Sāhitya Akādemī.
Shastri, D. (1978) *Āgney Tīrth Hiṅglāj*, Delhi: Lokālok Prakāśan.
Sircar, D.C. (2004) [1973] *The Śākta Pīṭhas*, Delhi: Motilal Banarsidass.
Stausberg, M. (2010) *Religion im modernen Tourismus*, Berlin: Insel Verlag.
Swatos, W.H. (ed.) (2006) *On the Road to Being There. Studies in Pilgrimage and Tourism in Late Modernity*, Leiden: Brill.
Tambs-Lyche, H. (1999) 'Introduction', in H. Tambs-Lyche (ed.) *The Feminine Sacred in South Asia*, Delhi: Manohar.
——— (2004) *The Good Country*, Delhi: Manohar Publishers.
Tod, J. (1920) *Annals and Antiquities of Rajasthan*, London et al: Oxford University Press.
Verkaaik, O. (2010) 'The Sufi saints of Sindhi nationalism', in M. Boivin and M. Cook (eds) *Interpreting the Sindhi World*, Karachi: Oxford University Press.
Westphal-Hellbusch, S. and Westphal, H. (1974) *Hinduistische Viehzüchter im nord-westlichen Indien*, Vol. 1, *Die Rabri*, Berlin: Duncker und Humblot.
——— (1976) *Hinduistsiche Viehzüchter im nord-westlichen Indien*, Vol. 2, *Die Bharvad und die Charan*, Berlin: Duncker und Humblot.
White, David Gordon (1996) *The Alchemical Body*, Chicago and London: The University of Chicago Press.
Zizek, Slavoj (1989) *The Sublime Object of Ideology*, London: Verso.

Gazetteers & Lexica

ERE – *Encyclopedia of Religion and Ethics*, 1913, New York: Scribner′s.
Baluchistan District Gazetteer Series, 1907, vol. 8, *Las Bela*, Allahabad: Pioneer Press.

Newspapers

Newsline, Karachi.
The Telegraph India, Calcutta.
Anandabazar Patrika, Calcutta.

10 Sacred journeys, worship and reverence

The Sufi legitimation of the *ziyārat* in Hyderabad

Mauro Valdinoci

At present, some South Asian Muslims oppose the legitimacy of the pious visit to a Sufi saint's grave (*ziyārat*), although many studies testify that it is common practice, and a significant element of the Muslim culture of the Subcontinent.[1] On the one hand, numerous Muslim scholars and activists that embraced reformist types of Islam criticize the *ziyārat* as a reprehensible religious innovation (*bid'at*) and an obstacle to the social reform of Muslim society.[2] On the other hand, Sufis continue to uphold the legitimacy of the beliefs and practices related to the *ziyārat* through ritual performances, and occasionally through speeches and writings.

Although a great number of scholarly works mention the criticism of the *ziyārat*,[3] the Sufi responses have not been fully investigated. Christopher Taylor has dealt with the legal defense of the *ziyārat*, but his study is limited to the late mediaeval period (1999: 195–218). Both Usha Sanyal's monograph on Aḥmad Riḍā Ḫān Barelwī (d. 1921) and his movement (1996: 118–20, 163–65, 172–88) and Arthur Buehler's article on the Naqšbandī response to the detractors of Sufism (1999: 480–91) explore the justification of Sufi devotional practices in modern times; however, they discuss it in general terms and draw almost exclusively on texts. I hope to enrich this area of study by focusing specifically on the rituals of the *ziyārat*, especially the *fātiḥa*, and by taking into account both texts and ethnographic context.

From an interdisciplinary framework theoretically based on Critical Discourse Analysis (CDA) (Fairclough 1989, 1995; Wodak 1989; Van Dijk 1993, 2001) and drawing on analytical tools from the socio-semiotic approach developed by Halliday and Hasan (1985), this study focuses on the textual strategies used to legitimate a controversial practice in Islam, namely the *ziyārat*. CDA scholars have made a valuable contribution to the study of legitimation of contested actions (Rojo and Van Dijk 1997, Van Leeuwen 2007, Van Leeuwen and Wodak 1999, Reyes 2011), especially by highlighting strategies of legitimation.

This chapter aims to examine the performance of the *ziyārat* by a branch of the Qādiriyya based in Hyderabad (Andhra Pradesh, India), and analyse the justification of the *ziyārat* by the masters (*pīrs*) of this branch using a few texts written by them.[4] Drawing on the categories developed by Van Leeuwen (2007), this chapter seeks to identify specific strategies of legitimation and relate these particular texts to other Sufi discursive strategies. This study argues that the response of Indian

Sufism to criticism by Islamic reformist movements is not monolithic, and points to some differences in the Sufis' views. Even though this particular topic cannot be fully covered here, as it requires further research, this chapter shows that these Qādirī masters' stance slightly differs from that of other Sufis, such as the renowned Aḥmad Riḍā Ḫān Barelwī (d. 1921). Indeed, even though the respective apologetic discourses appear quite similar as far as arguments and strategies of legitimation are concerned, nevertheless they diverge at the stylistic and rhetoric level. Whereas Aḥmad Riḍā and his followers frequently apply labels such as 'idolaters' and 'unbelievers' to Muslims that have different stances, drawing sharp boundaries within the Muslim community, 'Abd al-Qadīr Ṣiddīqī stresses the need to overcome misunderstandings among Muslims and refrains from branding other Muslims as unbelievers.

Theoretical and methodological framework

This is a study of an Islamic apologetic discourse about a particular social practice, namely the pious visit to Sufi saints' tombs. It is placed in the framework of CDA, an approach developed within the area of Discourse Studies. In CDA, discourse – language used in speech and writing – is considered a form of social action or practice (Wodak 1996, Fairclough 1995, Van Leeuwen and Wodak 1999),[5] a reflection of the power relations in society, and a constitutive factor of social relations and belief systems (Fairclough 1989; Van Dijk 1993, 2001; Wodak 1996).

According to Norman Fairclough (1993, 1995), discursive events should be analysed simultaneously at three levels: the level of social practice (the situational and institutional context), the level of discursive practice (the socio-cognitive aspects of text production and interpretation) and the textual level (the content and form of the text). This approach is based on the socio-semiotic method elaborated by Halliday and Hasan (1985), according to which there are three aspects of discourse: ideational, interpersonal and textual meaning. Halliday and Hasan stress that every piece of discourse should be studied in its social context, that is, in the culture and situation in which it takes place. The three aspects of discourse parallel three aspects of the social context: field, tenor and mode. According to Halliday and Hasan, it is meaning that connects discourse to the context; consequently the connection between discourse and context is placed on the semantic level (Halliday and Hasan 1985).

From a discursive perspective, legitimation is understood as a process that addresses specific issues and yet has broader social implications (Rojo and Van Dijk 1997, Van Leeuwen 2007, Van Leeuwen and Wodak 1999). Legitimation 'refers to the process by which speakers accredit or license a type of social behavior. In this respect, legitimization is a justification of a behavior' (Reyes 2011: 782). At the same time, such process is concerned with broader social practices and the power relationships between the social actors involved (Rojo and Van Dijk 1997, Van Leeuwen and Wodak 1999). The analysis of legitimation is based on the premise that legitimacy is formed in relation to specific discourses: discourses provide the frameworks in which people understand particular issues and give meaning to them (Fairclough 1989). Within any given 'order of discourse', defined as 'the totality of discursive practices of an institution and relationships between them' (Fairclough 1993: 138), discourses greatly constrain social actors involved in processes of production of meanings and interpretation.

This chapter applies Fairclough's approach to the analysis of legitimation in discourse using a set of categories put forward by Van Leeuwen (2007). Van Leeuwen points out four main categories of legitimation: *authorization* (reference to authority figures or tradition), *moral evaluation* (reference to a value system), *rationalization* (reference to goals and uses of social action) and *mythopoesis* (narratives that reward legitimate actions) (Van Leeuwen 2007: 92). These categories have been applied to the study of the discourses of political figures (Van Dijk 1993, Van Leeuwen and Wodak 1999: 104–11, Reyes 2011: 785–88), whereas I apply them to the investigation of a piece of apologetic discourse in Islam, concentrating on religious figures. Moreover, I combine the method of CDA with an ethnographic approach in order to provide an interdisciplinary perspective on the ways in which the visit to Sufi saints' tombs is justified. Before describing the performance of the *ziyārat* at a Sufi shrine of Hyderabad, and discussing its justification, I would like to introduce the controversy over the *ziyārat* providing a brief historical overview.

What's wrong with the *ziyārat*?

The disputes over the Islamic legitimacy of the *ziyārat* are long-standing. As is well known, prominent legal attacks on the *ziyārat* came from the Hanbalī jurist, Aḥmad ibn Taymiyya (1263–1328) and his student Ibn Qayyim al-Jawziyya (1292–1350). However, anti-Sufi ideas such as those of Ibn Taymiyya and his students, particularly in regard to the *ziyārat*, 'constituted a minority and distinctly unpopular position among the *"ulamā"* of their time' (Taylor 1999: 195). It has to be remembered that in the mediaeval period, the criticism over the *ziyārat* was directed toward its excesses and improper manifestations, and 'the legal basis in the *šari'a* for the *ziyāra* was never seriously in question' (Taylor 1999: 216).

A radical break from mainstream Sufi tradition by modernists and fundamentalists started in India in the second half of the nineteenth century, when the *ziyārat* began to be condemned as a practice against the principles of Islam (Gaborieau 1999: 452–53, Sirrieh 1999: 174). The criticism mainly focused on two points: the status of the living and dead saints, and the rituals connected to them. The most influential movements in the dissemination of this criticism were the Deoband Academy, the *Ahl-i Ḥadīṯ*, the *Tablīġī Jamā't* and the circle of Sayyid Aḥmad Ḫān (1817–1898), while a fairly determined defense of Sufism came from Aḥmad Riḍā Ḫān Barelwī (1856–1921) and his successors.[6] Any contemporary research about *dargāhs* must confront the fact that, at present, anti-Sufi tendencies have a following in Hyderabad. The *Ahl-i Ḥadīṯ* and other *wahhābī*-oriented groups strengthened their presence in the city by building or managing mosques and establishing educational organizations. Moreover, an important branch of the

Tablīġī Jamā't has been established in Hyderabad, with a well-organized network of mosques, and headquarters in the area of Mallepally.

The condemnation of the *ziyārat* revolves around three types of arguments: 'theological ones, legal ones about ritual rules, and finally, a more general argument which enjoins Muslims to avoid resembling non-Muslims' (Gaborieau 2003: 221). Besides, it is worth saying that for the *Salafīs* and *Ahl-i Ḥadīṯ*, the very existence of the graves is a reason for scandal (Gaborieau 2003: 222–23). The theological arguments concern the attributes the saints are credited with by the devotees, such as the gift of miracles and the power of intercession (Buehler 1999: 477; Gaborieau 2003: 221–22). In this perspective, such attributes only belong to Allah, and all human beings are equal in matters of spiritual powers. To deny these principles is *širk fi'l-'ilm* (polytheism in matters of science) and *širk fi'l-tasarruf* (in matters of power). According to the legal arguments, most of the rituals performed at graves are objectionable in respect to place, time and form (Buehler 1999: 479–80; Gaborieau 2003: 223). Such rituals are condemned as *širk fi'l-'ibādat* (polytheism in matters of ritual observance), since they make the saints the objects of worship which is due to Allah alone. They are also branded as innovations (*bid'at*) which did not exist in the time of the Prophet and the first two generations of his followers. Finally, all these practices are described in a way that makes them appear similar to Hindu devotional rituals and beliefs. These practices are condemned as *širk fi'l-'ādāt* (polytheism in matters of customs) and *kufr* (unbelief) (Buehler 1999: 479–80; Gaborieau 2003: 224–28).

It is important to note that these charges are not formulated from a position of power in the socio-political sense, as the discourse of Islamic reformism is by no means hegemonic in India. Apparently, those who adhere to any version of Islamic reformism are in the minority, whereas the large majority of Muslims follow the traditionalist doctrines and practices. The discourse of Islamic reformism does not identify with an official view on Islam, since India is a secular country that does not sponsor any particular form of Islam. However, it benefits from the political and economic power of Saudi Arabia, especially in terms of material resources and visibility in the media. The reformist and traditionalist discourses coexist within the Islamic discursive tradition as competing and conflicting discourses since in Islam there is not any centralized authority that could ultimately be referred to in matters of legitimate religious practices. Having summarized the controversy over the *ziyārat*, I turn now to the Sufi justification. Drawing on the analytical approach developed by Fairclough (1993, 1995), I explore the justification of the *ziyārat* by some *Qādirī* masters of Hyderabad as a discursive event. In the following pages, I try to analyze the three key dimensions of this discursive event: the level of sociocultural practice, the level of discursive practice and the textual level.

The *ziyārat* in practice

I begin with the level of the sociocultural practice, focusing on the institutional context and the nature of the social action that is taking place. This chapter describes the performance of the *ziyārat* at the *dargāh* of 'Abd al-Qadīr Ṣiddīqī, which is located in the area of Bahadurpurah (Hyderabad). First, it should be pointed out that the *Qādirī* masters of this branch justified the *ziyārat* implicitly, by permitting people (Muslims as well as non-Muslims) to visit the tombs of 'Abd al-Qadīr and his descendants. Second, these masters justified the *ziyārat* through both verbal and non-verbal communication. Ritual is a combination of verbal and extra-linguistic actions.

The present *pīrs* of this branch regularly performed the *ziyārat* to the grave of 'Abd al-Qadīr and his descendents and 'Abd al-Qadīr himself used to visit his own *pīr*'s tomb and those of other Muslim saints. At the *dargāh*, the collective *ziyārat* to the graves of 'Abd al-Qadīr and his spiritual successors was a recurring event of the ritual programme during the weekly, annual and monthly gatherings. It was led by the *sajjāda našīn* or by other *pīrs* of the Ṣiddīqī family. The collective *ziyārat* started from 'Abd al-Qadīr's grave. Flowers were offered and put on the grave, then the ritual of the *fātiḥa* was performed, followed by a supplication (*du'ā*) uttered by the *sajjāda našīn*. Finally, the participants respectfully greeted the saint by touching and/or kissing the grave. Then the same sequence of rituals was repeated at the graves of 'Abd al-Qadīr's successors. The collective *ziyārat* took place at definite times and lasted for a few minutes, whereas the individual *ziyārat* could be performed every day by devotees at any time, and could last from a few minutes to some hours.

The ordinary, individual *ziyārat* appeared more informal than the example described above, and pilgrims might perform other activities beside those already mentioned. In addition to flowers, devotees occasionally offered embroidered sheets and money as religious tributes (*nazrana*), and lit incense sticks and small earthen lamps. Some pilgrims brought water bottles or incense sticks, which they placed near the grave for some time in order to make them absorb the flow of blessing (*baraka*) emanating from the grave, and then carried them home to use them for therapeutic and propitiatory purposes. They often picked up a few flower petals from the grave and ate them on the spot or took them home for the same purposes. Some devotees recited portions of the *Qur'ān*, and sometimes those initiated to Sufism performed spiritual exercises of remembrance and contemplation. Some devotees expressed a vow to the saint, in hopes that the saint would help them to overcome everyday problems. Devotees used to beg the saint's help for any conceivable purpose: health, job, family, marriage, school and judiciary problems. When their wishes were fulfilled, they returned to the *dargāh* to thank the saint and to distribute food and money to the poor and needy. The ritual variations were all tolerated by the *pīrs* of the Ṣiddīqī family, provided that the former remained within the limits demarcated by *adab* or Muslim code of conduct.

Concerning a crucial ritual of the *ziyārat*, namely the *fātiḥa*, it has to be pointed out that at the time of my fieldwork, it was considered one of the most controversial matters within the Muslim community of Hyderabad and was undoubtedly a factor of division. Even if the issue of the *fātiḥa* did not create a radical separation among Muslims, like the one between Sunnī and Šī'ī, the reciprocal criticism between the parties was quite harsh and sometimes resulted in serious accusations. The *fātiḥa* is the first *sūrah* of the *Qur'ān* and is composed of seven verses. Its recitation, combined with other activities, is also called *fātiḥa* and can be performed on a number of different occasions, as there are different types of *fātiḥa*. For example it is recited at a funeral, on the fortieth day after somebody's death, before the distribution of some food or on the saints' death anniversaries, but in this chapter, I focus on the *fātiḥa* as a particular ritual of the visit to a saint's grave. The prevalent method of recitation of the *fātiḥa* according to this *Qādirī* branch is as follows: first, one should recite the *sūrat al-fātiḥa* once, then the *sūrat al-ikhlas* three times, then the Quranic verse (33:56), then the *durūd šarīf* three times, and finally, one should recite a supplication for the dead and send him the reward of the recitations.[7]

The *pīrs* of the Ṣiddīqī family did not restrict access to the *dargāh*. It was open to everybody, without distinction of religion, social class or gender. People who came for the *ziyārat* to this *dargāh* performed it directly, without the mediation of any religious specialist. Unlike many *dargāhs* of Hyderabad, women had direct access to the saints' tombs, and were allowed to sit in front of the tombs and touch them. In this *dargāh*, like most South Asian *dargāhs*, participants are supposed to cover their heads with a cap or a veil and to remove their shoes while entering the courtyard.

Sufi discourse vs. reformist discourse in *Luzūm-i fātiḥa* and *Tafsīr-i Ṣiddīqī*

Here, I explore another dimension of the justification of the *ziyārat* as a discursive event: the level of discursive practice. By addressing issues of text production and interpretation, I concentrate on the participants or the addressers and addressees of the message. I am particularly interested in discussing the participants' statuses and roles and the relationship between them.

In this case study the addressers are Muḥammad 'Abd al-Qadīr Ṣiddīqī (1871–1962) and his grandson and *khalīfa*, Muḥammad Anwār al-Dīn Ṣiddīqī (1923–1992). The former, besides being a Sufi master of the Qādiriyya, was a scholar in the field of Islamic religious sciences, in particular a *mufassir*, an expert of Quranic exegesis. He taught religious sciences first at the Dār al-'Ulūm of Hyderabad and then at Osmania University (Hyderabad), and has numerous literary works to his credit, both in poetry and prose. Along with his descendants, he has an unquestionable reputation for orthodoxy. The latter was initiated into the Qādiriyya by 'Abd al-Qadīr and received the *ḥilāfat* (spiritual deputyship) from him. He taught religious sciences at different institutes of Hyderabad and authored several tracts in addition to a monumental biography of 'Abd al-Qadīr.

I analyze here two particular texts produced by them. The first one is entitled *Luzūm-i fātiḥa. Fātiḥa bid'at nahīṇ, sunnat hay* (*Necessity of the Fātiḥa. The Fātiḥa is a Tradition not a Reprehensible Innovation*) and was written by Anwār al-Dīn Ṣiddīqī. It was published in 1958 and reprinted in 2010. The other is *Tafsīr-i Ṣiddīqī* (*Ṣiddīqī's Quranic Exegesis*), 'Abd al-Qadīr Ṣiddīqī's Urdu translation and exegesis of the Qur'ān. 'Abd al-Qadīr Ṣiddīqī started writing his *tafsīr* at the beginning of the 1930s and the writing process took several years. Portions of it were first published monthly in the periodical *Al-Qadīr* under the title *Dars al-Qur'ān*, whereas it was published as a single book – entitled *Tafsīr-i Ṣiddīqī* – only after 'Abd al-Qadīr Ṣiddīqī's death. The introduction to the *Tafsīr* and the first chapter have been translated into English and published in 2000 with the title *Introduction and Tafseer of Surat-ul-Fatiha*. I have selected the former because it is a pamphlet entirely devoted to the legal defense of a particular ritual of the *ziyārat*: the *fātiḥa*. Concerning the latter, I have selected the introduction and first chapter, since this portion of the text includes an attempt to rebut the charges of *širk* (idolatry), *kufr* (unbelief) and *bid'at* (reprehensible innovation in religion). Both texts offer a unique perspective on the personal view of the *pīrs* of the Ṣiddīqī family.

Luzūm-i fātiḥa (LF) is a short text composed of twenty-one pages that belong to the genre that we can tentatively call *religious-legal tracts*. The main purpose of such tracts is to provide a legal defense of controversial religious practices. This is not a modern genre, as we find instances of tracts devoted to the justification of the *ziyārat* written in Damascus as early as the first decades of the fourteenth century (Taylor 1999: 195–218). However, the extensive production of treatises that criticized traditional Islamic practices during the nineteenth and twentieth centuries gave particular impetus to the genre of *religious-legal tracts*. Like the genre of Sufi hagiographic literature, the production of *religious-legal tracts* certainly benefited from the development of printing in India (Green 2005: 617–21).

LF was published by Anwār al-Dīn Ṣiddīqī, reprinted by the publishing house of the *dargāh* (Hasrat Academy Publications) in a limited edition, and distributed free of charge by the *pīrs* of the Ṣiddīqī family on the occasion of the annual gatherings at the *dargāh*. LF did not have a large circulation; it was read mainly by the disciples and followers of the *pīrs* of the Ṣiddīqī family. It is a highly specialized text, which deals with a specific topic, namely the *fātiḥa*.

Tafsīr-i Ṣiddīqī (TS) is a voluminous work composed of six volumes, which belongs to the genre of *tafsīr* or Quranic exegesis. The *tafsīr* plays a prominent role in the discursive tradition of Islam as a well-established discipline within the Islamic religious sciences and literary genre, and its roots reach back to the formative period of Islam (Ohlander 2009, 620). As a discursive genre, the major aim of *tafsīr* is to interpret the text of the *Qur'ān* in order to apply it to the requirements of different socio-historical conditions. Usually, any *tafsīr* offers a remarkable perspective on its author's views about various issues.

Unlike LF, TS had a relatively large circulation among the learned religious circles of Hyderabad and beyond. Moreover, it was taught by 'Abd al-Qadīr's spiritual successors during the Sunday lectures at the *dargāh*, which are still taking place. As a *tafsīr*, TS is of greater import than LF, and covers a wide range of topics. It is mostly concerned with general issues and even though it attempts – among other things – to refute the charges of *širk*, *kufr* and *bid'at*, it does so without examining specific practices in detail.

Both LF and TS relate to other texts in their respective genres and were composed in response to those texts; moreover, both of them were written in reply to texts produced within the framework of the reformist discourse. In both LF and TS, we find quotations from other tracts and references to particular Sufis and reformist theologians.

It is important to note that although both LF and TS were composed as written texts, the discussion of their form and function should not be limited to the area of written communication. Rather, they should be regarded as written and spoken texts at the same time, since they were taught orally by the *pīrs* of the Ṣiddīqī family. In this way, far more people – including the uneducated and poorly educated – had access to them, not only those who had the time, competence and inclination for reading religious treatises. Most of the addressees, in this case the readers of the texts or the audience of the same texts transmitted through lectures, are Muslims, Sufis as well as non-Sufis, who largely agree with the addressers' basic doctrinal assumptions. The relationship between addressers and addressees is dialogic in nature. The latter might appear as passive receivers who can only accept or reject the message, yet they are always involved in a process of interpretation (Fairclough 1993). They interpret the message on the basis of several factors, such as the conventions of the genres, the cultural context and their own presuppositions and expectations.

The Muslim addressees of this message were provided by the *pīrs* of the Ṣiddīqī family, whom they accepted as authoritative voices, with a sound justification of the controversial practice. The *pīrs* reassured their followers about the legitimacy of a practice that was being carried on for centuries by means of a persuasive rhetoric and a personal authority based on religious esoteric and exoteric knowledge and adherence to the *sunna* (tradition) of the Prophet Muḥammad. These reflections help explain the legal defense of the *ziyārat* at the level of discursive practice, and highlight the 'interpersonal meaning' of discourse (Halliday and Hasan 1985), but a further dimension of discourse still needs to be explored, namely that of the 'textual meaning'.

The main arguments

The third level of the discursive event is that of the 'textual level' (Fairclough 1993). Looking specifically at the content and form of the two texts that I have introduced above, I make a few general considerations about the symbolic organization of the texts, style, rhetorical mode and function in the context. I do not embark on a detailed textual linguistic analysis, as this is more of a preliminary study. Rather, I limit myself to identify some linguistic devices which are instrumental in conveying the message and stance of the texts. My aim here is to highlight how the *fātiḥa* and, by extension, the *ziyārat* are justified, and identify the strategies of legitimation.

I would like to begin by briefly outlining the content of one of the texts in question, in order to provide an instance of the argumentative structure. I omit the summary of the introduction and first chapter of the *Tafsīr-i Ṣiddīqī* (TS) for the sake of brevity, as TS is a richly informative text that deals with numerous issues and would require much more attention. Nevertheless, I will discuss select excerpts from TS related to the justification of the *ziyārat*. In *Luzūm-i fātiḥa. Fātiḥa bid'at nahīṇ, sunnat hay* (LF) the author states the main purpose of the tract directly in the cover; here follow the three lines that serve as a subtitle:

> A reply, grounded in the Qur'ān, *Aḥādīṯ* and practice of the Companions of the Prophet, to the following accusation [advanced] by the opponents of the *fātiḥa* (*muḫallifīn-i fātiḥa*):
>
> The practice of performing the *fātiḥa* in congregation, encouraged by the innovators (*ahl-i bid'at*) does not belong to the Prophet's teachings, therefore it is a reprehensible innovation (*bid'at*) and as such, it is wrong
>
> (Ṣiddīqī 2010: cover).

As the author states, this text aims to counter the accusations against the *fātiḥa*, in particular the claim that the *fātiḥa* is an innovation. Similarly, in *Tafsīr-i Ṣiddīqī*, 'Abd al-Qadīr reveals that the purpose of his *tafsīr* is not only to translate and interpret the Quranic text as thoroughly as possible, but also to reply to the charges advanced by reformist Islamic movements:

> Throughout the translation, I have been trying my best, not only to translate Quranic passages according to Arabic idioms, but also to answer the objections of the enemies of Islam. This part of work is of scholastic philosophers. Times have changed. Objectors of older days are no more. Modem objectors object differently. The replies also should be according to the objections.
>
> (Ṣiddīqī 2000: 101)

Through the phrases 'objectors of older days' and 'modem objectors' Abd al-Qadīr alludes to the changed nature of the controversy over the *ziyārat*: e. g. while pre-modern theologians criticized the excesses in the performance of the *ziyārat*, modern reformist theologians and activists reject the *ziyārat* altogether. Both texts aim at justifying a specific sociocultural practice and, by extension, 'a certain status quo', thus we can say that 'perpetuation and justification' (Van Leeuwen and Wodak 1999: 92) is their main function.

LF is composed of twenty-one pages and divided into twenty-two chapters. The tract begins with a discussion of the concept of *bid'at* (innovation in religion) (chapter 1). Then it goes on to explain why the fātiḥa was not an established practice at the time of the Prophet (chapters 3–5).[8] After that, it asserts that though the *fātiḥa* was not common practice, the Prophet performed it and taught it to his Companions (chapters 6–7). Muhammad clearly intended to encourage this practice, but he did not make it obligatory so that it would not become a burden for the believers. In this way, the text stresses that the *fātiḥa* is not an innovation. Next, the text enlarges on the meaning, virtues and benefits of the *fātiḥa* (chapters 8–18). It claims that the *fātiḥa* is not only permissible, but necessary. The text also provides practical instruction on how to perform the *fātiḥa* correctly (chapters 12–13 and 17). Subsequently it provides further proof for the legitimacy of the *fātiḥa* (chapter 19), tries to show that the view of the opponents of the *fātiḥa* is in conflict with the scriptural sources (chapters 20 and 22), and mentions a few supplications to be used for practical purposes (chapter 21). This synopsis sums up the author's main argument.

Strategies of legitimation

Now I go on to address the issue of legitimation. The starting point of my analysis is the set of categories proposed by Van Leeuwen (2007: 92). The category of *authorization* refers to legitimation by reference 'to the authority of tradition, custom and law, and of persons in whom institutional authority of some kind is vested' (Van Leeuwen 2007: 92). In the discursive tradition of Islam, the supreme authorities are the *Qur'ān* and the *Aḥādīṯ*. Traditionalist Sunni Islam, to which Abd al-Qadīr Ṣiddīqī and his followers subscribe, besides the *Qur'ān* and the *Aḥādīṯ*, recognizes the authority of the four legal schools, and the principles of *qiyās* and *ijmā'*. In both LF and TS, the authors repeatedly refer to these sources of legal authority, and quote extensively from the *Qur'ān* and the canonical collections of *Aḥādīṯ* in support of their arguments.[9] Here follows an instance from LF:

> These things are not invented. Such accusation is without foundation. It is a calumny. [. . .] As stated above, it is clear that the present method of the *fātiḥa* is exactly in accordance with the conduct of the Messenger of Allah. Its confirmation is found in the *Aḥadīṯ*, in the sayings of Ḥaḍrat 'Ali, 'Abdullāh bin 'Abbās and Ḥaḍrat Abū Hurayrah.
>
> (Ṣiddīqī 2010: 16)

From the perspective of textual analysis, this excerpt also tells us something about lower levels of text. Concerning the choice of words (level of the *lexis*), it can be noted that the terms *be-baniyād* (without foundation) and *bahtān* (calumny), used to refer to the opponents' statement, has a negative meaning. At the level of *modality*, we find a pattern recurring throughout the text in which markers of 'high' *modality* are used. This shows a strong commitment by the writer, who fully supports the true value of his assertions. These markers are the modal adverbial *'ayn* (exactly), and the absence of modal verbs, such as can, must, etc.

Concerning TS, it is quite obvious that the text, belonging to the genre of *tafsīr*, is replete with quotations from the *Qur'ān* and the *Aḥādīṯ*. For example 'Abd al-Qadīr rejects the charge of *širk* in relation to the request of saintly intercession by the believers, by quoting evidence from the *Qur'ān*, (19:19) and (5:110), the *Aḥādīṯ* and the tradition of the first generations of Muslims (Ṣiddīqī 2000: 148). Concerning the permissibility of placing food (or other things) to be given in alms in front of the man who recites the *fātiḥa* over it, and the permissibility to do it at fixed times, he replies interpreting two *Aḥādīṯ*:

> Placing the food or the thing to be given in alms in front of the man is to set a limit to the thing to be given in charity. As far as *fātiḥa* is concerned, it is proved by tradition that 'anything of importance that does not begin with

> (*al-ḥamdu lillāhi*) 'Praise be to Allah' is unprosperous, and becomes vitiated'. Though placing the food or whatever it may be, in front of the reciter of the *fātiḥa* is admissible, what is the aim of preparing the same kind of food or stuff, when the *fātiha* is recited for the particular saint? We know that 'The best kind of work is that which has perpetuity, repetition and continuity'.
>
> (Ṣiddīqī 2000: 145)

In one passage of TS, 'Abd al-Qadīr asserts the lawfulness of kissing hands and feet out of respect. This principle is applied by analogy to the kissing of the graves. He supports his statement through two *Aḥādīṯ* (Ṣiddīqī 2000: 152–53):

> Kissing [the] hands of someone is similar to bowing up to the knees (*rukū'*), and kissing [the] feet is similar to prostration (*sajdah*). Are they unlawful (*ḥarām*)? Both these acts are *sunnat* (tradition), and so cannot be unlawful (*ḥarām*). No Muslim dare call a tradition unlawful. Whatever the Prophet said, did or an action done before him and [which] he kept going [on] without forbidding it, is tradition (*sunnat*).
>
> (Ṣiddīqī 2000: 152)

Similarly, the author rejects the charge of *bid'at* for the practice of celebrating saints' death anniversaries (*'urs*) and placing flowers on graves.[10] In the following excerpt, he discusses another crucial point of the anti-Sufi criticism: is it not idolatry to revere and to prostrate to others beside Allah? In his answer, he emphasizes a major argument used by all his living spiritual successors to justify the *ziyārat*, namely the difference between worship (*'ibādat*) and reverence (*ta'zīm*) (Ṣiddīqī 2000: 151–52):

> Worship of things beside Allah is idolatry, but not reverence. (48:9) 'So that you may assist and honour him [Muhammad]'. (17:24) 'And, out of kindness, lower to them [your parents] the wings of humility'. 'Get up, stand up for your chief'. Worship is nothing but revering and adoring one to the highest degree, thinking him to be perfect in himself and the personification of divinity. Worship is the action of the heart, a matter of belief. Prostration (*sajdah*), either for worship or for reverence, beside Allah is strictly forbidden in Islam.
>
> (Ṣiddīqī 2000: 151)

The writer remarks that the acts of worship, such as prostration (*sajdah*), are only due to Allah, yet he supports the legitimacy of revering individuals or things through quotations from the *Qur'ān*. Human beings can worship no other but God, but they can, or should, revere Muhammad (48:9), their parents (17:24) and the symbols of Allah (22:32). The 'symbols of Allah' is a loose expression which defines a broad category of persons and things which, in the author's view, deserve reverence: for example the *Qur'ān* and the *Aḥādīṯ*, mosques, religious scholars, Sufi saints, the *Ka'aba*, etc.

The category of *moral evaluation* refers to legitimation by 'reference to value systems' (Van Leeuwen 2007: 92). This strategy links a specific activity to a discourse of values. The strategy of *moral evaluation* is abundantly used in both LF and TS since they are religious texts. The *ziyārat* and the *fātiḥa* are evaluated in the light of the ethical principles of traditionalist Sunni Islam. These practices are presented as pious deeds and praiseworthy devotions. In the last page of LF, the writer makes a recapitulatory list of the positive qualities of the *fātiḥa*, which I quote below:

1 By the recitation of the *fātiḥa* the darkness of our heart is removed.
2 By the three-fold recitation of the *sūrat al-iḫlās* one receives the same reward as for the recitation of the whole Qur'ān.
3 Those spirits on whom one [will transfer] the spiritual reward of the *fātiḥa* in order to have his/her own sins pardoned, all of them, and especially the Prophet, will intercede for him/her in the court of Allah. This is the most important blessing.
4 By the three-fold recitation of the *durūd šarīf*, [that is to say by requesting God to send blessings upon Muhammad] we receive the same mercy (*rahmat*) [that God is supposed to bestow upon Muhammad] multiplied by thirty.
5 By means of this *fātiḥa*, the torment of the grave is kept far from the spirits of our beloved and intimate relatives and friends, or it is reduced, or their status is elevated. [. . .]
6 Good news. A Muslim is one who earns spiritual reward by reciting the *fātiḥa* on behalf of the spirits [of the deceased]. That is a virtuous practice. As a verse of the Qur'ān states (12:10), 'Verily the virtuous deeds erase the sins'. According to this, this form of piety is also the cause of the reduction of our sins. Therefore, every time we recite the *fātiḥa*, there is a reduction in our sins.

(Ṣiddīqī 2010: 21)

The first line of the excerpt includes a metaphor, 'the darkness of our heart is removed', which lays emphasis on the purificatory effect of the *fātiḥa*. At the level of *lexis*, some particular patterns in the choice of words can be identified. For example a symbolic opposition is created: negative things, such as 'the darkness of our heart, the torment of the grave, sins', are 'removed, pardoned, kept far, reduced, erased', whereas positive things, such as 'mercy, status, spiritual reward' are 'received, multiplied, elevated, earned'. At point 6, the *fātiḥa* is represented as a central element of the Muslim identity. The extensive use of the possessive adjective 'our' throughout the list aims at establishing a rapport with the readers.

The purpose of strengthening the rapport between writer and reader, both in LF and TS, is also achieved through linguistic 'constructive strategies', that is, 'utterances which constitute a "we" group and a "they" group' (Van Leeuwen and Wodak 1999: 92). Moreover, such strategies enact a process of *moral evaluation* that implies the positive representation of the 'us-group', composed of the writers and readers, and the negative representation of the detractors of the *ziyārat*, who are pushed into the 'them-group'. These two complementary strategies are crucial for the discursive process of legitimation (Van Dijk 1993: 263–64; Rojo and Van Dijk 1997: 539–40; Wodak 2001: 72; Reyes 2011: 785–86). Defining the strategies which are functional to the representation of the 'us-group' and 'them-group', Wodak (2001: 72) stresses the importance of asking some crucial questions, such as how are persons named and referred to? What characteristics are attributed to 'them'? By means of what arguments, linguistic structures and rhetorical devices do social actors try to delegitimize 'them'?

With these considerations in mind, let us turn back to our texts. In LF and TS, when referring to the detractors of the *ziyārat*, the writers use phrases such as *munkirān-i fātiḥa* (those who deny the *fātiḥa*), *ġayr muqallidīn* (non-conformists), *muḫāllifīn-i fātiḥa* (the opponents of the *fātiḥa*), *mu'tariḍ* (objectors), *muḫāllifīn-i Islām* (opponents/enemies of Islam), *mādda parast mū'aḥḥid* (materialist monotheists), etc. Such words stress the detractors' 'otherness' and lack of concern for spirituality, and emphasize that the latter do not comply with the principles established by the four legal schools. Despite all these words having a negative semantic load, they are not outrageously insulting. By using such phrases, the writers want to refer to the stance of the 'them-group' rather than situating 'them' out of the boundaries of Islam. The authors could have attributed a more radical otherness to the detractors of the *ziyārat* by using *kāfir* (unbeliever), as other Sufis commonly do. However, 'Abd al-Qadīr purposefully refrains from using that word and advises his readers to adopt the same attitude; perhaps he considered it important to diminish the controversy (Ṣiddīqī 2000: 204–05). 'Abd al-Qadīr was very critical of Muslims effortlessly accusing other Muslims of idolatry and unbelief, especially for non-incumbent things (*ghayr wājibat*), like the *ziyārat* and the *fātiḥa*, yet he always adopted a sober style while discussing the different points of the controversy.[11]

What characteristics are attributed to the detractors of the *ziyārat*? They are portrayed as *sinners*, as they accuse innocent people (Ṣiddīqī 2010: 2), or *bold*, as they usually descend to scurrilous language (Ṣiddīqī 2010: 3). It is stressed that they mislead innocent and uneducated persons (Ṣiddīqī 2010: 2), apply *Aḥādīṯ* inappropriately (*be-mūqe'*) (Ṣiddīqī 2010: 3) and have created a strong divergence between those who do the *fātiḥa* and those who reject it (Ṣiddīqī 2010: 3). However, more than everything else, LF and TS lay emphasis on their ignorance and incompetence. As an instance: 'Ignorance coupled with obstinacy results in ruin' (Ṣiddīqī 2000: 92).[12] The attempt to de-legitimate the 'them-group' is a central element in the Sufi legitimation of the *ziyārat*. In this respect, LF and TS make no exception. The main arguments against the detractors of the *ziyārat* are: a) their view clashes with the sayings of the Prophet and b) they are incompetent in religious matters. Unfortunately, it is not possible to discuss all the linguistic structures and rhetorical devices used to support these arguments, due to the limits of this chapter, and I shall deal with this topic in a future article.

The category of *rationalization* applies to legitimation by reference 'to the goals and uses of institutionalised social action, and to the knowledge society has constructed to endow them with cognitive validity' (Van Leeuwen 2007: 92).

This strategy of legitimation is also found in LF and TS. In LF, the writer stresses the benefits of each of the parts composing the ritual of the *fātiḥa*. The spiritual reward (*ṯawāb*) of reciting the *sūrat al-iḫlās* (chapter 112 of the *Qur'ān*) is equal to the reward of reading one third of the *Qur'ān* (Ṣiddīqī 2010: 9–10). Thus, the reward for its threefold recitation is equal to the reward for a recitation of the whole *Qur'ān*. By the recitation of the *durūd šarīf*, a ritual request to God to send blessings upon Muḥammad, one receives the same mercy (*rahmat*) that God is supposed to bestow upon Muḥammad increased tenfold. By the threefold recitation of the latter, one receives the same mercy multiplied by thirty (Ṣiddīqī 2010: 15). According to the sequence of the ritual, the cumulative spiritual reward obtained with these recitations is immediately transferred, by a specific supplication (*du'ā*), to the spirits (*arwāḥ*) of Muḥammad, the other prophets, the members of his family, his Companions, the following generations of Muslims and anyone whose name be put at the end of the supplication. This is the method of sending spiritual reward (*isāl-i ṯawāb*) to the spirits of the dead, and it is supported through one *Ḥadīṯ* (Ṣiddīqī 2010: 14).

In another passage, Anwār al-Dīn Ṣiddīqī describes the *fātiḥa* as an extremely suitable tool for the modern age, when people are generally quite busy and have little time for spirituality. Indeed, it allows people to obtain great spiritual benefits in a couple of minutes.[13] Throughout the text, *figures of speech* are used for rhetoric effect, emphasizing different concepts, in this specific extract, that the *fātiḥa* is a means of obtainment of a great reward. The writer uses a *simile*, comparing the *fātiḥa* to the *Laylat al-qadr* (the night of Power), the blessed night that falls on the month of *ramaḍān*.

The category of *mythopoesis* refers to legitimation 'conveyed through narratives whose outcomes reward legitimate actions and punish non-legitimate actions' (Van Leeuwen 2007: 92). In LF and TS this type of legitimation strategy is almost absent, unless we view *Aḥādīṯ* as stories. In that case, we should state that narratives abound in the two texts. Besides *Aḥādīṯ*, however, I have found a story in TS in which 'Abd al-Qadīr Siddīqī reports an anecdote on some unidentified 'internal enemies of Islam', who were irritated by reading some passages from TS:

> Once they approached Mr. Grigson, the Member in charge of Police and Public Affairs of the Executive Council of H.E.H. The Niẓām of Hyderabad, Deccan, complaining against my refutation referred to above. He asked them whether I had written a pamphlet. They replied in the negative. He asked them again where was the matter they were complaining about. They answered that it was in the *Tafsir-i Siddiqi*. Mr. Grigson said: 'That is the place where an exegete would express his views on religion. If you have any objection to his views, better avoid looking into it. So let me not be bothered with such meaningless matters'. Thus Allah saved me from the mischief of the enemies.
> (Siddīqī 2000: 101–02)

The fact that the writers do not systematically resort to the *mythopoesis* strategy, in part, may be explained by considerations of genre. LF is a *religious-legal tract*, while TS is a *tafsīr*. In general terms, tales are not a constitutive element of these genres. Readers would expect arguments to be substantiated by solid evidence and punctual references to the sacred scriptures, and probably would not look for stories in similar texts. It follows that in both texts the strategies of *authorization*, *moral evaluation* and *rationalization* predominate.

Conclusion

This chapter argued that the response of Indian Sufism to criticism by Islamic reformist movements is not monolithic. By analysing the arguments, linguistic structures and rhetoric devices used in Sufi texts, it is possible to highlight some differences in the Sufis' views. This preliminary study showed that 'Abd al-Qadīr Ṣiddīqī and his descendants carried out the justification of the *ziyārat* both implicitly and explicitly, through verbal and non-verbal communication. The texts I have analyzed justify the *ziyārat* first by rebutting the charges against it; second, by showing that not only is the *ziyārat* not an innovation, but it is also a virtuous and beneficial practice; third, by claiming that the opponents' arguments are conflicting with the *Qur'ān* and *Aḥādīṯ*.

Both the detractors of the *ziyārat* and the Sufi masters whose writing I have analyzed rely on the *Qur'ān* and *Aḥādīṯ* in their criticism and defense of the *ziyārat*. However, they do not agree on the other sources of religious authority or on the methods applied in the authentication of *Aḥādīṯ*, so their views are irreconcilable and their respective arguments are mutually seen as invalid. As Buehler states, 'there do exist at least two conflicting paradigms of Islamic practice which have been in tension long before the nineteenth century' (Buehler 1999: 491).

This preliminary study suggests that the modern Sufi defense of the *ziyārat* does not speak with a single voice, but includes different approaches. Similarly to other traditionalist Sunni Muslim leaders, including Aḥmad Riḍā Ḫān Barelwī, 'Abd al-Qadīr Ṣiddīqī's justification of the *ziyārat* is characterized by the profusion of quotations from the *Qur'ān* and the *Aḥādīṯ*, and emphasizes the difference between worship (*'ibādat*) and reverence (*ta'zīm*): while worship is only due to Allah, it is legitimate to revere the saints. The main strategies of legitimation are *authorization, moral evaluation* and *rationalization*. Whereas 'Abd al-Qadīr Ṣiddīqī's arguments are similar to those of Aḥmad Riḍā Ḫān Barelwī and other Sufis, a preliminary analysis showed that the respective discourses differ as far as linguistic structures and rhetoric devices are concerned. On the one hand, Aḥmad Riḍā and his followers are known for frequently applying labels such as 'idolaters' and 'unbelievers' to Muslims that are, according to them, on the wrong track, drawing sharp boundaries within the Muslim community, in a similar manner to the detractors of the *ziyārat*. On the other hand, 'Abd al-Qadīr Ṣiddīqī stresses the need to overcome misunderstandings among Muslims and to teach his followers to avoid branding other Muslims as unbelievers, even if they have divergent opinions. Further researches may highlight other differences among the Indian Sufis' views about the justification of Islamic practices.

Notes

1 See Gaborieau (1978), Ahmad (1981), Chambert-Loir and Guillot (1995), and Troll (2003).
2 For the purposes of this chapter, I use the adjective 'reformist' in the broad sense of the term, applying it to those Islamic movements that support any form of Islamic reformism, Islamism or fundamentalism. I use 'traditionalist' to refer to Muslims who, besides the *Qur'ān* and the *Aḥādīt̲*, recognize the authority of the four legal schools (*mad̲hab*), and accept the principles of *qiyās* (process of deductive analogy) and *ijmā* (the consensus of the community of the learned).
3 See, for example, Gaborieau (1999: 456–63, 2003: 198–239), Sirrieh (1999: 46–51, 148–67), Taylor (1999: 168–94), Baljon (2003: 189–97).
4 Data were collected during my fieldwork in Hyderabad between 2008 and 2010.
5 'Describing discourse as social practice implies a dialectical relationship between a particular discursive event and situation(s), institution(s) and social structure(s) which frame it: the discursive event is shaped by them, but it also shapes them' (Wodak 1996: 15).
6 For a discussion of the controversy surrounding Sufi devotional practices, see: Taylor (1998: 168–218), Sirrieh (1999), Buehler (1999: 468–91), Gaborieau (1999: 452–67, 2003: 198–239), Baljon (2003: 189–97).
7 This method is not rigidly codified, as some masters, even within the same order, use slightly different methods.
8 He claims that Muhammad did not need 'to recite a few words from the *Qur'ān*, get the reward and later send the reward to any spirit', as his supplication (*du'ā*) 'was so effective as to reduce the torment (*'azāb*) of the sinners, to grant them salvation (*najāt*) and to generate peace (*sukūn*)' (Siddīqī 2010: 4). Regarding the four caliphs and the companions, according to the author they were mainly concerned with compiling and preserving the *Qur'ān* and protecting Islam. One of their chief aims was to wipe conflict off the face of the earth and they were often engaged in war (*jihād*). Since they spent time in the company of Muhammad, experiencing his charisma and spiritual powers directly, and they were such virtuous persons and led such exemplary lives, 'why they should have worried about the *fātiḥa*?' (Ṣiddīqī 2010: 5).
9 In LF, the author quotes from the *Qur'ān* eight times, and cites eleven *Aḥadīt̲* in total, ten strong and one weak (not confirmed by the six canonical *Aḥadīt̲* collections).
10 The Messenger of Allah used to visit the grave of Ḥaḍrat Hamzah every year. This is the source of the 'death anniversary' (*'urs*). He once cut a date leaf into two and put it on two graves, saying: 'So long as these leaf pieces are fresh, they will be praising Allah and there is a hope that the torments the inmates of the graves are undergoing may be lessened'. This is the source of placing wreaths of flowers on the graves [. . .] (Ṣiddīqī 2000: 162).
11 For example, in another work he states: 'Remember: when an issue is being interpreted with the involvement of human mind (*ijtihād*), we cannot pronounce each other as infidels' (Ṣiddīqī 1996: 40).
12 'Being equipped with neither necessary nor complementary knowledge, by claiming to be master of *ijtihād* one does not become a wise man. One cannot read correctly four sentences in Arabic but calls himself *Ahl-i Ḥadīt̲* and believes each end every incompetent *Ahl-i Ḥadīt̲* without verifying or assessing what he says. This is nothing but imitation or believing unconditionally in others' (Ṣiddīqī 2000: 93).
13 'Please consider that today, in the fourteenth century [according to the Islamic calendar], the scientific age has superseded the spirituality. On one hand, from the radio we hear the news from all over the world; on the other hand, there are planes ready to carry nuclear bombs. In such an age, who has the free time or the bent to find time for studying the *Qur'ān*? Or to recite it and send the reward to the spirits of the forefathers and try to have their sins pardoned? Thus the knowledge of this practice is extremely

necessary, as it can become a means of obtainment of the greatest reward, like the *Laylat al-qadr* (the night of power), which is just one night but it is better than a thousand months. Indeed, he [Muhammad] gave a method in the form of the *fātiḥa*, in order that even the busiest man is not completely precluded from obtaining the reward of a recitation of the whole *Qur'ān*, and that both he and the spirits of his elders may benefit' (Siddīqī 2010: 11–12).

References

Ahmad, I. (ed.) (1981) *Rituals and Religion among Muslims in India*, Delhi: Manohar.

Baljon, J.M.S. (2003) 'Shah Waliullah and the Dargah', in C.W. Troll (ed.) *Muslim Shrines in India: their Character, History and Significance*, pp. 189–97, New Delhi: Oxford University Press.

Buehler, A.F. (1999) 'Charismatic versus Scriptual Authority: Naqshbandi Response to Deniers of Mediational Sufism in British India', in F. De Jong and B. Radtke (eds) *Islamic Mysticism Contested: Thirteen Centuries of Controversies and Polemics*, pp. 468–91, Leiden: Brill.

Chambert-Loir, H. and Guillot, C. (eds) (1995) *Le culte des saints dans le monde musulman*, Paris: École Française d'Extrême Orient.

De Jong, F. and Radtke, B. (eds) (1999) *Islamic Mysticism Contested: Thirteen Centuries of Controversies and Polemics*, Leiden: Brill.

Fairclough, N. (1989) *Language and Power*, London: Longman.

——— (1993) 'Critical Discourse Analysis and the Marketization of Public Discourse: The Universities', *Discourse and Society*, 4 (2): 133–68.

——— (1995) *Critical Discourse Analysis: The Critical Study of Language*, London: Longman.

Gaborieau, M. (1978) 'Le culte des saints chez les musulmans au Népal et en Inde du Nord', *Social Compass*, 25 (1): 477–94.

——— (1999) 'Criticizing the Sufis: the debate in early nineteenth century India', in F. De Jong and B. Radtke (eds) *Islamic Mysticism Contested: Thirteen Centuries of Controversies and Polemics*, pp. 452–67, Leiden: Brill.

——— (2003) 'A Nineteenth-Century Indian "Wahhabi" Tract Against the Cult of Muslim Saints: Al Balagh al-Mubin', in C.W. Troll (ed.) *Muslim Shrines in India: their Character, History and Significance*, pp. 198–239, New Delhi: Oxford University Press.

Green, N. (2005) 'Making a "Muslim" Saint: Writing Customary Religion in an Indian Princely State', *Comparative Studies of South Asia, Africa and the Middle East*, 25 (3): 617–33.

Halliday, M.A.K. and Hasan, R. (1985) *Language, Context and Text: Aspects of Language in a Social-Semiotic Perspective*, Victoria: Deakin University.

Ohlander, E. (2009) 'Modern Qur'anic Hermeneutics', *Religion Compass*, 3 (4): 620–36.

Reyes, A. (2011) 'Strategies of Legitimization in Political Discourse: From Words to Actions', *Discourse Society*, 22 (6): 781–807.

Rojo L.M. and Van Dijk T.A. (1997) 'There Was a Problem and it Was Solved! Legitimating the Expulsion of « Illegal » Immigrants in Spanish Parliamentary Discourse', *Discourse and Society*, 8 (4): 523–67.

Sanyal, U. (1996) *Devotional Islam and Politics in British India: Ahmad Riza Khan Barelwi and his Movement (1870–1920)*, Oxford: Oxford University Press.

Ṣiddīqī, M.A.Q. (1996) *Tafhīmat-i Siddīqī*, trans. by Mir Asedullah Shah Quadri, *Siddiqi's Elucidations*, Hyderabad: Izzat Publishing House.

——— (2000) *Tafsīr-i Siddīqī*, trans. by Khwaja Abdul Ghani, *Introduction & Tafseer of Surat-ul-Fatiha*, Karachi: Idara-e-Tafseer-e-Siddiqi.

——— (2010) [1958] *Luzūm-i fātiha*, Hyderabad: Hasrat Academy.

Sirrieh, E. (1999) *Sufis and Anti-Sufis. The Defence, Rethinking and Rejection of Sufism in The Modern World*, London: Curzon Press.

Taylor, C.S. (1999) *In the Vicinity of the Righteous: Ziyara and the Veneration of Muslim Saints in Late Medieval Egypt*, Leiden: Brill.

Troll, C.W. (ed.) (2003) [1989] *Muslim Shrines in India: their Character, History and Significance*, New Delhi: Oxford University Press.

Van Dijk T.A. (1993) 'Principles of Critical Discourse Analysis', *Discourse and Society*, 4 (2): 249–83.

——— (2001) 'Critical Discourse Analysis', in D. Schiffrin, D. Tannen and H.E. Hamilton (eds) *The Handbook of Discourse Analysis*, pp. 352–71, Oxford: Blackwell Publishers.

Van Leeuwen, T. (2007) 'Legitimation in Discourse and Communication', *Discourse and Communication*, 1 (1): 91–112.

Van Leeuwen, T. and Wodak, R. (1999) 'Legitimizing Immigration Control: A Discourse-Historical Analysis', *Discourse Studies*, 1 (1): 83–118.

Wodak, R. (1989) *Language, Power and Ideology*, Amsterdam: Benjamins.

——— (1996) *Disorders of Discourse*, London: Longman.

——— (2001) 'The Discourse-Historical Approach', in R. Wodak and M. Meyer (eds) *Methods of Critical Discourse Analysis*, pp. 63–94, London: Sage.

11 An ambiguous and contentious politicization of Sufi shrines and Pilgrimages in Pakistan

Alix Philippon

It was partly as an engine against the system of meanings and practices centred on shrines that the Ministry of Religious Endowments (*awqaf*) and religious affairs was created in Pakistan in 1959 under the regime of the modernizing and military dictator Ayub Khan, causing many shrines to subsequently be nationalized. At that time, the path to 'progress' was only thought possible once these alternative centres of power had been harnessed by the authorities and their powerful religious appeal channelled into allegiance to the State. As influential religious and political actors, living *pirs*[1] were delegitimized in modernizing discourses and, through this, their authority was meant to be curbed. As stated in an official document of the Punjab ministry, one of its core functions is to 'make holy places centres of social, cultural and spiritual inspiration', as if the *pirs* themselves were unable to achieve this task.

But by that very bid to bring it under control, the State actually strengthened, rather than reformed the shrine culture. Shrines, as sites of mass pilgrimage centres, became platforms whereby the State was able to relay its ideology to the masses and, by showing allegiance to the buried saints, to gain a source of Islamic legitimacy for its own authority. In the context of 'the war on terror', the universe of Sufism, deeply embedded in Pakistan's ethos, has been constructed as an ideological alternative to Islamism and instrumentalized by those in power. Hence, the State remains politically dependent on the traditional institutions and practices it was originally intent on reforming and has somehow ended up re-legitimizing them. These typical paradoxes of post-colonial States have not gone unnoticed in the Muslim world and can be observed in many different fields. 'With the view of insuring a proper foundation for its legitimacy, the State should, on the one hand, appropriate a field of solidarity which transcends it in order to neutralize it and, on the other hand, activate it in order to benefit from the reception of its symbols' (Camau, Geisser 2003: 75). Under Pervez Musharraf's military regime (1999–2008), and in a more systematic way than under any other government, Sufism has truly become what the philosopher Slavoj Zizek calls a 'sublime object of ideology' (Ewing 1997: 67), which has been energetically popularized through the media. The long despised 'popular' aspect of Islam present at the shrines has become part of the 'true face' of Pakistan. However, traditional Sufi actors such as *gaddi* (or *sajjada*) *nishins*, the heirs of spiritual lineages who are often the descendants and custodians of the shrines of past Sufi saints, were not always directly involved by the government in the new promotion of Sufism. Confronted with a new wave of violent activism, the Pakistan People's Party-led coalition government that came to power in 2008 has more actively co-opted and supported Sufi-based groups than the Musharraf regime ever did.

These complex and often contradictory dynamics are manifest at a local level in the way relations between the *awqaf* administration (the employees of the ministry whose main function is to manage and control *waqf* properties[2]) and custodians of shrines are unfolding. Consistent with the ideology underpinning the creation of the *awqaf* ministry, the State has taken control of shrines and often expropriated *gaddi nishins*, some of whom have resisted the move through different strategies. Pilgrimages and rituals have notably been at stake between these contending actors fighting to impose their authority. This is precisely the case at the shrine of the seventeenth-century Sufi saint Mian Mir in Lahore. On the basis of interviews and participative observations conducted from 2004 to 2012 at Pakistani shrines and at the Punjab ministry of the *awqaf* in Lahore[3], I intend to show some contradictions between the modernist ideology on the basis of which this nationalization was undertaken, and its implementation. After highlighting the rationale behind this public policy and the hiccups and ironies manifested in the administration of shrines, I intend to focus more specifically on the struggle for the control of the shrine of Mian Mir before eventually analyzing the contentions between competing authorities concerning the rituals taking place there during the annual pilgrimage (*'urs*).

Nationalizing the shrines: a failed public policy?

As Jamal Malik has convincingly shown in his work (Malik 1990, 1998), in Pakistan, and probably elsewhere in the Muslim world, traditional Islamic institutions (Sufi shrines, *madaris* or mosques) have been identified as the expressions of a 'tradition' that secular and modernizing elites, strongly influenced by Western colonial thought, were more than willing to transform in order to turn Pakistan into a 'modern' Nation State. In their bid to implement modern strategies of development, Pakistani modernists perceived indigenous local cultures as archaic remains of the past in need of urgent reformation (Malik 1998: 3). Katherine Ewing has also emphasized the fact that the tradition/modernity dichotomy has been pervasive in the public policies of the young Pakistani State, the latter being assigned the task of replacing the former in the shape of a new 'cosmology': 'Traditional cosmology was viewed as constituting a static, traditional subject which had no place in the modern world. And its ritual practice, which placed the common man in a position where God was inaccessible except through spiritual mediators, was congruent with the "traditional" social, political, and economic structure. The new cosmology; by contrast, was intended to give a universally acceptable content to Islam that was the founding signifier of Pakistani nationalism' (Ewing 1997: 89).

The *gaddi nishins*, among other 'traditional' actors, were identified as the corrupt representatives of a declining, backward and perverted Sufi tradition. As local notables in the British control system, Sufi leaders had been deeply involved in the political activities of the *Raj*. Over time, they had gradually developed from religious leaders to powerful landlords and influential politicians to the extent of accumulating spiritual and temporal powers (Ansari 1992). When Pakistan was created, the *gaddi nishins*, and more specifically the *pir zamindars*, i.e. those among them who were landlords, emerged as the dominant social class, along with other feudal lords with whom they had contracted alliances or marriages. As Sufis, feudal lords and politicians, these powerful leaders with a composite authority appear until today to be some of the main players in the Pakistani local power structure. However, they have not entered the political scene as a social class, but have been active in all the parties, often jumping ship from one to the other (Aziz 2001). Thanks to their disciples, most prominent *pirs* possess a 'spiritual constituency' potentially convertible into a vote bank. If the adequacy between the spiritual and the political allegiance is not always complete, since some disciples might not vote according to their *pirs'* wish, the latter, whether they are politicians or not, enjoy a great capacity to mobilize the masses. Each election is the opportunity for clientelist practices involving disciples/citizens and *pirs*/notables.

The judge Javaid Iqbal, following the footsteps of his illustrious reformist father Muhammad Iqbal who did not consider contemporary *pirs* as potential vectors for an Islamic modernization, deplored as early as the 1950s the decadence and corruption plaguing Sufi orders. In his *Ideology of Pakistan*, that was to greatly influence Ayub Khan, he promotes the idea that it is about time to reform or even get rid of these '*Mutawallis, Mujawars, Sahibzadas, Gaddi-Nishins, Sajjada-Nishins, Pirs* etc.' whose self-proclaimed spiritual functions in Sufi institutions have notably prospered thanks to feudalism (Iqbal 2005: 47,48). He suggests the creation of a ministry of 'religious affairs' and of the '*awqaf*' that should nationalize shrines, monasteries and tombs of the saints of Pakistan and appoint administrators, whose legitimacy was secular (Malik 1998: 60), to manage them. In 2004, I met the secretary/chief administrator of the *awqaf* for the Punjab, Javaid Iqbal Awan. His modernist discourse is an exemplary sample of the way the elite perceives the cult of the saints performed at shrines in Pakistan and considers the *gaddi nishins* as 'fake Sufis' with no spiritual power:

> 'Anybody who leads the religious ceremonies enjoys a lot of social, religious and even political influence in these areas. (. . .) These pirs, the gaddi nishin, they carry a lot of political influence also. The minister who is sitting here (there was a minister sitting here whom he designates), he cannot be insensitive nor oblivious to any of these pirs because if they give a call to their followers which are generally in thousands, not to vote for Mister the minister, then he will be in big trouble! (The two men laugh.) It is just like that. All the political names, they have to carry them along and seek their blessings while they are campaigning politically. (. . .) So the pirs get a lot of influence in South Punjab and interior Sindh, mainly in these areas where there is a big concentration [of shrines]. I didn't say they have a spiritual power because that is entirely a different world, but they have influence. (. . .) That devotion

> or that belonging of the people is to the saint buried in the shrine and not to them. But they are the main beneficiaries, some of them not even qualifying for it by their own virtues (laughter of the minister). They do not exactly fall in line with the saint but because of that lineage that they have, people still attach a lot of their devotion, dedication, love, affection to that family but basically they take them as symbols of these saints. (. . .) The saints buried in shrines are believed to be still alive. So to be in their good books, they want to keep their direct descendants, their children happy[4].'

This effort of nationalization had certainly been instituted for more than one reason. Besides its ideological underpinning, and the aim to bureaucratize the shrine culture and curb the autonomy of these institutions (Malik 1998: 54), this public policy also implied great financial benefits for the State, even though its enrichment was not the main aim originally (Malik 1990: 75). Popular donations constitute a major benefit from the nationalization of shrines. According to Pakistani anthropologist Adam Nayer: 'When Pakistan was in full economic crisis right before 9/11, the only ministry which had no deficit was that of the *awqaf* in Sindh and Punjab. Every bureaucrat was fighting to be its secretary. (. . .) It is managed in such a way that only a few persons have access to the enormous amounts of money which are pouring into these shrines.[5]' The official annual revenue of the ministry in Punjab was 590 million rupees (about 6 million euros) in 2007 (Daily Times 2007) and over a billion rupees in 2011[6].

The official communiqué of the mission of the ministry under Pervez Musharraf notably mentioned the resolve to better administrate the *waqf* properties, to improve the quality of religious services and the facilities for public leisure at the shrines and mosques, to promote 'harmony', 'religious unity' and 'interreligious cordiality', to propagate the teachings of Sufi saints and to support the Pakistani heritage and . . . 'popular beliefs'[7]. In many ways, State interventionism in shrines re-legitimized the practices associated with popular Sufism. Under the Musharraf regime, the provincial *awqaf* minister, Sahibzada Saeedul Hassan Shah, was a *pir*, the *sajjada nishin* of the shrine of Chiragh Ali Shah, and a politician of the party then in power, a faction of the nationalist party, the Pakistan Muslim League (Q). The secretary of the minister described him as a Naqshbandi and a Qadiri *pir*, but also as 'a descendant of the Prophet, a *sayyed*, not by blood but by action[8]', thus avoiding any hasty assimilation of the minister with the usually discredited *sajjada nishins*. The minister is therefore endowed with a religious legitimacy whereas in theory, *awqaf* employees are supposed to be legitimized by secular means. As a representative of 'Sufi Islam', he almost transformed the ministry into a bureaucratized Sufi order. When he met the American Consul in 2007, he explained that there are two Islams: the 'Islam of *mollahs*' and the 'Islam of saints', the latter clearly being promoted as 'a blessing. (. . .) As far as terrorism is concerned, we should emphasize the education of the saint; bombs are not the solution. Nobody likes bombs. The Consul agreed with me[9].'

Hence, the great narrative of modernization did not necessarily have all the anticipated effects. The bid to intervene in the political subjectivity of Pakistanis by shaping them into 'modern citizens' and secularized subjects, freed from traditional allegiances, was probably partly a failure, or at least, it did not materialize in the way its promoters had desired. Malik evokes the 'colonization of Islam' undertaken by the post-colonial Pakistani State and he insists on the success of the 'colonial sector' in absorbing and 'secularizing' these autonomous institutions, and imposing its ideology on the masses (Malik 1990: 97). Indeed, Ewing evokes the willingness manifested by Ayub Khan to use shrines as a 'vehicle for modernization' (Ewing 1983: 252). These pioneering studies have offered detailed and rich analysis of the intentions of the State and of the means implemented to insure its predominance and social control in society, that is to say its ability to impose new norms, rules of behaviour and ways of life. However, they have probably taken these official discourses for granted and might have assumed a bit too quickly that the 'State' has succeeded in refashioning the behaviour and identity of 'society' with little resistance. Indeed, the practices of the State can be incoherent and can promote contending forms of social control. The historian K.K. Aziz, despite the normative tone of his work on *pir zamindars*, has analyzed the real impact of the creation of the *awqaf* ministry more accurately by suggesting that it has made *pirs* a 'central aspect of the government' (Aziz 2001: 71).

Therefore, the laws and rules of the State might be producing unexpected results, both for the State and for the society it is intent on ruling. The implementation of public policies may have had effects which were not foreseen in the initial project (Migdal 2001: 12). As Joel Migdal puts it: 'the State is a contradictory entity that acts against itself' (Migdal 2001: 22). Successive governments have implemented 'eclectic strategies' (Migdal 2001: 22) according to their own ideology and political imperatives, which have not always been consistent with the initial spirit of the reforms. One could almost talk of a 'creeping recolonization' of the bureaucracy of the *awqaf* by the structures of the traditional institutions it intended to reform. My hypothesis is that far from 'modernizing people's consciousness', the State became the paradoxical promoter of this popular Sufism it aimed to reform. This 'recolonization' of the *awqaf* staff by Sufism has been expressed by many high-ranking employees of the ministry. Even the most skeptical bureaucrats end up believing in these saints. According to the administrator of the shrine of the patron saint of Lahore, Hadhrat Syed Ali Bin Uthman al-Hujweri (1010–1072), popularly known as Data Ganj Bakhsh: 'My prime job is administrator. But I can't do this job unless I have the devotion in my heart. (. . .) Each and every one of the *awqaf* employees here has faith in the power of the saint. (. . .) And if some of the people working here didn't have that kind of devotion, they developed it over time when their prayers were answered[10].' More generally, the *awqaf* secretary/chief administrator can be considered, according to the *waqf* ordinance and the explanation of the high court on some special cases, as the unofficial *gaddi nishin* of the shrines under the control of the ministry.

> There was a case once of a *gaddi nishin* who came to the court and said "I am the *gaddi*, I have to perform the spiritual activities because *awqaf* cannot perform the spiritual duties, they are just civil servants." The high court had

> to give the explanation that the chief administrator is the actual *gaddi nishin* of all the shrines under his control. It was a way to dismiss the claim of the *gaddi nishin* and legitimize the *awqaf* Department[11].

Furthermore, the 'dissolution of traditional institutions' (Malik 1998) has generated, among some *gaddi nishins* whose status and resources had been appropriated by the State, a defensive and reactive form of modernization. This public policy has also contributed to the politicization of the Barelwi movement, which emerged in the nineteenth century in reaction to reformist attacks on *pirs* and shrines, whose doctrines notably revolve around the cult of the Sufi saints – whether dead or alive.

The struggle for the control of the shrine of Mian Mir

The shrine of the *qadiri* Sufi saint Mian Mir, who died in 1635, is one of the most significant in Lahore, along with that of Ali Hujweri and Madho lal Hussain. Altogether, they attract thousands or even hundreds of thousands of pilgrims each year. Mian Mir is still famous today for having been the shaykh of the imperial prince of the Mughal court, Daruh Shikoh, and for his close relations with the Sikh gurus: he laid the first stone of their golden temple in Amritsar, the holy Sikh city in India. One of the present *sajjada nishins* of the Mian Mir shrine is Chan Pir, who claims to be the descendant of the first *khalifa* (spiritual lieutenant) of the saint and the nineteenth spiritual successor of the saint Mian Mir.

Chan Pir was born in Lahore on 13 May 1953 in a Sayyed family. One of his ancestors, a descendant of the Sufi Abdel Qader Gillani, Khwaja Abu Saeed Fateh Ullah Masoom Al-Gillani, came to Lahore during Mian Mir's lifetime and became his disciple, before being entrusted with the status of *khalifa.* Since the saint himself never married, it was to be in the family of this disciple that the spiritual legacy was handed down from father to son until Chan Pir. He received both a traditional and a modern education: he went to several *madrasas* in Lahore and Multan, and received a BA degree from the University of Punjab. As Chan Pir's spiritual authority is being defied in Pakistan by the *awqaf* administration, the *pir* attempts to self-legitimize by extending his mission of 'peace' and 'harmony' between religions in foreign countries. In Malaysia, where he went to lay the first stone of a Sikh temple, as Mian Mir had done in his own time, Chan Pir enjoyed quasi royal protocol: he was welcomed by the Prime Minister and the numerous cars forming his entourage were graced with stickers bearing his image. In Malekota, in India, he was welcomed by a huge crowd of both Muslims and Sikhs, and in Lucknow by Shias[12]. Furthermore, Chan Pir not only frequently attracts rich and powerful people who need help and advice, but also commoners for whom he practises a spectacular *dam*[13]. If he acts as a mediatory Sufi, mainly responding to worldly demands from people, the *pir* also initiates his disciples on the Sufi path. He claims to be endowed with spiritual powers and the Sufi double vision (*kashf*), experiences ecstasy (*wajdan*) and receives illuminations from Mian Mir and other deceased Sufis. He claims he can also perform miracles by healing people and moving in space and time[14] (by taking part in some of the prophet's wars). Hence, in his self-representation, Chan Pir refuses to be simply labelled as a hereditary *pir*. He presents himself as a 'true Sufi' who has undergone a serious spiritual training, and as the 'ambassador of peace, love and harmony between religions[15].'

However, the *pir* has been caught up in highly conflicting interactions with the *awqaf* administration, as well as with a group of influential figures who have formed under the umbrella of the 'Mian Mir committee' through the impetus provided by the *awqaf* ministry. Deprived of his traditional resources (the shrine, the land attached to it, the donations) which were confiscated by the *awqaf* ministry, Chan Pir had to open some schools as early as 1985, called *Crescent Schooling Systems*, to provide for his and his family's needs. As a matter of fact, the *awqaf* ministry has taken control of the most profitable shrines, that is to say the most central and popular in the sacred geography of Pakistan. Generally, when the ministry decides to nationalize a shrine, there is very little chance of the *gaddi nishins* winning a legal victory in court. Until 1985, a dozen *pirs* had made appeals before the Supreme Court against the ministry of the *awqaf*. Only three demands have been accepted (Malik 1998: 65). The most famous case remains that of the *gaddi nishin* of the shrine of Golra Sharif, near Islamabad. In order to protest against the ministry's decision to take over his properties, he called on his disciples to go on strike and not to make any offerings that would have ended up in the State's coffers. He also resorted to his powerful connections, hired a good lawyer and eventually won the trial against the ministry (Matringe 1995: 196). In 2011–2012, the Punjab *awqaf* ministry was officially fighting 525 court cases, but according to an assistant administrator, there are more than 600 today[16]. After being submitted to the district and sessions courts, the cases are sent to the Lahore high court. But it is the decision of the Supreme Court which is final and, as a matter of fact, the offices of the ministry are located right next to the Lahore bench of the Supreme Court. According to Khaled Chaudhry, considered the 'legal eagle' of the ministry:

> 'These *gaddi nishins* are not fulfilling the spiritual requirements, they don't have the same level as the saint; they are all anti-*awqaf* elements so we are always angry and aggressive at each other, they want to get benefit from the *awqaf* Department. This type of situation is constant, everywhere, in every shrine there is a case. We fight with each one of them because we took over their property. They all claim it is their right to have the shrine. We give them notices, we write to the police station to say that they are interfering. They can go to the shrines to get money from the pilgrims saying *awqaf* Department is not the legal heir of this property, telling them not to put the money in the boxes, so it is our loss if people don't put money in the box, we are struggling for the people to put it in the box. We are the managers, all expenditures are up to us. The *gaddis* don't have the level of the saint, they cannot prove their function. So many are not good, they are drinking, etc.'

It should be remembered that such actions are not specific to the Pakistani field but are also attested elsewhere in the Muslim world, notably in Egypt (Meriboute

2004: 278). As for Chan Pir, he is running his *khanqah*[17] at his own place, which is located very far from the shrine. In 2010, the Chief Justice of Punjab gave a decision in his favour, stating that he was the only legitimate *gaddi nishin* of Mian Mir. However, he can only go to the shrine as a regular pilgrim and he does so only once a week or once a month. 'A Sufi is strong when he is on his shrine, but far from his shrine, he is baseless. All my disciples don't come to my place, it is too far. There are thousands of them but if I could go to the shrine as a real *gaddi nishin*, there would be many more. And the annual income goes to the government, not to me[18].' Hence, since there is a great deal of social and religious prestige, as well as a high monetary value attached to these shrines, litigants have continually faced a struggle. At times, certain *gaddi nishins* request the help of high-ranking politicians to defeat the ministry's designs. Those who are powerful politicians have often retained informal control over their shrine. In many cases, a *modus vivendi* has been found, and the *awqaf* administration grants them permission to perform religious duties and rituals. The sums of money generated by the shrines usually go to the ministry's coffers, but at times they can be shared with the *sajjada nishins*. In Multan, the 'city of Sufi saints' located in Southern Punjab, the most prominent shrines do not generate much revenue for the *awqaf* ministry because the powerful *pir zamindars* receive the donations directly from the pilgrims[19]. And they officially perform the rituals at the *'urs*.

In Pakistan the veneration of saints takes on a spectacularly festive turn during the '*urs*, which means marriage in Arabic, designating the death anniversary of a saint. From a mystical perspective, it is his union with God and thus his true birth, which becomes the occasion of a popular annual pilgrimage. It is truly an immersion in the beating heart of Pakistan. One prays, reads, sleeps or goes to the *mela*, a huge fair with extravagant animations. In nationalized shrines, these popular festivals are generally managed by the Ministry of Pious Endowments. Emile Durkheim's analysis, which perceives ritual as a gathering, the cement crystallizing social solidarity and integration (Durkheim 1991), applies to many '*urs* in Pakistan. Michel Boivin has shown how the pilgrimage to the shrine of Lal Shahbaz Qalandar in Sindh is 'a process favouring the integration of different publics through the performance of rituals' (Boivin 2005: 312) and I have studied how the celebration of the union of the patron saint of Lahore (Ali Hujweri, popularly known as Data Sahib) with God somehow becomes the yearly opportunity for the sacred union between the Pakistani State and society (Philippon 2012). In the case of Data Sahib, the State has invested massive amounts of money, and the shrine has become one of the architectural landmarks of the old city. Hujweri *'urs* constitutes one of the largest religious gatherings in the Pakistani calendar. Heavily loaded with nationalist and political symbols, the ritual is legitimized as a key element of national identity and conversely, serves to legitimize the government and its administrative machinery. Hence, the State implements this pilgrimage as a political platform in order to communicate with the population, through emotional and symbolic means. The nationalization of this shrine has not been thwarted by the resistance of a traditional religious leadership who might have contested the legitimacy of the *awqaf* administration and so the latter took control of it easily[20]. For the 2012 *'urs*, more than 7 million rupees were allocated by the *awqaf* ministry to organize the event. A great number of activities contributed to turn the festival into a grand national Sufi gala. High profile guests from the political world, the media, academic institutions, the army, charitable institutions and the judiciary were invited to the festivities. Many religious and spiritual leaders from Pakistan and abroad also participate in the activities as official guests of the ministry meant to bestow a legitimizing spiritual stamp to the event. Others take part in the ritual system without being officially acknowledged.

In the Mian Mir shrine, the situation is slightly more complex because of the contentious relations between the administration and the *gaddi nishin*. In this case, John Eade and Michael Sallnow's analysis, envisaging the ritual as an 'arena' (Eade and Sallnow 2000: 5), where multiple and polysemic discourses are expressed, and where tensions can arise between the various actors involved, seems more appropriate. Friction can arise when officials, in this case the *awqaf* employees, try to control practices and the production of meaning. The 'sacred' may indeed be 'contested' among competing authorities (Eade and Sallnow 2000). The *awqaf* secretary Javaid Iqbal defended the idea that: 'Wherever we have direct descendants available, we associate them with the performance of religious ceremonies. And this is exactly about their role. Nothing more, nothing less. (. . .) No privileges or anything. But there is a lot of social prestige attached to it[21].' But as a matter of fact, in the case of Mian Mir, there is more enmity than cooperation between the 'descendants' and the administration. This hostility is most apparent in the discourses of the protagonists: 'We are not in good terms with Chan Pir . . . this man supports a gang of land robbers. He certainly does not have the virtues and qualities of his ancestors[22].' This sounds like the typical accusation of corruption and imposture usually directed at *pirs*. It aims to discredit Chan Pir and reinforce the bureaucratic and modernist position represented by Javaid Iqbal Awan. On the other hand, Chan Pir deemed the *awqaf* provincial minister in 2007, Saeedul Hassan Shah, who is a *sajjada nishin* himself, to be a 'puppet' and a 'drug dealer[23]'.

Chan Pir is extremely critical of the nationalization of shrines. In the case of Mian Mir, as in many others, it has put an end to his traditional material resources and weakened his status as a *sajjada nishin*. The argument invoked to discredit the *awqaf* ministry is precisely that, by disturbing the traditional social order, its creation has favoured terrorism by destroying the 'love factories' that shrines are purported to be. According to Chan Pir, the only way to tackle the fundamental problems of the day, most notably violent activism, is to reactivate the system of the shrines. 'In the 1970s, the population was 90% Barelwis. Now, militant groups are very powerful. The Sufis in shrines have been replaced by *maulwis* accusing everyone of *kufr* (infidelity). Today, shrines don't produce love because they are not under the control of Sufis anymore. The *awqaf* people are just interested in their salaries[24].'

Besides heading his own *tariqa* (Sufi order), Chan Pir has brought his programme of 'peace and love' into play through the creation of numerous organizations. In 1999, he founded *Sai Mian Mir Ji Welfare Trust*, an international charity association, as well as *Sain Mian Mir Sahib Ji Foundation*, an association aiming to promote the teachings of Mian Mir. He is also the Patron in Chief of the *International foundation of Sain Mian Mir* in Amritsar, India, and of a welfare society in Lahore. Since 2001 and the beginning of the 'war against terror', Sufism and the saints gradually became the symbols of the fight undertaken by the government against creeping 'talibanization', deemed to threaten the very fabric of the nation. Given the emphasis placed by Musharraf on the importance of Sufism and Sufi shrines in fostering peace and tolerance in Pakistan in the face of radical Islamism, Chan Pir might logically have been supported in his efforts by the government.

On the contrary, until 2008, the *pir* could hardly get into the shrine. His presence was systematically interpreted by the administration as a will 'to interfere with the government[25]'. During the '*urs*[26], when disciples and pilgrims visit the shrine in huge numbers and pay homage to Mian Mir, as well as to Chan Pir as the living representative of the saint, 'The *awqaf* are agitated because they do not want problems of public order[27].' Hence, the power ratio between the two competing authorities fighting over the shrine is particularly visible during the '*urs*, a time when Chan Pir is often kept away from rituals which are traditionally fulfilled by him.

Rituals at stake during Mian Mir '*urs*

During the fieldwork I conducted in this shrine in 2004 and 2007, I have witnessed several examples of the conflicts between Chan Pir and his challengers.

1/ Every year, the Mian Mir shrine was the centre of a special ritual, called *palki*, which used to take place during the first day of the '*urs*: Chan Pir was supposed to sit on a porters' chair, along with a politician eager to show the people his devotion to the *pir* and the buried saint. In 2004, this ritual was interrupted by the *awqaf* administration in order to curb the influence of Chan Pir and to prevent politicians from the opposition, such as Jehangir Badar who belongs to Pakistan People's Party (PPP) and has his constituency on the territory of the shrine, from benefiting from his support. In Pakistan, at the time of every general election, famous *pirs* are indeed approached by political parties who wish to increase their vote banks by obtaining the *pirs*' disciples' votes. From a modernist point of view, these are backward practices which are partly responsible for the undemocratic political system. According to the historian Aziz, and many modernist minds in Pakistan, the disciples are caught in a double-faced 'feudal' system, where they can only have access to their salvation through political vassalage. The master/disciple relationship (*piri-muridi*) is a powerful instrument to ensnare a *pir*'s 'captive electorate'. 'Piri muridi dominates Pakistan's politics on every level and, in tandem with feudalism, rules it. (. . .) Piri-muridi paints the face of feudalism with the cosmetic of religious sanction' (Aziz, 2003: 163).

2/ During the 2004 '*urs*, the *qawwali* group Faiz Ali Faiz was invited to perform next to the tomb during a ceremony organized by the *awqaf* administration and presided over by its secretary at that time, Javaid Iqbal Awan. *Qawwali* is a poetical and musical mode formalized by the Sufi and scholar Amir Khusrau in the fourteenth to fifteenth centuries from different musical traditions. A *qawwali* session, a rite of spiritual hearing called *mehfil-e sama*, is traditionally directed by a Sufi shaykh. It has recently been popularized by the great Pakistani singer Nusrat Fateh Ali Khan, and it can provide secular listening material. But its initial aim was to transmit a mystical message and to help devotees to enter into a trance in the framework of a ritualized communal assembly. The shaykh's position is pivotal, both in space and in the ritual. He is traditionally a centre (*markaz*), an intermediary between the message of the *qawwals* and the audience, and between the latter and God.

In the 2004 *'urs*, when the *awqaf* secretary arrived, the massive audience suddenly stood up as a sign of respect. With his neck loaded with pink flowers and golden garlands, the bureaucrat forced his way through the crowd in a solemn way. He walked very slowly, his eyes modestly turned to the floor. He adopted the same behaviour throughout the evening, as the old practice consisting of donating money by showering bills on a musician during a *qawwali* concert was directed towards him, and small notes rained on his head. In a traditional setting, these donations, destined to the *qawwals*, operate 'through the intermediary of the *gaddi nishin* who will "purify" the money before it is thrown to the musician or laid down before them' (Baud 2008: 21). If the main actor of 'tradition' (Chan Pir) is absent, his substitute (Awan) fulfils the traditional duties in his place: the notes are thrown on him, and he then purifies them before they are given to the *qawwals*. At the same time, on the other side of the shrine, Chan Pir appeared to ignore the concert he had not even been invited to. He was sitting next to the mosque and welcomed the pilgrims and disciples who had come to benefit from his supposed *baraka*. Hence, the shrine appeared to be the focal point of a conflict of authority between the bureaucrat and the *gaddin nishin*, each drawing a territory of his own. The behaviour of Javaid Iqbal Awan evoked, without any ambiguity, the attitude of a *pir* among an assembly of disciples. Don't political actors have to 'pay their daily tribute to drama' (Balandier 1992: 13)? Awan had found his own repertoire: that of the *pirs* he is so critical of in his discourse. In a very ambivalent way, the modernist promoter of a bureaucratic order aiming to replace the traditional one, is forced to 'act as a Sufi' in order to impose his authority. Awan embodies the failure of the policy of secularization he is supposed to represent, and instead the *awqaf* action has seemingly resulted in a re-legitimization of the shrine practices. Such symbolic irony does display the difficulties faced by State representatives in controlling the popular appeal of shrines and the authority of the *pirs* or at least to break free from their symbolic apparatus and repertoires of action.

Ewing has observed how competing ideologies can be embodied in individual experiences, often in inconsistent ways. Despite the conscious will of the subject to belong to a given ideology, he or she can at times manifest his or her attachment to another competing one without even realizing it (Ewing 1997: 107). This subtle analysis sheds light on the seemingly inconsistent behaviour of Awan during the *qawwali* concert in Mian Mir. Was he even aware of the contradictions between his ideological anti-*pir* discourse and the virtuosity with which he invested the

Sufi repertoire? A quick interpretation might have been that of a conscious manipulation of the Sufi repertoire to legitimize himself in the shrine, and delegitimize Chan Pir. But was he really conscious of his own movements within competing frames of reference? Similar ambiguities have been observed during an interview with his wife, Ambreen Javaid, a professor of political science at the University of Punjab. She expressed her amazement at the vigour of popular Sufism and especially at the fact that many devotees and *pirs* were 'modern'. She strongly condemned the religious practices performed at shrines, in a clearly reformist line. However, in a moment of inconsistency, she evoked her own visitations to Sufi shrines . . . before immediately denying it:

> 'I don't believe somebody who is dead, one thinks that he is still alive. But then, what I do when I visit a shrine . . . which I don't! (Silence, and uncomfortable laughter.) I just believe that I visit the shrine only to pay homage or to thank the person who helped in spreading Islam. But people beg for everything from them, for money, for a job, for children, for health *we* are asking somebody else other than the God, which actually the religion does not say that. Islam says we should ask everything to God only. Not from anybody else. The contribution of these saints . . . yes, they helped making Islam more popular. We should regard that, yes. But we should not ask for our needs from them[28].'

3/ Parallel to the presence of the *awqaf* administration is the 'Mian Mir committee'. The *awqaf* ministry has gradually appointed a Religious Purposes Committee (RPC) to each and every nationalized shrine. Officially, these RPCs are consultative bodies. In the case of prominent shrines, the RPC members are those taking the most important decisions. In Mian Mir, the committee is composed of influential figures, including politicians and judges. The previous president (Mohammad Akram Bittu) and the president in 2007 (Rana Shaukat Mehmood) were judges, which is an important detail, keeping in mind the fact that Chan Pir was engaged in a lawsuit with the *awqaf* administration. 'They want to keep me at a distance[29]', he says. In 2006, an 80-member delegation of this committee from Pakistan, including former ministers and three members of the National Assembly, went to Amritsar in Indian Punjab to participate in a festival in honour of Mian Mir and it raised a great deal of controversy by questioning the credentials of Chan Pir as the nineteenth descendant of Mian Mir. Justice Mohammad Akram Bittu said Chan Pir could not claim to be a direct descendant of Mian Mir as the saint never married. He also said the *pir* had been removed from the primary membership of the shrine (Tribune News Service 2006a). He further described the Sikh artefacts possessed by Chan Pir as 'bogus' (Tribune News Service 2006b).

The RPC expressed the will to 'exploit' the strong symbolic resources of Mian Mir, the herald of 'harmony between religions' and 'love', but also to maintain a distant relationship with Chan Pir, who had already created organizations aiming to promote the thought of the *qadiri* saint. Indeed, this committee harbours the ambition of 'imitating' the activities of the *pir*. During the 2007 *'urs*, the *langar*[30], which traditionally falls under the responsibility of the *pir*, was financed by the committee. It involved a Sikh Non Government Organization, NGO, Guru Nanak Ji Mission, promoting interreligious collaboration, which helped the committee to distribute the food. The committee's modes of action are thus meant to reactivate the 'friendship' between Muslims and Sikhs as Mian Mir had done in his own time. The committee also uses the shrine as a backdrop for cultural meetings between the Punjabi Sikh and Muslim communities. A few days after the 2007 '*urs*, the committee invited a Sikh delegation from India. *Bhangra*[31] sessions were performed by Indian Sikhs at Mian Mir shrine, and the Sikh guests also took part in Sufi rituals. Hence, the committee appears to be a new weapon for the ministry to curb Chan Pir's authority. Therefore, religious rituals are at stake between competing authorities calling on the spirit of Mian Mir.

4/ According to Chan Pir, the committee also aims to replace him to the extent of accomplishing some ancient rituals in his place, or even to change some details of tradition. Every year during the '*urs*, a ritual bath (*ghusal*) of the Sufi tomb is carried out by the *gaddi nishin*. Chan Pir claims he has been taking responsibility for this since he took charge of his spiritual duties in 1978. In 2006, it was not the *pir* who accomplished the ritual but the committee, who decided to change its timing. The *ghusal* had always been done at 2:15 in the morning but, judging the hour too late, the members of the committee unilaterally decided to carry it out at midnight[32]. Chan Pir protested, and he impressed upon them that the timing of this ritual could not be changed. Twisting the tradition would amount to a lack of respect for the saint and defiance of Sufi authority. But Chan Pir went further than just words. He threatened the then president of the committee since 2004, Mr Bittu, with a move to block his promotion. At that time, according to Chan Pir, Bittu was session acting judge in a district court. He was soon to become judge of the high court and was waiting for his promotion. Chan Pir supposedly challenged Bittu: if he insisted in changing the timing of the ritual, he would not get his promotion. If he obtained it, Chan Pir swore that he would shave his beard and leave his *silsilah*[33]. Bittu in fact never got his promotion, as the *pir* had predicted. In 2007, when I met him, he was working in the Lahore *zakat* (compulsory alms) committee. Is this an effect of the spiritual powers of the *pir* or simply an activation of his networks in political circles? Chan Pir had asserted he was continuously visited by important political figures who wished to benefit from his spiritual powers[34]. He might have called on his social capital to retaliate.

Conclusion

A swing in the power ratio between the *awqaf* administration and Chan Pir took place after the new government came into power in February 2008. Youssaf Raza Gilani, the Prime Minister chosen by the PPP which won the general elections, happens to be a close relative of Chan Pir: the *pir*'s son is married to the minister's niece. Gilani belongs to a prominent *gaddi nishin* family from Multan, like many other politicians in the PPP. Chan Pir informed him about the 'agitation' provoked by the action of the *awqaf* administration in the shrine and the Prime Minister instantly ordered the ministry to stop hindering the efforts of the *pir*, and to assist him in his work. Gilani also offered his full support to Chan Pir's promotion of 'peace' and 'love'. In 2010, Chan Pir headed the *'urs* of Mian Mir as the chairman of the shrine. In the 2012 *'urs*, however, he was not present at the shrine. His son welcomed the disciples without taking part in the official ceremonies.

These latest developments further illustrate the complexity of the politics of Sufism in Pakistan: despite the nationalization of shrines, *pirs*, especially of the feudal variety such as Mr Gilani, are still, as they have always been, influential political figures. In the case of Chan Pir, thanks to family connections, this reality has been instrumental in allowing him to partially regain his authority over the disputed shrine of Mian Mir. Furthermore, the new government in power in Islamabad has decided to pursue and even intensify the promotion of Sufism, commenced under the previous regime to fight extremism in all its forms. If Musharraf had not really associated Sufi actors with his bid to change mentalities, the new regime has started promoting Sufi and Barelwi actors and institutions to give teeth to its 'fight against terror'. Therefore, successive governments have implemented eclectic strategies tailored to their own ideologies and political imperatives, not always consistent with the initial spirit of the *awqaf* reforms.

Notes

1 In the academic literature on South Asian Islam, different definitions are given for this term, all evolving around Sufi tradition: a religious leader, a spiritual leader, a Sufi master who has disciples (murids), a guide and a professor of Sufism, the descendant of a Sufi saint, or even the politico-religious leader of a tribe, as *pirs* are often political leaders and Sufi orders are often structured on segments of population (tribes, clans, etc.)

2 *Waqf* is the singular form of *awqaf*. '"*Waqf* property" means property of any kind permanently dedicated by a person professing Islam for any purpose recognized by Islam as religious, pious or charitable (. . .) If a property has been used from time immemorial for any purpose recognized by Islam as religious, pious or charitable, then in spite of there being no evidence of express dedication, such property shall be deemed to be *waqf* property' (Arif 2003).

3 Some facts about the Punjab ministry of *awqaf* and religious affairs drawn for official documents communicated to the author at the ministry in Lahore: its total staff amounts to 2736 people, the total properties are 1403 (including 534 shrines and 418 mosques), and the total land owned by the ministry is 76,625 acres.

4 Interview with the *awqaf* secretary for Punjab, April 2004, Lahore.

5 Interview with Adam Nayer, February 2006, Islamabad.

6 Official budget of the *awqaf* ministry communicated to the author.

7 See the official site of the Punjab government, http://pportal.punjab.gov.pk

8 Interview with the secretary of the Punjab *awqaf* minister, April 2007, Lahore.

9 Interview with the *awqaf* minister for Punjab, April 2007, Lahore.

10 Interview with Rasheed Khan, administrator of Data *darbar*, January 2012, Lahore.

11 Interview with Dr Ghafoor Shazad, principal architect of the Punjab ministry of *awqaf*, January 2012, Lahore.

12 Interview with Chan Pir, April 2007, during which he showed me pictures of his many travels abroad.

13 A healing ritual that is widespread in Pakistan. In 2004, I witnessed such a *dam* at Chan Pir's house: one of his *khalifas* brought a knife heated to melting point, and put it on his tongue several times. The *pir* invited my friend and me, after giving us some blessed water, to try it too and we performed it without feeling any pain.

14 Interview with Chan Pir, April 2004, Lahore.
15 See his website, www.mianmir.com
16 Interview with Muhammad Youssaf, January 2012, Lahore.
17 Sufi lodge.
18 Interview with Chan Pir, March 2012, Lahore.
19 Official budget of the *awqaf* ministry communicated to the author.
20 In 2012, as I was interviewing the administrator of that shrine, the descendant of shaykh Hindi, the saint's disciple, came to his office and asked him to give her 100 pieces of blessed clothes which had been donated to the shrine during the *'urs* in order to organize a spiritual gathering at her place. The manager was very embarrassed that I witnessed the scene, because it meant the administration communicated with the *gaddi nishins* and did unofficial favours for them.
21 Interview with Javaid Iqbal, April 2004, Lahore.
22 *Ibid.*
23 Interview with Chan Pir, April 2007, Lahore.
24 *Ibid.*
25 Interview with Chan Pir, May 2004, Lahore.
26 The Mian Mir *'urs* generates about 1 million rupees for the *awqaf* ministry, and about 6 million rupees yearly (Daily Times 2007). According to the 2012 *awqaf* budget, Mian Mir shrine generated more than 8 million rupees that year.
27 Interview with Chan Pir, May 2004, Lahore.
28 Interview with Ambreen Javaid, April 2004, Lahore.
29 Interview with Chan Pir, April 2007, Lahore.
30 Free blessed food distributed in shrines.
31 Punjabi folk dance and music.
32 Interview with Chan Pir, April 2007, Lahore. I only succeeded in getting Chan Pir's version of the story, as Mr Bittu, whom I only interviewed once, avoided a second meeting and seemed reluctant to reply to my questions.
33 Spiritual chain of Sufi saints and their disciples going back to the Prophet.
34 Interview with Chan Pir, April 2007, Lahore.

References

Ansari, Sarah F.D. (1992) *Sufi Saints and State Power: the Pirs of Sindh, 1843–1947*, Cambridge: Cambridge University Press.

Arif Raja, M. (2003) *Manual of Waqf Laws in Pakistan*, Lahore: Kausar Brothers Law Publishers.

Aziz, K.K. (2003) *Religion, land and politics in Pakistan, a study of piri-muridi*, Lahore: Vanguard.

Balandier, G. (1992) *Le pouvoir sur scènes*, Paris: Editions Balland.

Baud, P.A. (2008) *Nusrat Fateh Ali Khan. Le messager du qawwali*, Paris: Demi Lune.

Boivin, M. (2005) 'Le pèlerinage de Sehwan Sharif dans le Sindh (Pakistan): territoires, protagonistes et rituels', in S. Chiffoleau and A. Madoeuf (eds.) *Les pèlerinages au Maghreb et au Moyen-Orient, Espace publics, espaces du public*, Beyrouth: IFPO.

Camau, M. and Geisser, V. (2003) *Le syndrome autoritaire, politique en Tunisie de Bourguiba à Ben Ali*, Paris: Presses de Science-Po.

Durkheim, E. (1991) *Les formes élémentaires de la vie religieuse. Le système totémique en Australie*, Paris: Le Livre de Poche.

Eade, J. and Sallnow, M. (eds) (2000) *Contesting the Sacred: The Anthropology of Christian Pilgrimage*, Urbana-Chicago: University of Illinois Press.

Ewing, K.P. (1983) 'The Politics of Sufism: Redefining the Saints of Pakistan', *Journal of Asian Studies*, 42 (2): 251–268.

Ewing, K.P. (1997) *Arguing Sainthood. Modernity, Psychoanalysis, and Islam*, Durham and London: Duke University Press.

Iqbal, J. (2005) *Ideology of Pakistan*, Lahore: Sang-e-Meel.

Malik, J. (1990) 'Waqf in Pakistan: Change in traditional institutions', *Die Welt des Islams*, 30): 63–97.

Malik, J. (1998) *Colonisation of Islam: Dissolution of Traditional Institutions in Pakistan*, Delhi: Manohar.

Manan, Abdul. 'Auqaf meets its expenses with income from shrines' Daily Times, 27 August 2007.

Matringe, D. (1995) 'Golra Sharif', in H. Chambert-Loir and C. Guillot (eds) *Le culte des saints dans le monde musulman*, pp. 193–196, Paris: Ecole française d'Extrême-Orient.

Mériboute, Z. (2004) *La fracture islamique: demain, le soufisme?*, Paris: Fayard.

Migdal, J. (2001) *State in Society. Studying how states and societies transform and constitute one another*, Cambridge: Cambridge University Press.

Philippon, A. (2012) 'The *'urs* of the patron saint of Lahore: national popular festival and sacred union between Pakistani State and society?', *Social Compass*, 59 (3): 289–297.

Walia, Varinder 'Pak jatha arrives' Tribune News Service (a), http://www.tribuneindia.com/2006/20061112/punjab2.htm

Walia, Varinder 'Sikh gurus gifted artifacts to my forefathers, says Syed Qadri' Tribune News Service (b), http://www.tribuneindia.com/2006/20061113/jal.htm#5

Index

Abdal musa 21
Abdals 21
Abraham 20, 145, 146
Abū Bakr al-Ṣiddīq 64
Abû Bakr Jawlaqî Nîksârî 24
Abū Muḥammad Arghūn 67
administration 125, 139
Agarbattī 73
Agra 66Agwa 145
Ahir 90, 91
Ahl-i Ḥadīṯ 159, 160, 172
Aḥmad Riḍā Ḫān barelwī 157–9, 171
Ahwaz 18
Ajmer 66, 88, 108
Akbar merathi 86
Alchemy 64
Aleppo 64, 67
Alexander the Great 20
Amîr husaynî 21, 23, 24
Anatolia 3, 11, 21
Arabia 22, 160
Araul 67
ascetic 5, 16, 20, 21, 31, 35, 36, 44, 47, 49, 50, 57–9, 110
Ashik 28
authority 3, 6–8, 42, 47, 49–52, 56, 57, 59, 63, 64, 68–72, 75–7, 88, 108, 122, 128–30, 134–6, 141, 159, 160, 164, 166, 172, 175–7, 180, 185, 187
Awadh 21, 66
Awrangzīb 66, 67
Ayâzi 41

Bâbâ tâher 32
Badī' al-Dīn Shāh Madār 63
Baghdad 16, 18, 21, 24, 49
Bang 22
baraka 63, 76, 119, 123, 135, 160, 184
Barelwīs 70
Barzakh 17
Bâyazîd bistâmî 16, 18
Bektashi 21, 40
Bengal 65, 72, 77, 97, 116, 138, 144, 155
Benyâmin 42
Bhar 90
Bībī nānī 139, 145, 147, 154
Bid'at 157, 160, 162, 163, 165, 167
Bihar 70, 85
Bihishtî darwâza 15
Bilhaur 67
Bî shar' 24
Brahmins 75, 145
Bû 'alî shâh qalandar 22
Buddhism 38
Bukhara 22, 25
Bursa 25

*Cādar*s 67, 71, 72
Cairo 22, 24, 25, 29, 77
Cāraṇ 140–2, 147, 153
Cathay 22, 28
celibacy 35, 36
Central Asia 4, 11, 20, 25, 27, 28, 119, 138
charismatic qualities 70
China 22, 28
Cilla sharīf 107
Communitas 4, 9, 26
corporeal 56–8

Dafali 80, 89, 90, 92, 93, 95
Dam 74, 75, 180
Damascus 20, 21, 25, 163
Damietta 21, 24
Dam madār, beṙā pār 74, 75
Dâr al-islâm 21
Dârâ shûkuh 19
Darbar 55, 83, 187

Darbidar 22
Deccan 9, 22, 116, 170
Deg 67
Delhi 3–5, 8, 10, 11, 21, 27, 28, 65, 67, 82, 85, 88, 97–9, 103–9, 117, 118, 122, 127–30, 134, 138, 155, 156, 173, 174
Deobandīs 70
detachment 34
Devī 139, 156
devotee 1, 89, 150
devotion 1, 2, 17, 22, 23, 39, 56, 80, 124, 150, 177–9, 184
Dhamāl 52–4, 58, 59
Dhikr 19, 69
disciple 17, 42, 59, 73, 111, 115, 127, 128, 135, 180, 184
Dīwāngān 69
dogma 75
dream 36, 37, 52, 54, 55, 84, 87
Dutch East India Company 66

East Turkestan 18, 22
Eaton, Richard 10
Egypt 9, 21, 38, 59, 146, 174, 181
Elmalı 21, 22
embodiment 2, 56, 135, 141
ephemeral 10
essence 36
exoteric knowledge 64, 164
Eyüp neighbourhood 25

Fajr-prayer 73
Fakhr al-Dîn 'Irâqî 21
Fakīrī 47, 50–8
family 45, 46
Fana fi'llah 4
Faqir 9, 38
Faqr 20, 50
Faqrnâma 20
Farîd al-Dîn Ganj-i Shakar 15
Farrukh-siyar 67
Fars 18
Fātiḥa 72, 74, 106, 108, 109, 111, 112, 116, 157, 161–73
female 8, 47–51, 53–7, 59, 141, 147, 154
femininity 48, 53, 55–7
Forqân al-Akhbâr 32, 34, 35, 43
free prayers 72
Friday mosque 67
Fûta 18

gate 15, 42, 135
genealogy 40, 49–52, 71
Ghāzī miyān 66, 79–99
Girah verses 113, 115
God 80, 87, 90, 91, 139, 142, 143, 146
Grand Trunk Road 66
guide 16–18, 36, 49–51, 69, 95, 154
Gujarat 72, 129, 142
Gûristân-i Bilâl Habashî 20

Hafiz mehmed emin efendi 25
hagiographic tradition 64, 65, 70, 71
Hâjj ne'matollâh 32, 34
Hamîd qalandar 15, 24
Ḥanafī school of law 70
Haqiqat 42, 43
Haryana 22
Haydarî 21
Hijra 59
Hiṅgula 144
Hosayn 33
Ḥusayn shāh sharqī 67
Hyderabad 9, 10, 72, 117, 118, 145, 157, 159–63, 170, 172, 174

Ibrāhīm shāh sharqī 65, 66
Iftikhār aḥmad 107, 113, 117
imagination 61
Imami Asim shrine 28
Imâm Zayn al-'Âbidîn 20
India 6–, 19–22, 24, 26, 38, 40, 44, 58, 64–8, 70–2, 75, 80–5, 88, 90, 93, 95, 105, 106, 111, 112, 119–20, 126, 130, 133, 134, 140–5, 147, 149, 152, 153, 156–7, 159, 160, 162, 179, 184, 186
initiation 60
instruction in Islam 71
instructions about proper Islamic behaviour 69
intoxication 27
Iran 6, 8, 11, 16, 20, 23, 24, 31, 32, 39, 40, 58
Isfahan 24
Islam 1–3, 6–11, 15, 19, 27, 28, 38, 40, 57, 65, 68, 72, 77, 79, 86–90, 93, 96, 99, 105, 112, 113, 115–7, 119, 120, 138, 146, 157, 159, 160, 163, 165–70, 172, 173, 175, 176, 178, 179, 186
Islamic reformism 160, 172
Istanbul 22, 25, 27, 30

Jacob 20
Ja'far al-Sâdiq 16
Jalâl al-Dîn Rûmî 24
Jalâl bukhârî 19
Jalâl darguzînî 20
Jalâyirids 24

Jamāl al-Dīn Jaman Jatī 65
Jamâl al-Dîn Sâwî 20, 21, 24
Jâmî 24, 27
Jāti 82, 141, 153
Jaunpur 64–6
Jawqî qalandar 21
Jerusalem 6, 11, 15, 25, 27, 28
Jesus 20, 33
Jeth melā 80, 83
Jeyhûnâbâdi 32–4, 36, 37, 43
Jîruft 20
John the Baptist 33
Joseph 20
Jumādā I 68

Kabul 22
Kakori 24, 29
Kanpur 65, 77
Karnataka 72
Kashf 27, 103, 117
Kashmir 18, 22
Kaygusuz abdal 21
Kâzimî 24
Kerman 24, 27
Khadṛā 49, 51, 55, 59
Khâksâr 23, 31, 32, 40, 41, 43–6
Kharâbât 23, 25
Kharjard 24
Khâtun-e Asmareh 33
Khâvandgâr 42
Khilāfat-nām 74
Khurasan 16, 18, 24
Khusrau, amīr 136
Khwâja ‘abd allâh ansârî 19
Khwāja khizr 90, 97
Konya 24
Kufa 21
Kurdistan 32, 40

Langar 28
law 39, 42, 43,
Lucknow 65, 180

Maghrib-prayer 73
Maharashtra 72
Makan deo 65
Makan khān 65
Makhdoom jahâniyân 39
Mama ji sarkar 23, 27
Mâmilâ cemetery 24
Margalla mountains 23
Masjid al-harâm 18
Mawlânâ Jalâl al-Dîn b. Husâm Harawî 23
Mazâr-i anbîyâ 20
Mazâr-i awlîyâ 20
Mecca 6, 15, 16, 18, 64, 72
Medina 15, 114
Melā 124
Middle East 9, 26, 27, 44, 64, 139, 173
Mi‘rāj Aḥmad 107–10, 117
Moses 20
Muḥammad of Ghūr 65
Muhammad siddîq zalîlî 22
Muḥammad tughluq 65
Mullā muhammad ghaznavī 94
Muraqqa‘a 18
Murīd 72, 74
Muwallihs 21
Mystics 2, 15, 17, 19, 25, 48, 57, 63, 97

Naḍr 66
Najaf 9, 11, 21
Naqshbandiyya 19
Na‘t 74
Nûrâii 39
Nûrbakhsh 34
Nurpur 23

Pakpattan 8, 119, 120, 122, 125–33, 135–8
Pandā 90, 92
Panipat 22, 49
Parwāna 66
path 7, 8, 15, 16, 19–22, 25, 39, 40, 43–5, 53, 54, 69, 71, 74, 76, 88, 175, 180
performance 6, 25, 53, 58, 59, 74, 89, 103, 104, 107, 108, 110–16, 149, 151, 157, 159, 161, 165, 182, 183
Persia 22, 24, 153
Pîr balkhî 24
Pīr-i murīdī 69
Pir zamindar 177, 179, 182
power 4–6, 8, 41, 53, 63, 68, 70, 71, 73, 76, 84, 88, 95, 126–8, 130–2, 140–3, 158, 160, 173, 175–9, 184, 187
prayers 1, 17, 22, 66, 72, 106, 179
proper Islamic behaviour 63
public 10, 49, 51–7, 59, 67, 74, 110–12, 115, 120, 126, 152, 154, 176, 178–80, 184

Qadiri 178
Qalandar 5, 8, 15, 20, 24, 32, 48, 49
Qalandarkhâna 24, 25, 30
Qalandar sarâ 24
Qannauj 65
Qâsim trabîzî 24
Qaum 82

qawwali 103–8, 110–17, 184, 185
qawwals 103, 106–15, 117, 185
qualities 26, 31, 73, 75, 168, 183
Quṭb 71

Raj 53, 61, 138, 177
Rajasthan 72, 120, 130, 131, 142, 148, 156
Rājpūt clans 65, 129, 141
Rak'at 16
Rawalpindi 23
Razbâr 42
Remonstrantie 66, 77
Rend 5, 33
Ribât 18
Rihla 15
ritual 1, 8, 21, 38, 41, 48–50, 53, 57, 59, 63, 66, 69, 70–6, 79, 80, 82–4, 86, 87, 89–92, 95, 96, 106, 108, 115, 135, 139, 140, 143, 145, 148, 149, 157, 160–3, 170, 176, 182–5, 187
ritual prayers 66
Rudauli 84, 94
Rukhas 18

sacred 3–6, 23, 25–6, 28, 32, 44, 48, 49, 63, 65, 67, 68, 75, 125, 139, 141, 145, 150, 171, 181–3
sacred character 63
sacred place 3, 4, 6, 23, 63, 65, 68
Safarnâma 22
Sahâk 36, 41, 43
Sahibzada 178
Śākta pīṭha 156
Śakti 156
Ṣalāt al-jamāʿa 73
Samā' 103–5, 107, 108, 111, 112, 114, 116–8
Samarkand 22, 25
Sanskrit formulas 75
Sar-sepordan 41
Sayyed sālār mas'ūd ghāzī 80, 86
Sayyid Ashraf Jahāngīr al-Simnānī 64
Schimmel, Annemarie 11
Sehwan sharif 3, 4, 8, 59–61
Sevā 82, 151
sexuality 57
Seyyed abolwafâ 33
Seyyed jalâl bokhârâi 39
Seyyed Jalâl ed-Din Heydar 40, 43
Seyyed Jalâl ed-Din Hosayn 39, 40
Seyyed Qotb ed-Din Heydar 'Alavi 40
Shâh 'Abbâs ii 24
Shâh 'Abd al-Latîf 15
Shahid 45
Shāh Jahān 67
Shâh khoshin 42, 43
Shâh Mohammad Qalandar 33, 34
Shâhnâmeh Haqiqat 32
Shahr-e Zur 32
Sharqī kingdom 65
Shath, pl. *Shatahât* 17
Shattâriyya 19
Shaykh 69, 71, 86, 180, 185
Shaykh Ibrâhîm al-Qalandarî 24
Shaykh Shihâb al-Dîn Qalandar 23
Shihâb al-Dîn Qalandar 24
Shīr shāh sūr 67
Shiva 48, 58, 67
shrine 1–9, 11, 15, 17, 19–26, 29, 36, 47–51, 53–5, 57–9, 63, 64, 66–73, 75–7, 79–83, 85, 86, 88, 91, 97, 103–9, 111, 113–7, 119, 120, 122–36, 138–54, 159, 175–89
Sîbak fattâhî nishâpûrî 23
Sikandra 66
Sindh 6, 10, 18, 22, 48, 58, 116, 142, 148–50, 154, 177, 178, 182
Sīnī-prasād 81
Širk 160, 163, 166
Sistan 18
Soltân 36, 41–3
Somnath 85, 87
South Asia 1–4, 6–11, 26, 27, 50, 53, 57, 71, 76, 79, 99, 103, 104, 110, 111, 114–6, 134, 135, 139, 146, 157, 173
spirit 52, 55, 56, 59, 69, 86, 106, 111, 172, 177, 179, 187
spiritual qualities 70, 76
Sûf 18
Sufi 3–5, 7, 8, 10, 11, 15–19, 21–8, 31, 32, 38, 40, 43, 48, 49, 56–60, 64, 68, 69, 71, 72, 75–8, 86, 88–91, 94, 96, 103–20, 122, 124, 126, 127, 130, 131, 133–5, 137, 138, 156–60, 162, 163, 167, 169, 171, 172, 175–8, 180–90
Sufi poetry 23, 104, 111, 116, 124
Sufism 2–4, 7, 8, 11, 19, 27, 28, 44, 60, 63, 69, 75, 77, 78, 89, 94–7, 99, 103–5, 112, 113, 115, 116, 118–20, 130, 137, 138, 157–9, 161, 171, 173–6, 178, 179, 184, 186
Suhal deo 80, 83, 87, 90, 94
Suhba 24
Syrian Desert 16

Tablīġī Jamā't 159, 160
Tafsīr 163
Tahrîm al-makâsib 18
Takht-i nashīn 69, 74
takîya 24
Takîya sharîf 24
Talab al-'ilm 15
Ṭālibān 69
Tarim basin 22
Tariqa-e Muhamadiyya 2
Tark al-kasb 18
Tark-i dhawq-i râhat 20
Tashkent 25
Ṭayfūr shāmī 64
Tigris river 24
Transoxiana 18
Truth 34, 37, 40, 42, 43
Tustar 18

Uchh 39, 40
Uttar Pradesh 24, 29, 63, 70, 79, 80, 85, 86, 90, 94, 97–9
Uwaysī 64

validate 48, 50, 51, 55

Waḥdat al-wujūd 64
*Wakālat-nāma*s 66
Walaya or *wilaya* 5
Waqf 77, 83, 128, 130, 135, 175, 177, 178, 187

Xinjiang 22, 28

Yârsân 31
Yetim ali çelebi 22
Yūsuf malik qavvāl 113

Zangî 'ajam 24
Zâwîya al-hunûd 25
Zaynab 20, 47
Zayn al-'Âbidîn Shîrwânî 22
Zinda 8, 63, 65, 67, 69, 71, 73, 75, 77, 90, 92
Zinda shāh madār 90, 92
Ziyārāt-darshan 81
Zohra bībī 80, 83, 84, 88, 89, 92, 94, 95, 97